FROM IRISH ORPHAN

TO

V.C. HERO

The Life Story of
Major General Sir Luke O'Connor VC KCB
1931 - 1915
'IRISH TO THE CORE'

Researched and Compiled by

BRIAN HUMPHREYS

CONTENTS

ACKNOWLEDGMENTS

Many people who have helped me on this long road to culmination, the principal ones are: -

My brother-in-law, Alan Williams, the cause of my journey

Sean and Kathleen O'Dowd. Kilcroy, Elphin, Co. Roscommon and their children, Siobhan, Charles and Adeline O'Dowd (RIP Sean 2013)

Dr Lucille Campney student and author concerning Irish emigration to Canada

Jenny Cropper, now retired BBC producer, once a junior journalist reporting Luke's story.

Karen Murdoch Collections Manager for Wrexham Heritage Service

Dr Kevin Mason, Royal Welsh Fusiliers Museum, Caernarfon and Staff Shirley Williams and Keith Jones

Neil Lewis, a Warwickshire retired book publisher for his insight into the world of publishing

The Reverend Dr. Jason Bray, Vicar of St. Giles Church, Wrexham and Ann Owen, his administrator

Mrs Diana Bailey (R.I.P.) of Pershore. Descendant of Capt. E. Bell

Timothy Gaul of Wisconsin, USA descendant of Thomas O'Connor

Adrian Conner (R.I.P.) of Cardiff, another interested family historian

Colonel Mark Jackson, Worcestershire Regiment Museum.

Those proof-readers from Droitwich Golf Club who have suffered in silence - Craig Nichol, Jim Jackson and John Weston.

Mr Google, of course, of Internet fame.

Many more who will know who they are and have put up with me burying my head in Luke's fascinating story for far too long.

No one more than my wife Jo, who started me off on this, thanks to the legacy of Luke's photograph, left by her grandmother, Elizabeth Brennan, said to be Luke's great niece.

INTRODUCTION

This marathon journey of research commenced due to the author's discovery about this soldier, Luke O'Connor, said to be a great uncle of his wife's grandmother, Elizabeth (Bessie) Clabon. Although maybe attractive to military historians, the book reflects the social history surrounding the 'Great Irish Hunger' of the 1940s decade and the approach of the 'potato famine'.

His research soon made him realise that Luke and his siblings, all possessed a remarkable survival trait and a realisation that although he had been physically separated from his siblings for almost sixty years, that their antecedents had disclosed remarkable similarities of character and determination.

Elizabeth (Bessie) Clabon (nee Brennan) was raised in Dublin and died at Kington Herefordshire in 1958. Following her death, a framed photograph of a smart, heavily decorated soldier which had been on display on the mantle shelf of her country cottage, was removed from its frame to reveal an eye-opening revelation about the soldier in question.

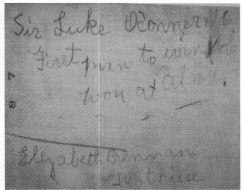

Sir Luke O'Conner VC. First man to win VC. Won at Alma. (sic)

NB. Surname should be spelt 'O'CONNOR'.

He was the first 'soldier' to win the VC

The photograph of Major General

Sir Luke O'Connor

Amazingly, the photograph, remembered on display by the author's wife, Josephine, when she was a little girl, had remained in the possession of her brother for over 50 years until, in 2008, he sent it to her, for her husband, the author Brian Humphreys to further his genealogical hobby, by investigating the history, of what transpired to be, this remarkable man.

It was the reverse of the photograph which set him on a journey of research. In particular, that which Bessie had written in faint pencil, as can be seen above. The signature was in her maiden name of Brennan; it was therefore likely to have been made prior to her marriage which occurred 51 years after the medal was won.

He was 'driven' to learn more and soon discovered that although much had been recorded about his military accomplishments, hardly any reference could be found about his family, nor their horrific voyage to Canada, during which, the six O'Connor children lost their parents and a 'babe in arms' sibling to disease. Suddenly, they were orphans, standing on foreign soil, often not being able to understand the French language being spoken around them.

James O'Connor == Margaret C. Gannon

Margaret	Catherine	Patrick	Thomas	Luke	Daniel	James
1820-1902	c1816-1907	c1822-1869	c1828-1889	c1831-1915	c1834-1925	c1840-1840
Married	Married	Married	Married		Married	
4/3/1844	App. 1847	12/2/1848	26/11/1849		16/08/1876	
John Bell	John Hute	Katherine Kelly	Ann Kearns		Mary Ann Reilly	

Margaret — John Bell
- Sarah J. Bell 1845-1886
- Robert D. Bell 1847-1926
- Mary E. Bell 1850-1927
- William E Bell 1852-1934
- Margaret A. Bell 1854-1932
- Anna M. Bell 1856-1945
- Agnes Bell 1860-1936

Catherine — John Hute
- Jane (Jennie) Hute 1849-1906
- David Hute 1850-1917
- Isabel (Belle) Hute 1852-1941
- Charles J. Hute 1854-1945

Patrick — Katherine Kelly
- Anastasia 1849-1857
- John 1851-1933
- James P. 1853-1855
- Ambrose 1858-1924
- Mary 1860-1923
- Katherine (Kate) 1862-1955

Thomas — Ann Kearns
- Charlotte A. 1850-1920
- John 1852-1874
- Margaret 1854-1932
- Charles J. 1856-
- Frank 1859-
- Evelyn P. 1860-1916
- Ellen Lucretia 1864-1914
- Mary (Mollie) 1866-1949
- Katherine 1868-1955
- Theresa (Tracy) 1870-1941
- Edmund (Eddie) 1872-1907

Luke — Mary Ann Reilly
- Maie 1877-1971

ANCESTRY AND EARLY DAYS

Luke died a bachelor in 1915, with no direct 'blood line' descendants, nor are there any known living witnesses who can confirm or deny anything about him.

The first of such facts produced, though without provenance, concerns Luke's ancestry. This newspaper clipping written by Mr. W.A. Jones J.P., was published following Luke's death.

The only piece of direct evidence found, concerns an article titled, *'In the days of my youth'* which was written by Luke in the form of a short autobiography in a magazine called, 'Mostly about People' (M.A.P.), published on 6th October 1900 in which he says:-

"I come from that part of Ireland, the country of O'Connors, where both rich and poor claim to be descended from the O'Connors who were anciently Kings of Connaught."

Unfortunately, his article was written very much in general terms, without dates or names of siblings etc. Mr. Jones JP isn't the only author who suggests that Luke's family bore such regal links. Indeed, the research conducted by the author, suggests that he was a member of the O'Connor Roe and O'Connor Don clans, but principally of the 'Roe' clan indicating the 'red haired' side.

The generations recently traced, include those going back from Luke, to Hugh O'Connor of Cloonfree Castle, but, with no documentary evidence to warrant authenticity, as much as Mr Jones is probably correct, no one can claim accuracy, without documentary proof.

There being no available proof of Luke's birthdate, complications have arisen because two separate dates have been tendered. They are 20th January 1831 and 21st February 1832. Luke himself, in his memoirs, said that he was born in 1832, the 21st February having later been attributed. Whether by accident or design, the author suggests that one of these dates has been manufactured. Here they are below, in 'table form' which makes it easier to see how they form a pattern.

It can be seen that in the lower (February) date, each element of the birthdate in January, had been increased by one!

20th becomes 21st, January becomes February and 1831 becomes 1832.

20th	January	1831
21st	February	1832

The earliest 1831 date would make him older, perhaps to join the Army and the 1832 year would present himself to be younger, coupled with his good looks, maybe to impress in later life. Only Luke can benefit by such manipulation and therefore, it is suspecting that this was a clever move by him.

However, the fact remains, that he was born in that small farming cottage shown here in the townland of Kilcroy, Hillstreet, Elphin, County Roscommon, Ireland.

Kilcroy as it was. Origin: Adeline O'Dowd - Unknown Irish newspaper

Kilcroy as it was in 2009

Kilcroy's owners, Sean and Kathleen O'Dowd, had unwrapped the fact that this was, indeed, the very house in which Luke was born. It is now a fantastically modernised and extended farmhouse, as can be seen above. The O'Dowd family are said to be descendants by marriage to Luke's family and they were pleased to host the author and his wife at their home and to show them the points of interest, concerning Luke's influence, in that area. Sadly, Sean passed away in 2013.

The comfort and splendour of the house as it stands, it now, however, nothing to compare with the poverty and depravation which existed in Ireland during the early years of Luke's life.

Luke's Family

Just like the O'Dowd family, Luke's and most others in that part of the world, were devout Roman Catholics. In Luke's words, his family were *"**Irish to the core"***.

Luke's father was James and his grandfather had been another Luke, from whom, we presume, Luke had inherited his name. It was his grandfather who was from Rathmore, Strokestown and who allegedly stemmed from the ancient Kings of Ireland. Luke's father and grandfather were also born in that cottage at Kilcroy. Luke Snr. was the second eldest of five boys born to their mother, Mary (nee Fox).

One of Luke's uncle's, a brother of his father James, became the Parish Priest of Croghan. He was Peter, who died there on 11th November 1838. Sean and Kathleen O'Dowd accompanied the author and his wife, to this church during their morning visit to it.

The area concerned, is nestled within the county of Roscommon; this was of steep Irish nationalist country, and so, as to gain an appreciation of the places of family interest, the area is included in the area on the Google map below. Elphin, the nearest town to the small township of Kilcroy, (sometimes Killcroy) is in the mid-west of Eire and about 8 miles SW of Carrick on Shannon.

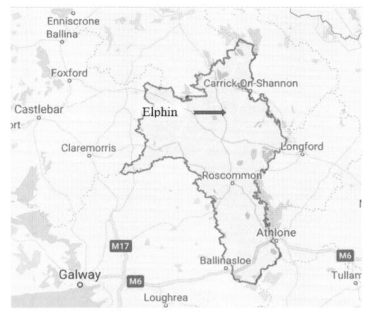

Luke's father, James married Margaret Catherine Gannon (sometimes known as Mary or Kathrine) circa 1815-16. The identity and number of their children has variously been recorded, however, the consensus of opinion believed to be correct, is that they had seven children, named Catherine 1816 – 1907, Patrick 1819 – 1869, Margaret 1820 – 1902, Thomas, 1828 – 1899, Luke 1831 – 1915, Daniel 1834 – 1925 and a baby James who was to die with his mother as a "babe in arms'. The gap between Margaret born in 1820 and Thomas in 1828 is, unusually long for those days and hence draws suspicion that maybe a birth is missing.

It was the poor conditions existing in Ireland during the 'great hunger' and the approach of what was to be the potato famine, that caused this family, and possibly many others of their extended family, to set sail from Galway for America in the period 1838 - 1841. This would have been in a wooden sailing vessel, which, like most others carrying these Irish emigrants, would make Quebec its port of destination. This was due to the sea captains knowing that docking charges were far less in Canada, than those in America.

Disease was rife and the children's father, James was to die before they reached Canada. He was buried at sea and no sooner than they landed on Canadian soil at Quebec, their mother and the baby, James both died. This left a family of orphans comprising two girls and four boys in a foreign land, with a population, the majority of which, spoke French as their first language. They were stranded alone more than 4,000 miles, and an ocean away from the home and the land they knew, but now, had abandoned.

As the story unfolds, it becomes logical that their parents had intended to reach the area in North America, later to become the state of Wisconsin, to the west of Lake Michigan, where probably, others of their extended family had previously settled.

The object of this book, therefore, is to capture the stories of these siblings by exploring their lives following them disembarking their ship in North America, as orphans.

It must have been quite soon after their landing, or at least prior to their onward trek to Wisconsin, that Luke was returned to Ireland by an elder sister. He had a younger brother, Daniel, so the mystery as to why he was returned and not Daniel, to be left with a guardian uncle, in Boyle, Roscommon, was the first of many mysteries to attempt to unfold. Sadly, nothing concrete has been discovered and the only conclusion drawn, was that Luke had suffered the most with 'homesickness'. This subject is just one example where Luke could have been more explicit when writing his memoirs, particularly as to the identity of the sister, who had repatriated him and as to why it was only him wo was repatriated?

Whichever sister it was, quickly returned to her siblings in North America. So, this was to be the start of a sixty year separation for Luke and his siblings. A joyous occasion for him when he finally made the trip to the USA to meet up with them again, however, had he not stopped for a long period with Daniel, he would have met up with another brother, who died not many days prior to arriving at his door. What a sad occasion that would have been.

In his short memoire.Luke says : -

"I was born near Elphin, Co. Roscommon, in 1832 and owing to the troubles in those days my parents, with a large portion of their numerous family, emigrated to Canada in order to go in for farming, and took me, being one of the youngest children, with them". [sic]

His words**, "my parents, with a large portion of their numerous family",** maybe suggests that members of their extended family travelled with, or before them.This is believed, to be the cause of the doubts expressed by some, as to the identities of his siblings. Names of 'Michael' and 'Owen' have been introduced by others, but following extensive research, it is believed that these are children of their extended family.

One of the most difficult facts to ascertain, was the exact year when this emigration took place. The absence of records and the apparent enigmatic need seen by most of the siblings to provide differing dates of birth, has hindered that research, beyond belief. Ignoring the baby James, who was to die with his mother shortly after their arrival in Canada, we can be sure that Luke was one of the youngest, but not the youngest, because that was his brother, Daniel, who was born on 16th July 1834.

Margaret and Catherine were undoubtedly the eldest of the remaining six. Assuming that the baby, James was born around 1838, Luke would have been around 7 or 8 years of age or perhaps a little older. So it can be seen, that the object of ascertaining their ages, is to attempt to fix, as acurately as possible, when it was, that this emigration from Ireland occurred.

There is little to be gained in explaining the many occasions when age variations have been found. Taking everything into consideration, including the details found in American Censuses and other vital records of births, marriages and deaths, the author has merely left a year or two as a margin for error, when attempting to 'nail down' the year of their emigration. It would have been in or around the 1838 to 1841 period. This was a very dark period in the history of Ireland, indeed, in the run up to the potato famine, when, not even to mention the O'Connor family, many thousands of Irish took part in a mass immigration to many parts of the world. Their intended destination, probably identified by earlier emigration of members of their extended family, was the virgin plains of North America, which had only hitherto been occupied by various tribes of Indians.

And so, using all the collective evidence amassed, with 1939 used as a focus of their emigration, the best stab as to the ages of the family setting sail from Galway, in that year, would be as follows:-

Father James – 49, Mother Margaret – 44, The Children - Catherine – 23, Margaret – 19, Patrick – 17, Thomas - 11, Luke – 7 or 8, Daniel – 5 and baby James – 1.

Ireland - Pre Potato Famine

Just prior to the Irish potato famine of 1845 over a million Irish people emigrated and during it, another million died. Land ownership was gradually being transferred to absent English landlords and failed crops were reasons why those who owned land and properties on it, were being forced to sell. If you were a tenant, heaven knows what would happen to you by unscrupulous landlords. The below is an extract from that published in **'The History Place'**

During the Famine period, an estimated half-million Irish were evicted from their cottages. Unscrupulous landlords used two methods to remove their penniless tenants. The first involved applying for a legal judgment against the male head of a family owing back-rent. After the local barrister pronounced judgment, the man would be thrown in jail and his wife and children dumped out on the streets. A notice to appear was usually enough to cause most pauper families to flee and they were handed out by the hundreds.

The second method was for the landlord to simply pay to send pauper families overseas to British North America. Landlords would first make phony promises of money, food and clothing, then pack the half-naked people in overcrowded British sailing ships, poorly built and often unseaworthy, that became known as coffin ships.

The additional restrictions placed on Catholics were particularly harsh.

With Luke's family having departed before 1845, most people in Ireland no longer owned their land. Much of it had been turned into English plantations. Land-owning Irishmen who worked for themselves became English tenants overnight. The only money that changed hands, of course, was the rent largely paid to the new landlords.

Those who emigrated, required quite a heavy monetry investment and one wonders, whether there may have been a need to sell their land, property and belongings, to raise the funds required.

FROM EMIGRATION TO IMMIGRATION - The Voyage

The earliest of immigrants from many countries to the unclaimed prairies in North America, were sending word to their loved ones at home, about the better opportunities which existed there. Although the masses of unclaimed land had yet to be tilled for farming purposes, huge stretches of it had been occupied by bands of native Indian tribes. Sadly, they were being chased off by American forces. The amalgamation of the Souks with the Meswakis and Kickapoo tribes which formed the 'British Band' were defeated in 1832 and moved from Iowa Indian territory, eastward across the Mississippi into what became the state of Illinois.

The brutal movement of these indigenous people opened the door for mostly European land grabbers from initially, the Netherlands, Norway, and Germany, who were purchasing large swathes of prairie land to which their countrymen could immigrate. It wasn't long before they were joined by neighbouring Canadians and Americans from further south in their own country.

Similar conditions and Indian movements were experienced in lands now known as the states of Wisconsin and Minisota. Iowa had been included in Wisconsin territory from 1836 to 1838 and Minnesota was not separated from Iowa until 1846. It's difficult to imagine that during the first three decades of the nineteenth century that part of the Upper Mississippi Valley including the present State of Wisconsin, remained practically in its primitive condition.

A debt of gratitude is owed to the author and historian Dr. Lucille Campey who has written many books about European immigration to Canada. Her research suggests that it may have been on the 225-ton sailing ship *'Midas',* captained by a Thomas Moore, in which the O'Connors sailed from Galway, in the April of 1841. This vessel had 83 passengers aboard and whilst this information is nothing like corroborated, its description contained within agents records held at Aberdeen University, does indeed, coincide with the O'Connor experience, particularly concerning the fact that three of the same families were aboard, with a desire to travel onwards to America to settle in the prairies of Illinois and that one of them died and was buried at sea.

It is also here, that, in 1967, a young journalist, Jenny Cropper, employed by the Reveille newspaper, was tasked to write an article on Luke. Her story covered many pages but unfortunately, her research and resultant article, occurred some 52 years, following Luke's death. The author has spoken to Jenny whose career rose to the dizzy heights of being a BBC film and drama producer. She has, of course, used a great deal of journalistic licence in producing it. In her words, she describes the situation she wrote **"As he would have remembered it".**

The first landing of their ship, would have been at the immigration and isolation island, Grosse Isle. The O'Connor family had been torn apart by the environment they left and the dreadful conditions prevailing on board that ship and on Grosse Isle. How they must have been relieved when they finally reached Quebec but how sad were they after losing their parents and the baby?

In order to gain a better appreciation of what faced them, the next section, discloses various unattributed accounts of the hell which pertained on Grosse Isle.

These sailing ships crossing the Atlantic, were sometimes aptly referred to as 'coffin ships, which immediately paints a portrait of the blackest scenario ever imagined. It can only be hoped that maybe the O'Connors had beaten the worst of the experiences to come, but by reading an article, again published by 'The History Place' in which this awful situation, is vividly described, and taking into account the deaths of the parents and the baby sibling, makes that hope, rather despairing.

> *"The first coffin ships headed for Quebec, Canada. The three-thousand-mile journey, depending on winds and the captain's skill, could take from 40 days to three months. Upon arrival in the Saint Lawrence River, the ships were supposed to be inspected for disease and any sick passengers removed to quarantine facilities on Grosse Isle, a small island thirty miles downstream from Quebec City.*
>
> *But in the spring of 1847, shipload after shipload of fevered Irish arrived, quickly overwhelming the small medical inspection facility, which only had 150 beds. By June, 40 vessels containing 14,000 Irish immigrants waited in a line extending two miles down the St. Lawrence. It took up to five days to see a doctor, many of whom were becoming ill from contact with the typhus-infected passengers. By the summer, the line of ships had grown several miles long. A fifteen-day general quarantine was then imposed for all of the waiting ships. Many healthy Irish thus succumbed to typhus as they were forced to remain in their lice-infested holds. With so many dead on board the waiting ships, hundreds of bodies were simply dumped overboard into the St. Lawrence.*
>
> *Others, half-alive, were placed in small boats and then deposited on the beach at Grosse Isle, left to crawl to the hospital on their hands and knees if they could manage. Thousands of Irish, ill with typhus and dysentery, eventually wound up in hastily constructed wooden fever sheds. These makeshift hospitals, badly understaffed and unsanitary, simply became places to die, with corpses piled "like cordwood" in nearby mass graves. Those who couldn't get into the hospital died along the roadsides. In one case, an orphaned Irish boy walking along the road with other boys sat down for a moment under a tree to rest and promptly died on the spot.*
>
> *The quarantine efforts were soon abandoned and the Irish were sent on to their next destination without any medical inspection or treatment. From Grosse Isle, the Irish were given free passage up the St. Lawrence to Montreal and cities such as Kingston and Toronto. The crowded open-aired river barges used to transport them exposed the fair-skinned Irish to all-day-long summer sun causing many bad*

sunburns. At night, they laid down close to each other to ward off the chilly air, spreading more lice and fever.

Many pauper families had been told by their landlords that once they arrived in Canada, an agent would meet them and pay out between two and five pounds depending on the size of the family. But no agents were ever found. Promises of money, food and clothing had been utterly false. Landlords knew that once the paupers arrived in Canada there was virtually no way for them to ever return to Ireland and make a claim. Thus, they had promised them anything just to get them out of the country.

Montreal received the biggest influx of Irish during this time. Many of those arriving were quite ill from typhus and long-term malnutrition. Montreal's limited medical facilities at Point St. Charles were quickly overwhelmed. Homeless Irish wandered the countryside begging for help as temperatures dropped and the frosty Canadian winter set in. But they were shunned everywhere by Canadians afraid of contracting fever.

Of the 100,000 Irish that sailed to British North America in 1847, an estimated one out of five died from disease and malnutrition, including over five thousand at Grosse Isle.

Up to half of the men that survived the journey to Canada walked across the border to begin their new lives in America. They had no desire to live under the Union Jack flag in sparsely populated British North America. They viewed the United States with its anti-British tradition and its bustling young cities as the true land of opportunity. Many left their families behind in Canada until they had a chance to establish themselves in the U.S.

Americans, unfortunately, not only had an anti-British tradition dating back to the Revolutionary era, but also had an anti-Catholic tradition dating back to the Puritan era. America in the 1840s was a nation of about 23 million inhabitants, mainly Protestant. Many of the Puritan descendants now viewed the growing influx of Roman Catholic Irish with increasing dismay."

Grosse Isle

And so, with their father having been buried at sea before their arrival in Canadian waters, their ship would have docked at Grosse Isle and held in quarantine until allowed to carry on to Quebec.

The 'Google' map below shows the Island located well into this wide river, 28.5 miles downstream from Quebec city. It measures just under two miles long by 0.62 miles wide, with its physical location ideally serving as an immigration station and quarantine. In that context, it had often been termed, the 'Ellis Island' of Canada. It was first established in 1832. During that period until 1848, the very period when the O'Connors would have made their voyage, thousands of Irish migrants were quarantined on it, having contracted, or about to contract typhus or cholera.

With father, James already buried at sea, his wife, Margaret and their baby, were two of the believed over 3,000 Irish who died on the island. (If not at Quebec) Over 5000 are currently buried in the cemetery. Despite Luke suggesting that his mother and brother died of smallpox and fever, it has been widely reported since, that most who had died on the island were infected with typhus.

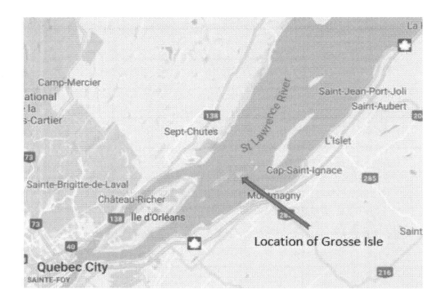

Location of Grosse Isle

Much has been written about the lack of medical resources and accommodation deployed there. Some believed that washing and airing out the ships would be enough to stop the spreading of disease between infected passengers. There are also reports of instances where overworked doctors simply walked the lines of passengers, glancing at the tongues of those who looked feverish.

It is no surprise to learn that many people with latent fever could pass as healthy beings, only to succumb to their sickness once they had left Grosse Isle. One can imagine how these immigrants were shunned by locals, nurses, doctors, and potential employers, who were in fear of contracting their diseases.

With the O'Connor children witnessing their parents' deaths, the picture of that era painted above, is perhaps, the blackest imaginable. The story of what happened to those orphaned children plus the knowledge that Luke was returned to Ireland to be raised by an uncle, makes one feel that they were lucky to have escaped themselves, but what were they going to do now?

Bearing in mind that Luke was a very young boy, the following is his account taken directly from his short memoire: -

> *"Crossing the Atlantic was a tedious business then, and we did it in a slow sailing vessel. During the long voyage my father died at sea. My widowed mother reached Quebec in the middle of an epidemic of small-pox and fever, when she, too, was taken ill and died, also one of my brothers, leaving me to the care of an elder sister, who brought me back to Ireland."*

If his account is accurate, it does appear that their mother and the baby had indeed, reached Quebec where they died. At such a tender age, Luke describes his journey as just a "tedious business", which, of course, hardly matches with the bleak picture painted by the publisher of 'The History Place'. But with their father dying of disease during the voyage, it would have been necessary for them to have experienced the Grosse Isle tortuous procedures described.

The island rapidly became overwhelmed. Tents were set up to house the influx of people, but many new arrivals were left lying on the ground without shelter. Hundreds were literally flung onto the beach, left amid the mud and stones to crawl onto the dry land.

An Anglican Bishop recalled seeing people lying opposite the church screaming for water, while others lay inside the tents without bedding. One child he saw, was covered in vermin; another who had been

13

walking with some others, sat down for a moment, and died. Many children were orphaned, as were, of course, the O'Connor children of James and Margaret who had taken them there for a better life.

Conditions were so terrible that a 'Senate Committee' was assembled and reported on the filthy and crowded situation existing. They found patients lying in double tiers of bunks which allowed dirt from the top bunk to fall onto the lower. They saw two or three invalids were placed together in one berth, irrespective of age or gender.

This Celtic cross built on Grosse Isle in 1909 stands there, as a memorial of the memory of the Irish who perished.

There was no bread and meals consisted of tea, gruel or broth served three times a day. There was never enough drinking water for the fever patients. A Catholic priest, a Father Moylan, reported giving water to invalids in a tent who had not been able to drink for 18 hours.

Because of the lack of personnel and space, the invalids lay in their own excrement for days and there were insufficient staff to take away those who had died. The hospitals themselves had very little equipment and planks for bedding, were not always available, meaning that they were spread on the ground and became soaked.

As well as a shortage of accommodation, there was a serious lack of medical personnel to care for the sick. Attempts were made to enlist healthy female passengers as nurses with the promise of high wages. However, the fear of disease, meant none accepted. Nurses were expected to sleep alongside the sick and share their food; they had no privacy, often caught the fever themselves and were not helped when they fell ill.

Prisoners from the local jail were released to carry out the nursing, but many stole from the dead and the dying. All the medical officers involved became ill at some stage, with four doctors dying of typhus. Under the Passenger Act of 1842, ships were not obliged to carry a doctor, and only two doctors arrived as passengers. One of these, Dr. Benson from Dublin, volunteered to help the sick, contracted typhus himself and was dead within six days.

FROM CANADA TO AMERICA

The French were the original 'white' of the immigrant inhabitants, they were already settled in the **Fox River Valley,** where most probably, the family were aiming for, and where they first settled. This was also the place where one of the elder siblings, Margaret was to remain, she having married a Scotsman, John Bell who was to develop a farm and nursery business there.

However, before delving into any of the other siblings lives, there was that move to be made from Quebec, to Wisconsin, the place their parents had been aiming to settle.

The southwestern part of Wisconsin was the first to receive American settlers in around 1819. They came in large numbers for several years until the southern section of Wisconsin contained practically all the population found within the borders of the present State. The magnet drawing them there, was the mining of lead ore which had been worked by white French Canadians at around the time of the American Revolutionary War.

Following continued increases of immigrants, came the rush of 1827, the Indian uprisings, the treaties made with them, and the ever-increasing number of immigrants into Wisconsin. In those very early days, the sending of letters to homelands was key to this influx and by 1830, many post offices were in existence at what were, frontier villages. It may well have been the case that earlier O'Connor settlers found their way to this area and that they were the 'pull factor' behind this later O'Connor family's immigration. However, our O'Connor siblings would not have arrived until approximately a decade later.

Letter writing home, would have been a prime necessity when one imagines that moving hundreds of miles on foot or by horse, would entail letting folk back at home, know exactly where they were and their progress in general. Skipping many years ahead, this was what those O'Connor orphans must have done. For a start, arrangements would have had to be made to return Luke to Ireland. In addition, the fact that after Luke's retirement, he made visits to America to meet up with his siblings, only goes to prove that communications were maintained between the travelling sibling orphans and those back at home.

Whilst it would have been a very long journey for the earlier individual settlers to make it to a post office by horse, many settlers would have been in the same situation and a rota system of taking and collecting the settler's post, had emerged.

The below Google map may be helpful to readers in order to acquaint themselves with the possible route taken by the O'Connor siblings from Quebec. Whether Luke would have been returned to Ireland following their arrival in Wisconsin is doubtful.

The geographical situation and the need for rapid 'back and forth' communications with their homeland, was paramount. Though one cannot be totally sure, it is far more likely, that his repatriation was made before the final push to Wisconsin had commenced and the sister repatriating him, had returned. This would not have been a rapid process and it must be borne in mind that their letters sent, required a reply, and so having sent a letter, unless they provided advanced addresses, they would be required to remain where they were to receive each response. One exchange of mail would most likely, have taken many months to complete and it adds more weight in theorising that Luke would have been returned from Canada, early in the process.

The below map shows the locations of their starting point at Quebec to where they at first settled at Spring Prairie, Wisconsin. It was possible for them to have taken advantage of the Eerie canal or even the great lakes transportation, but their most likely mode of transport would be by horse wagon, most probably along with other freshly landed immigrants. Nearby Milwaukee would have been well established on their arrival but whilst the girls were to remain in Wisconsin for the early schooling of their brothers, at some later stage, these three boys, Patrick, Thomas and Daniel moved on to Illinois where postal services would have been comparatively easy to maintain.

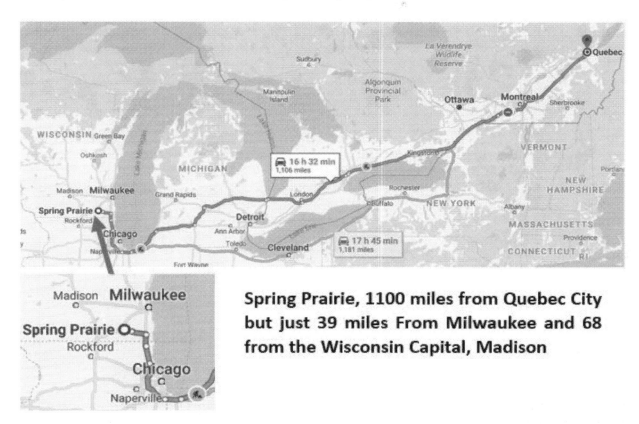

Spring Prairie, 1100 miles from Quebec City but just 39 miles From Milwaukee and 68 from the Wisconsin Capital, Madison

The Territorial Government was organised in Wisconsin in 1836 and it wasn't until then, that Madison, was chosen as the state capitol, even before it was built! It now stands on land occupied previously by thick forests. In a June 1839 edition of Madison's early newspaper, the *Enquirer,* mention is made of thousands of acres of land being purchased by large New York and Pennsylvanian companies. The comment was made that, **"Immigrants are expected during the course of the present summer and approaching fall."** Another indication that the year 1839 or thereabouts, was the period of the 'O'Connor family's immigration.

The influx of immigrants saw emigration companies emerging which were to have no small influence, either directly or indirectly, on the settlement of south eastern Wisconsin. One such example was the 'Western Emigration Company'. Their influence on immigration, took a foothold in late 1836 in an area, close to the shores of Lake Michigan, which wasn't far from where the O'Connor siblings had settled. One cannot discount the probability, that such services were planned to be used by the O'Connor parents and that their children would have taken advantage of their earlier planning.

The Iowa journal of History and Politics published in July 1919 states: -

> *'Wheat and corn were growing well, and oats, rye, barley, buckwheat, peas, and beans were to be found to a lesser degree. numbers of farmers in 1838 who were cultivating from one hundred to one hundred and fifty acres of land, and had imported good breeds of horses, sheep, cattle, and hogs. But these prosperous settlers with their fields of growing grain occupied the country in the southern and eastern parts of the Territory.'*

It is the circumstantial evidence contained within such clippings, that adds weight to be confident that it was during the period, 1838 -1841 when they moved on from Quebec, to their intended American destination seeking their new lives, the new lives that their parents had sought to achieve on virgin land to raise their family.

Admissions have been made by past British governments that not enough was done to assist the Irish with the situation existing which drove them to flee their homeland and take these desperate measures. That, now seems a massive understatement. Grosse Isle is now a Canadian national historic site, administered by 'Parks Canada' and is open to the public. How well had these siblings managed to survive and take themselves close to what was most probably, their parent's intended destination. With especially, the two girls, Margaret and Catherine being of young adult age, fate and their courage, appears to have been on their side.

In plotting how to record the lives of this brave family of orphans, advantage has been taken by now being able to reflect on their lives before deciding whether to continue to track Luke's progress after he was returned to Ireland, or to return to him later, having explored his siblings continued lives in America. The decision here, was taken to continue with Luke's life after he was returned to Ireland, albeit it would not be right to do so, without at least, reflecting a little on the other siblings.

In order to overcome this dilemma, the author has written another book which concentrates, from here on, with the alternative version, to swing the spotlight on the five other siblings who remained in America, particularly on Luke's closest sibling, Daniel, who fought bravely for the Union Army in the American Civil War. It was he, who was left for dead on the Missionary Ridge battlefield, to survive in a Confederate State to become one of Wilmington, North Carolina's best known citizens and businessmen. Although Luke was separated from his siblings by the Atlantic Ocean, their lives bore remarkable similarities and most definitely, needed to be explored.

To research and write about such a famous soldier and hero is both an honour and a pleasure but, the icing on the cake had been the discovery of his brief autobiography which had been lodged in the Wrexham archives. Its existence had also been brought to the authors attention by an Adrian O'Connor, of Cardiff, who for years, had believed that Luke was an ancestor of his brother, Patrick O'Connor. That turned out not to be the case and sadly, Adrian died in 2019, unfortunately before this book was published.

The front cover of the magazine M.A.P. (Mainly About People) dated week ending 6th October 1900, which carried Luke's memoirs, is shown on the next page. The editor, Thomas Power O'Connor (known as TP O'Connor) was not related to the family, but they became close friends. TP was a well-known journalist and in Irish politics, became a household name, especially concerning the subject of 'Home Rule'. He was also, an MP for many years.

His bust remains in Fleet Street, London today. The inscription reads, "His pen could lay bare the bones of a book or the soul of a statesman in a few vivid lines". The reproduction of the original copy of Luke's autobiography is so poor and faint, that for the benefit of clarity, and the fact that its importance for readers to read, is paramount, it has been transcribed, word for word, below.

It will also provide an understanding of what is missing. No doubt the editor would have wanted him to write concisely or maybe, could it have been Luke's embarrassment which caused various omissions. We shall never know. However, mention of various aspects of these memoirs will be touched upon later, so, the reading of it here, is a must. In any event, it is a most interesting document of great 'social history'.

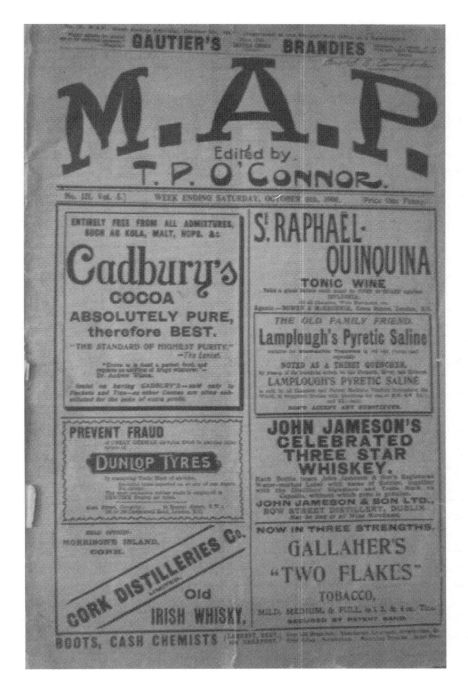

IN THE DAYS OF MY YOUTH

Chapters of Autobiography

Like my gifted namesake, the editor of this paper, I am an Irishman to the core.
I come from that part of Ireland, the country of O'Connors, where both rich and poor claim to be descended from the O'Connors who were anciently Kings of Connaught.
I was born near Elphin, co. Roscommon, in 1832, and owing to the troubles in those days my parents, with a large portion of their numerous family, emigrated to Canada in order to go in for farming, and took me, being one of the youngest children, with them. Crossing the Atlantic was a tedious business then, and we did it in a slow sailing vessel. During the long voyage my father died at sea. My widowed mother reached Quebec in the midst of an epidemic of small-pox and fever, when she, too, was taken ill and died, also one of my brothers, leaving me to the care of an elder sister, who brought me back to Ireland.

*   *   *   *   *

My first recollection in life is my return to Boyle, a military town containing barracks, and well known to the readers of "Charles O'Malley". Here, I was handed over to an uncle, as my sister returned immediately to America, where many of my relations still are; some of them attained to high positions during the American War. It was not strange that my earliest ideas had a military tendency, for Roscommon is famous for giving soldiers to the service, and, indeed, many of my own relatives have served in the Army all over the world. My first and greatest delight was in playing at soldiers and drilling other children in the street; also, occasionally making raids into the barracks, in defiance of the sentries, instead of attending school, for which I often received a severe thrashing. Little did I then think that later in life I should become a captain commanding a two-company detachment in the same quarters.

It was intended at first to make me a priest, and this notion sometimes took hold of my fancy. My uncle, however, wished me to return to Canada to join my people, but all at once, he died. There was a first cousin of mine, however, in London in medical practice, who had served as a military surgeon under Sir de Lacy Evans in Spain. I resolved to visit this relative, and see what he could do for me.

My cousin promised to do his best but said it would take some time. Meanwhile, having met some young fellows of my own age, we went about town and were soon attracted at Westminster by sergeants flaunting gay ribbons in their caps anxious to secure recruits. Being like most of my countrymen very fond of horses, I took the Queen's shilling for the 17th Lancers.

When I told my cousin of this the next day, he said, "I hope you'll do something better than that," and I got off by paying the "smart money" before being regularly attested.

In spite of this my wish to soldier became too strong for me, and shortly afterwards when again in Westminster I was struck by the gallant appearance of a fine looking recruiting sergeant of the Royal Welsh Fusiliers, a regiment I had never heard of before, and its title caught my fancy. I took the shilling once more, a few of my young friends followed my example and we enlisted in the same regiment. I said nothing to my cousin this time, and in a few days found myself in the barracks at Winchester, where the Royal Welsh were quartered in July 1849.

On joining I was told [sic] off to a Barrack-room and placed in charge of an old Welshman, Tom Jones by name, who was told to look after me. This veteran soldier took great interest in this duty and showed me how to clean my things and turn out smart for parade, and I felt much gratitude to him for his kind attention. In those days the soldier's rations were very bad, the bread served out to us was black and so badly baked it would stick to the wall. With spare money of my own I used to buy some of a better quality, which I shared with my elder comrade, besides standing him beer. The sergeant of my room, a fine tall man, who played the fiddle, was also very kind to me. Strange to say, years afterwards this sergeant, Kneightly by name, was my quartermaster when I commanded the regiment. Within a fortnight of joining, I had so mastered my drill that I was noticed by the adjutant and sergeant-major and called out to drill a squad in their presence to see if I could do it just as I had been taught.

Proud of the opportunity, I repeated the necessary cautions and gave the words of command completely to their satisfaction.

Next day I was brought to the orderly-room before my colonel, Arthur Wellesley Torrens, a man well known in the service. Formerly adjutant to the Guards, very much to the disgust of the older officers of the Royal Welsh he had been promoted to the command of their regiment. Yet, no doubt, he was a thoroughly clever, competent officer, and, I can now say, was very far advanced in military subjects for that period, for he had published "Six lectures by a Field Officer," a little treaties written fifty years ago, which is well worth the attention of some officers in high command in 1900. I may add that he was a great admirer of the tactics used in Crawford's celebrated Light Division during the Peninsula War, and, although very severe, seemed devoted to his profession, and loved to encourage young soldiers.

To my great delight, on that very day he gave me my stripe as a lance-corporal, which I am always proud to remember. It was the first step in my soldier's career, and I felt determined it should not be my last. In June, 1850, I was promoted full corporal and to lance-sergeant the same year, and twelve months later on, when the regiment was at Plymouth, I became a sergeant just two years after joining it.

In 1853 the Royal Welsh was garrisoning the old castle at Chester, when the militia were called out, which had not been done for many years past. In consequence, I was detailed to take two corporals and twenty men to Welshpool and drill the Montgomeryshire Militia. I took such interest in teaching these Welshmen their military work that I often acted as sergeant-major, even drum-major, for some of their staff were not very efficient.

Sir John Conway, a well-known man at Court, was the commanding officer. An Irishman by birth, and coming from Roscommon, he not only was very kind to me, but so were all his officers; indeed, I was often called out to drill the whole regiment on parade. After a month of this, I was ordered back to Chester when the militia not only gave us a farewell dinner but as there was no railway for twenty miles, hired conveyances to send us to the nearest station. Sir John further sent a favourable report to Colonel Torrens of my good behaviour of my command.

Soon afterwards I was sent to drill the Anglesey Militia and met with the same success. Then again, I went to the 3rd Lancashire at Liverpool. After finishing off three militia battalions I obtained six weeks' furlough, and visited Boyle in my sergeant's uniform, where I was hailed with delight by all my old friends and acquaintances.

*   *   *   *   *

I re-joined at Newport, Isle of Wight, and the following year was sent to drill militia once more. My next business was to proceed with my company, No. 6 of the Royal Welsh, under Captain Jack Evans, to the newly formed camp at Chobham. Here, under Lord Raglan, the first attempt was made at manoeuvring a British force in peace time. My company - distinguished by a sprig of heather in the forage caps - had to represent a skeleton enemy. This work was very hard, but I took such interest in it that at moments I imagined we were in earnest; yet after six weeks of such severe exercise, I was not sorry to rejoin my regiment. Colonel Crutchley was now in command of the old Royal Welsh Fusiliers, then a splendid body of tall, fine men, who stood a thousand men on parade.

In 1854 we moved to Portsmouth. At this moment there was much excitement about the impending war with Russia; but when we received orders to embark for the East, our colonel had to retire, owing to ill health, and was succeeded by Colonel Chester, a former officer, from the Half Pay List.

On April 4th (1854) we embarked at Southampton on the S.S. Trent for Turkey. I saw sad scenes on leaving, especially the parting of Sir William Young, of ours, from his young, newly married wife. The poor lady was so overcome, she was carried off the ship insensible.

The transport was overcrowded and furnished with none of the comforts of the present day. On 25th inst, we arrived at Constantinople, (now Istanbul) and encamped at Scutari (Uskudar). The state of the Turkish barracks there was filthy, but the beauty of the Bosphorus delighted me. (Bosphorus is a strait dividing Turkey at Istanbul) On May 29th the s.s. Victoria took us to Varna, and until June 4th. We were encamped at this miserable place. Then we marched to Ailhadin, in a lovely but unhealthy region. Here our Light Division, under Sir George Brown, was attacked by cholera. We lost men every day, and in my own tent two men were taken with it one night and immediately died. On July 2nd we marched to Devna, men, and even the soldiers' wives, dying on the way, for our unrelenting enemy followed us everywhere. We encamped at Monastir, and suffered much from long marches and great heat until we came back to Varna and glad of the change.

Here we embarked once more on the Victoria, when Captain Sutton and several men died on board. It was on September 14th we arrived opposite Old Fort in the Crimea, and there was great excitement in the expedition as to who would be the first to land. Our Major, Daniel Lysons, being a very active and intelligent officer, managed to do this, followed by my own company. Some Russian waggons *were captured; it poured with rain all night, and we had a wet bivouac with cold pork for our supper. The next day the French landed, lit large fires, and went foraging, while we were forbidden to touch a thing. I took a few men to get wood for a fire, but meeting Sir George Brown and his staff coming my way I dropped the faggots and fled. The cholera was still raging, and there was a little confusion from the picquets (pickets on guard) giving false alarms at night. On 19th we marched for the Alma River, and on the road had a slight skirmish with the enemy, who had hitherto kept out of our way. I was extended with my company, and some privates were hit, and I now saw men and horses lying dead before my eyes. It was my first acquaintance with the realities of war.*

*   *   *   *   *

Early on the morning of 20th. (Sept.) large columns of the enemy were to be seen in movements on the heights beyond the Alma; between us and the river were vineyards surrounded with loose stone walls. The Light Division was deployed into line, and halted for some time. Our adjutant came to my captain and asked him to let me go as one of the escorts for the colours. He replied I was wanted where I was. The adjutant returned with the colonel's commands that I be sent as directed. I went away delighted with the distinction of being with the colour party, and was appointed centre sergeant. On the line being ordered to advance, I took the usual six paces to the front as guide to the right brigade, of which the Royal Welch was the battalion of direction.

The general, however, called me back, as we were now under a heavy fire of shot and shell, and told me to take the usual place between the colours. On nearing the first vineyard, the order came to charge; we dashed over the wall and rushed through the vines, I plucking at the grapes as I went to quench my thirst, for the day was oppressively hot. We pushed through the river, which was deep in some places and took me up to my knees; here the men began to drop very fast. After crossing, Lieutenant Anstruther, carrying the Queen's colour, said to me : "The regimental colour and Lieutenant Butler are missing". I replied, "The closer we get to the enemy, sir, the safer we shall be". For we were now under severe musketry fire from the heights and, some of our officers being unfortunately close together, seven of them were just then shot dead, among them poor Sir William Young; so I further observed: "The shot drop thickly here at the bottom of the hill, but will go over our heads if we go on". We then ran up the slope until about eighty yards from the redoubt when I remarked: "If we go further the colours may be taken, for we are far ahead of the men". We halted; at that moment the poor officer was killed and I was knocked over at the same time by a bullet striking me in the breast and breaking two ribs. Private Evans came up and helped me on my legs; I then snatched up the flag, rushed to the earthwork and planted it on the parapet.

The silk standard was riddled with shot, but the redoubt itself sheltered my body. I did this to rally and encourage the men, the line being broken and the regiments mixed up in confusion, for the loss of life was great. I then heard cries giving false alarms, such as Cavalry! Look out for Cavalry! Retire!" And some bugles sounded the retreat. Colonel Chester, commanding my regiment, galloped up, shouting bravely, "No! No! No!" and casting a pained expression on me I never can forget, fell dead, shot off his horse. A crowd of men now appeared with Sir George Brown commanding the Division, and Sir William Codrington who commanded our Brigade; they both thanked me and permitted me to carry the colour until the fighting ceased, although I was now feeling very faint through the loss of blood. I then handed over my charge to Captain Bevell Granville, of my regiment, and was promoted to colour-sergeant on the spot. Lieutenant Butler who carried the regimental colour, was killed crossing the river.

After the action I wondered that the Russians, who moved about in large columns all the time, did not offer more resistance, for had they have done so we should have lost the battle.

It was a painful sight to see so many dead and to hear the poor wounded calling for help. After my wound was dressed, I slept that night on the field; I wished to remain with my regiment but the surgeon ordered me on board the transport, Columbo next day.

When there I found men without food or doctors to attend them on the upper deck, and, as they died, their bodies were thrown overboard at once. I reached Scutari Hospital on 26th and was discharged on October 20th. I again embarked for the Crimea, but caught a fever on board, was landed at the Balaclava Hospital and sent back to Scutari, where I received much kind attention from Miss Nightingale and the Sisters of Charity.

I was most anxious to rejoin my regiment, but when somewhat better was appointed acting sergeant-major to take charge of invalided British soldiers on board a Turkish man-of-war until I picked up more strength. Meanwhile in February, I received the good news I had been promoted to an ensign's commission in the Royal Welsh Fusiliers, and this was subsequently antedated to November 5th 1854.

On arriving in camp before Sevastopol I received the kindest welcome from Colonel Lysons, now in command of the regiment, and all the officers. Of my new colonel I cannot speak to highly; he did everything he could for the men.

       *   *   *   *   *

In the same month, February, promotion was then so rapid, I became a lieutenant. The weather was dreadful; cholera and other diseases pestered us, and the work in the trenches was continuous. Our troops suffered from want of clothes and food, and words can hardly describe our suffering during that winter.

The regiment being short of officers, I often went all night to the trenches, came off next morning only to go back after dark the same day, as by volunteering for the advanced works I could obtain 12 hours off duty. The Russians made frequent sorties, and I happened to be in the 'quarries' when they attempted to surprise us, and several men and officers were killed in driving them back.

On June 18th we made our first attempt to take the Redan. I volunteered with others for the storming party, but at the last moment, a newly arrived regiment – the 34th replaced us. We were all repulsed with great loss, and our colonel was wounded. No doubt, if we had assaulted at the same time as the French, who attacked the Malakoff we should have had a better chance but our allies had already been badly defeated.

That same evening, I went back to the trenches where Guards and Highlanders had been sent on duty for the first time. As they were new to the work, there was a false alarm followed by panic, during which they fired into my men holding the advanced works, wounding two of them. A guardsman charged at me in the dark with a fixed bayonet; it slightly wounded me but had I not struck it partly aside with my sword my leg would have been pierced through. Later on, we had a sharp affair when I was acting adjutant to Colonel Edgerton, 77th, in the attack on the 'pits' which bear his name where he was killed.

       *   *   *   *   *

On September 8th, we made our second attempt at the Redan; again, we allowed the French to go first at the Malakoff, and as the Russians, when driven back, immediately reinforced their comrades at the place we were to attack, our difficulties were doubled. I volunteered to command a storming party; we had to run 180 yards in the open under a terrific fire of shot, shell and musketry. I gave orders to our men not to draw a trigger until they reached the parapet, and then to use bayonet or ball as much as they pleased, but half of them fell before they got there. I arrived safely at the top of the work, cheering on the rest, when, I was shot through both legs, and, fortunately for me, fell back into the ditch. I remembered no more until I came to myself in camp some hours later, still grasping my broken sword. Seven of our officers were killed, including our gallant adjutant who was called 'Soldier Dynley' and five others wounded in this affair. Being young and strong, I escaped amputation, which at one time was thought necessary.

On 25th I was invalided home in the 'Robert Lowe'. We had a bad passage – little food, and that of inferior quality – and I did not reach Portsmouth until November 10th. I was then taken to Haslar Hospital, where I received the greatest kindness from the naval authorities, and although still very lame, I re-joined my regiment at Aldershot a year later.

The Royal Welsh were ordered to China in 1857, but owing to the Sepoy revolt landed instead at Calcutta. Here I joined them overland, having been detained to receive the Victoria Cross from the Queen in Hyde Park in June of that year. The decoration was not instituted until after the Crimean War, and it was my old Colonel, Daniel Lysons, himself the bravest of the brave, who recommended me for this honour, as well as for the Sardinia Order, the latter because I had served longer in the trenches than any other officer of the regiment.

In the Indian Mutiny I was present at the relief and capture of Lucknow, the defeat of the Gwalior contingent at Cawnpore, besides many other affairs, and escaped unscathed through the campaign, during which time I was promoted to Captain.

*   *   *   *   *

Here should end my youthful recollections, but I may add that I was one of the very few who have been fortunate enough to realise early ambitions before reaching middle age, and this was the luck of the service.

Luke O'Connor.

Now it can be realised, that the unfortunate part of this wonderful discovery, relates to the fact that whilst he has named many of his colleagues, Luke chose not to mention by name, any of his immediate family, nor the period of time when they had emigrated to America. Not even the names of his parents or any of his siblings are mentioned, which had they been so mentioned would have assisted the research conducted into the family by many years.

But who knows? Maybe this was fate because many other things have been unearthed about the family, during this research, which otherwise, may not have been discovered.

UNCLE BARTHOLOMEW GANNON

Although Luke made mention that the voyage to Canada was a 'tedious affair', he also suggests that his first recollection in life was his return to Boyle. This might suggest, therefore, that maybe he was so young, that he simply could not remember leaving Ireland in the first place, other than that 'tedious trip'. Is it possible that much of those memories on board the ship could have merged with his later, return voyage to Ireland and above all, his later visit to America to see his siblings in 1898? This was only a very short time before his story was published. He had only been back in England, four months prior to that.

We can therefore deduce that maybe Luke was either about to, or had just started his school days. He was certainly at school at some time following his return because he talks of playing at soldiers and drilling other children in the street. He says he was often being thrashed for trespassing into the barracks instead of attending school.

With the voyage suggested to have taken place circa 1839, all this tends to indicate that his memory of events, would have been very faint indeed. With him playing soldiers in the street, one might suggest that he had grown a year or two and would have been around 10 or 11 years of age, which again, places the year of his landing in Canada, to be around the suggested 1839 era. However, as always, even though this notion fits into the suggested order of events, it can only be regarded as a good hunch.

It was, indeed, his mother's brother, Bartholomew Gannon, the owner of a grocery shop and hotel in Boyle, who became Luke's guardian. This is also mentioned in Jenny Cropper's Reveille story, as is the fact that homesickness was the cause of Luke's repatriation. It must be remembered that Luke's new home in Boyle was about 20 miles away from the Hillstreet home and the friends he might have remembered. The shop and hotel where he helped his uncle, was in the centre of the town of Boyle and very close to the Barracks which housed the Roscommon Militia.

Unfortunately, an identification of the hotel in question has not been made, but below is an extract from the Directory, *'Ireland, City and Regional Directories 1847 – 1946'*. This is the 1856 edition.

Bartholomew was Luke's mother's second elder brother who was born in 1793 and in this 1856 entry below, he, or at least a Bartholomew Gannon, is shown as the owner of an Inn or Public House. This same Bartholomew is also mentioned in the Griffith's Valuation during the following year, 1857. However, both documents relate to the town of Dunmore, Galway which is over 20 miles from Boyle.

In 1856, Luke would have been 25 and two years earlier, had won his Victoria Cross in the Crimea.

The earliest available directories for Boyle are in 1847 and there are no members of the Gannon family living there then. All this tends to indicate that either the Bartholomew Gannon at Dunmore is not Luke's uncle, or it refutes his autobiographical version that he suddenly died, which was the reason for his departure to London. Unfortunately, death records have not, unearthed a date for Uncle Bartholomew's death, but the explanation given below, may throw light on the subject.

What isn't in doubt, is the fact that the hotel in question was very near to the Militia barracks in Boyle. The extract from Luke's autobiography concerning him 'drilling' his mates in the street, proves this. He was obviously a leader then and his playing at soldiers, made him proficient at drilling, which was later to earn him his first promotion.

The barracks at Boyle occupied a Georgian Mansion built in 1730 for the family of Sir John King. It is now a public building and houses the museum of the Connaught Rangers, then a regiment of the British Army. It must have been fate that brought Luke to live alongside these barracks, which later motivated his burning desire to become a soldier.

Connaught. — **DUNMORE.**

GENTRY AND CLERGY.	
Barratt John S. Esq. Balliutaba	O'Loughlin Patrick J. attorney
Bermingham John, Esq. Millbrook	Wynne Edward, clerk of petty sessions
Bermingham Mrs. Mary, Dalgan	**INNS & PUBLIC HOUSES.**
Blake Francis, Esq. Curaroe	
Blake Mr. Walter, Dunmore	Clancy John / Kelly Mary Ann, *Hotel*
Bodkin John James, Esq. Kilclooney House	Coen John
Duff Rev. Patrick, P.P. Dunmore	Collins John / King Michael
Gray Joseph B. Esq. Prospect Hse	Donnelan James / Loftus Martin
Griffith William D. Esq. J.P. Dunmore House	Dwyer Daniel / Murphy William
Handcock John S. Esq. Carentrily	Gannon Bartholomew / Quinn Patrick
Higgins James, Esq. Carrapadden Lodge	/ Reilly George
Jennings Mr. Matthew, Strawberry hill	Gilmore Bridget / Ryder Patrick / Ward Martin
Kealy Roderick J. Esq. Carokeel	**SHOPKEEPERS & TRADERS**
	Breheny John, baker
	Byrne Patrick, baker
	Clancy John, draper

There are circumstances which recently identified, which throws doubt on Luke's assertion that his move to London was due to his uncle's sudden death. Indeed, if the evidence found in the directory above is correct, then Bartholomew was far from dead. There are indications that Luke wasn't happy with Bartholomew extracting him from the grocery shop, where he had enjoyed his work, to transfer him to more menial work in the hotel. Also, he recalls that instead of following his own and his family's desire for him to become a priest, his uncle wanted him to return to Canada. That, in itself, is probably an indication of the lack of a bond between the two. Luke also spoke of receiving thrashings for truanting himself from school with his explorations into the nearby barracks.

Other accounts since handed down, make mention of him fleeing Boyle to live with another of his mother's brothers in London. The reason suggested, is that he was so unhappy about being a boot cleaner and porter at the hotel, that he ran away to London after turning on all the beer barrel taps in the cellar and flooding it with beer.

This account is constant in all others, though it must be said that the story, true or false, may well have been handed down from one to another. Whatever, there is no mention, or other evidence of his uncle's death being the reason for him taking off for London.

This alternative version also featured, not only in Jenny Croppers Reveille article, but in an article published in the Journal of the Connaught Rangers Association. No. 4. Vol. 1. January 2007, which was written by a Danny Tiernan and is reproduce below: -

> *At the tender age of 17 years, the hedge school educated Luke O'Connor left his home near Elphin, Co. Roscommon to learn the grocery trade from relatives in the town Boyle. The year was 1849 and advance education was out of the question for the young Luke. His hopes of learning the grocery trade were also dashed when Luke found himself degraded to the position of boots and porter in the hotel also owned by his relatives. The disappointed Luke took his revenge on his relatives by turning on the taps of all the barrels and absconding himself from the hotel.*

Clearly, in stating that Luke had left his home near Elphin to learn the grocery trade in Boyle, the author appears not to have known of Luke's terrible 'sojourn' to Canada, which casts doubt on the version it mentions. So, with Luke's relocation to London, to yet another of his mother's 'Gannon' brothers, this might be an appropriate time to introduce his maternal 'Gannon' relations.

The Gannon Family

Luke's mother, Margaret Catherine Gannon was the daughter of Joanne Gannon and Mary Fair. Here we immediately hit another obstacle involving the Latin and old Irish languages. Whilst Joanne is primarily, a female name, it was also the feminine name for John. We live in a different era, but why there should be a feminine name for a male child, is still difficult to understand.

Mary Fair's surname was also recorded as 'Fae' and her Christian name was sometimes Marie or Maria. From here henceforth, if it becomes necessary, they will be referred to as John and Mary.

Only four children of this union can be found and Margaret Catherine was the youngest of those. There may be more but of those found, only two baptisms match them. Here are the details of those discovered:-

1. John Gannon born c1790 (Eldest son takes father's name?)
2. Bartholomew Baptised 25th August 1793
3. Brigitta (Bridget) Baptised 15th June 1795 and
4. Margaret Catherine born c. 1795-6

It may be that John and Margaret Catherine weren't baptised, but that is unlikely or maybe the Latin and difficulty in deciphering the writing on some pages, could be the cause of the missing baptisms not being located.

So far as John, the apparent 'first born' is concerned, he is believed to be born circa 1790 and because of the known facts recited in Luke's autobiography, he has been the easiest to research. Reproduced below, is the excerpt from Luke's autobiography, relating to him.

There was a first cousin of mine, however, in London in medical practice, who had served as a military surgeon under Sir de Lacy Evans in Spain. I resolved to visit this relative, and see what he could do for me.

My cousin promised to do his best but said it would take some time. Meanwhile, having met some young fellows of my own age, we went about town and were soon attracted at Westminster by sergeants flaunting gay ribbons in their caps anxious to secure recruits. Being like most of my countrymen very fond of horses, I took the Queen's shilling for the 17th Lancers.

When I told my cousin of this the next day, he said, "I hope you'll do something better than that," and I got off by paying the "smart money" before being regularly attested.

In spite of this my wish to soldier became too strong for me, and shortly afterwards when again in Westminster I was struck by the gallant appearance of a fine looking recruiting sergeant of the Royal Welsh Fusiliers, a regiment I had never heard of before, and its title caught my fancy. I took the shilling once more, a few of my young friends followed my example and we enlisted in the same regiment. I said nothing to my cousin this time, and in a few days found myself in the barracks at Winchester, where the Royal Welsh were quartered in July 1849.

The 1849 which Luke quotes, is the first, and one of few times he has used such a clear landmark which provides us with some idea of how old he was at any given time. Being born in 1831, he would have been 18, or 17, as he sometimes suggested being born in 1832.

In this case, the 'Gannon' sibling in question would be his mother's brother, his uncle John Gannon born 1790. Therefore, the first cousin he mentions, would be John Gannon's son, John Palmer Gannon. The 2nd Christian name being taken from his Uncle's wife's maiden name, which was Sarah Ann Palmer. Her death was recorded in the third quarter of 1839, the same quarter as she gave birth to her only child, John Palmer Gannon whose birth, may have been a contributory factor in his mother's death.

So, Luke is obviously correct when he writes about this first cousin of his in London who was a surgeon. Yes, Uncle John Palmer Gannon was, indeed a surgeon. In 1861, he was a house surgeon at University

College hospital, London and in 1880, he had been a surgeon at sea being employed on the vessel Parthia. He was discharged from her when it docked in Liverpool on 20th February 1880.

BUT WAIT! This first cousin of his was born in the July quarter of 1839 so when Luke describes him as assisting him in his venture to join the Royal Welsh Fusiliers in 1849, this cousin, would have only been 10 years of age. So, there is obviously something very wrong here.

General Sir George de Lacy Evans

It was Luke's mentioning that his first cousin had served under General Sir De Lacy Evans which helps us sort out the confusion. Not only was his first cousin, John Palmer Gannon a surgeon and not only had he served at sea, but his father, John Gannon also fitted that same description. The difference here though, was that it was Luke's uncle who had served in the Royal Navy as a surgeon and who had served under General Sir de Lacy Evans in Portugal and Spain. (Not his cousin)

This General de Lacy Evans was born in 1787 at County Limerick, Ireland and was educated at the Woolwich Military Academy. He served as an MP for Rye in 1830 and for Westminster from 1833 to 1841. However, no doubt due to his military education, he longed to command a fighting force and amid seeing conflict at many places across the world, including some in America, and the Peninsula wars, as a member of the British Army, he volunteered to assist Isabelle 2nd of Spain in the first Carlist War.

Many in British high places regarded Evans and those he commanded, to be mercenaries but the British Government had formed an alliance with Spain and he had personally been sought by the Spanish, Premier, Juan Medizabal, that he should be the commander of the British Legion being sent to help his country. Evans had already expressed his commitment to the Spanish causes in Portugal and to cut a very long and interesting story short, he became very successful leader in this conflict.

He also fought in the Crimea where he commanded the 2nd Division of the British Army. Following his death in 1870, he was buried at Kensal Green Cemetery, the very same cemetery where Luke was buried some 45 years later.

And so, it was, in fact, Luke's uncle John Gannon himself, who assisted him to enrol with the Royal Welsh Fusiliers and that, was in 1849. His uncle John Gannon Snr. and his son, John Palmer Gannon were aged 59 and 10 years respectively. Luke would have been just 17 or 18.

As an aside, Luke's uncle must have led an interesting and dangerous life himself under General Sir George De Lacy Evans. Fever and dysentery swept through his troops in Spain. At one time, out of approximately 7,000 men quartered in or near Vitoria, 4,706 were admitted to hospital, 819 died and 787 remained incapacitated when they began their departure from Vitoria. It would have been much worse if Evans hadn't organised a large corps of doctors and surgeons who fought extremely hard to combat the sickness encountered.

No-one was to know that Luke was also to face the same type of enemy (Disease) that was experienced by his uncle. It was to be, that both had survived, against very short odds of survival against the sword, the shot and the diseases they faced.

LUKE'S EARLY MILITARY CAREER

Luke's early, but short-lived recruitment into the 17th Lancers came about through him and his pals venturing into Westminster where they were lured into the regiment by a keen recruiting sergeant. He states that it was a short time following this that he was, once again, similarly lured into the Royal Welsh, after his uncle had bought him out of the Lancers before he was attested.

It has become very apparent, that his immediate family had apparently fallen into what appears to have been the severe poverty of those times. However, his aristocratic, ancient family's antecedence and the mention of his uncle Bartholomew's shop and hotel, and now coupled with the knowledge of another uncle and a cousin who were surgeons, there can be no doubt that opinions will have been formed, that he may well have been regarded as having been born with a 'silver spoon' in his, or at least, his ancestor's mouths.

In his memoirs, he mentions that his spare money was spent on purchasing better quality bread and treating his soldier colleagues to beer and other 'goodies'. One can imagine that he quickly became the best mate of the whole regiment and indeed, as he says, he was being treated very kindly by his Sergeant Kneightly.

However, he was still having to do the 'business' on the drill square and no doubt, due to his earlier experiences, this attribute quickly surfaced and came to notice of his superiors. It was because of his skill that he gained his first promotion to Lance-Corporal. As he says, he became a sergeant only two years after joining the Army.

His drilling skills were quickly utilised in training recruits in the Militia and he was first sent to Welshpool to drill the Montgomeryshire Militia. Here, luck was on his side because having been raised in Roscommon, he fell into the lap of the militia's commanding officer, Sir John Conway, who by chance, also came from Roscommon. Luke hints at his luck by saying that he was treated very kindly by him. He also says that he was similarly treated by Sir John's other officers. Of course, he was! Which one of them was going to upset his commanding officer by treating his 'Roscommon Pet', Luke, with anything but kindness and undoubtedly, with kid gloves?

He returned to his Chester base with an excellent report for the information of his own commanding officer, Colonel Torrens. Surely, this amounts to 'being in the right place, at the right time'. It may also be recalled that Luke mentioned Colonel Torrens in his autobiography. He specifically mentioned how Torrens looked after the young soldiers in this quote.....

"I may add that he was a great admirer of the tactics used in Crawford's celebrated Light Division during the Peninsula War, and, although very severe, seemed devoted to his profession, and loved to encourage young soldiers".

The encouragement of young soldiers was also exactly what inspired Luke, who was often remembered for this attribute himself. This will be mentioned many times, later in his story.

Luke's success at Welshpool was quickly followed by similar successes at both Anglesey and the 3rd Lancashire's at Liverpool where he drilled further militia units. Now being the star sergeant drill instructor of the Welsh Fusiliers, he later paid a return trip to Boyle in his Sergeant's uniform. Of course, he was going to show off those three stripes. One can imagine how his acquaintances and old mates with whom he used to play soldiers, were amazed, and perhaps proud, at his rapid rise to fame. They were later to remember him in a very significant way. More on this later.

Having re-joined his regiment on the Isle of Wight, he became attached to No. 6 Company and following a further drilling of yet another militia, they became based at Chobham, Surrey. This was a newly formed camp under the overall command of Lord Raglan where numerous soldiers were trained in military manoeuvres which were to become extremely beneficial in the upcoming Crimean War. Luke says that his company were utilised by playing the enemy and that he became so interested in what he was doing that *"at moments, I imagined that we were in earnest"*.

The 1851 census of England was the first English census in which Luke can be found. The whole regiment were currently based at the Plymouth Citadel, the fort built to protect Plymouth during the Dutch Wars of 1664-67. Lieutenant Colonel Arthur Wellesley Torrens was still the commanding officer at this garrison.

This census was taken only a few months after the Reserve Battalion had suffered a tragic loss in the deaths of its assistant surgeon, three sergeants, two corporals, nineteen privates and eight wives who were all drowned in one of the Great Lakes of North America, Lake Erie. when their steamship, 'Commerce', was involved in a collision with another vessel.

It is interesting that Luke has recorded his birth at Boyle, Roscommon, and not at Elphin, where he was born. This was possibly due to him being so young as having no memories of his early life at the cottage they had left behind at 'Kilcroy' Hillstreet. It is entirely understandable, that his later memories of being with his uncle at Boyle, had superseded them.

Now fully trained in war time manoeuvres, the British Army were becoming confident that their resources would be required in the Crimea. The Russians had threatened to crush the power of the

Turks, and to take possession of Constantinople. (Now Istanbul) This was the cause of the declaration of war by England and France against Russia. The Royal Welsh moved to Portsmouth and as Luke puts it, *"There was much excitement about the impending war with Russians"*.

THE CRIMEAN WAR – 5th October 1853 – 30th March 1856

The Crimean War had started on 5th October 1853, long before British involvement. However, although parliament had long been concerned about Russia's encroachment into the countries bordering on the Black Sea, whilst nerves were jangling both in Britain and in France, members of parliament were at odds to decide what exactly to do about the situation.

Coincidentally, it was the hitherto mentioned, MP Sir George De Lacy Evans, Luke's uncle John Gannon's commander, who fervently roused parliament into eventually deciding that we should declare war. There were still many dissenters to this course of action, ironically including Lord Raglan, Luke's commanding officer at Chobham, who was to become the British Commander in Chief in the Crimea.

Also, in opposition, was General Sir John Burgoyne who, coincidentally was to become Lord Raglan's chief engineer. He referred to the invasion as a desperate undertaking and in doing so, rightly quoted the Cholera epidemic and the lack of land transport as major critical disadvantages. They had no proper plan of campaign for a war in the Crimea and none of its future leaders believed in it. Not a good starting point!

Three of the eventual five Divisional Commanders, General Sir George Brown, Sir George Cathcart and HRH the Duke of Cambridge, were against the invasion for the same reasons. That would mean that exactly half of the highest ranked in the eventual command team, were all against the idea. With that level of resistance, what sort of inspiration were they going to provide for their troops?

Sevastopol, on the Crimean Peninsula was already a Russian port, the home of the Tsar's Black Sea Fleet. The port, which had been strengthened by Russia over many years, was an ideal launching pad for its fleet to threaten the Mediterranean. This was, therefore, a strategic port and as such, crushing the fleet and pushing the Russians out of Sevastopol, became the principal objective which led to the declaration of war.

Much has been written about the alliance between the British / French / Turkish and Sardinian countries to fight the Russian Imperial Army, but the conclusions drawn, were that as much as Russia needed to have her wings clipped to stop her further incursion south, this was an unwanted alliance which, at the outset, caught both parties in a state of really not knowing what to do!

Turkey and Sardinia formed final members of the alliance when war was eventually declared on March 27th, 1854. It having already commenced a year past, saw British and French fears heighten when Russian troops began expanding into the Danube region (Rumania).

There hadn't been a war fought by the British since the Battle of Goojerat in 1849 (the 2nd Sikh War) and so, not a great deal of confidence or experience could be placed in the Crimean War Commander, Lord Raglan, who, as stated above, wasn't at all excited about the prospect of war, in the first place.

The principal commanders

LORD RAGLAN   PRINCE MENSHIKOV   JACQUES L. de SAINT--ARNAUD

Lord Raglan

Lord Raglan (Fitzroy James Henry Somerset) was viewed in many of the higher circles as a one-armed old soldier without much experience in the field, let alone a commander of troops in operation.

Educated at Westminster School, he quickly rose through the ranks but much of his service was in a secretarial position. He served in the Peninsula wars, as the aide-de-camp to Sir Arthur Wellesley, (Duke of Wellington) who saw him as a loyal servant and once said of him that, "he wouldn't tell a lie to save his life".

In 1852, Raglan became Master-General of the Ordnance. He was appointed as a Privy Councillor and was elevated to the peerage as Baron Raglan of Raglan, Monmouthshire, on 12 October 1852.

Prince Menshikov

The Russian Commander in Chief, Prince Alexander Sergeyevich Menshikov was a year older than Raglan, and like him, had little experience in the field of battle.

Starting his career in 1809, he rose through the ranks becoming a major general in 1816. He was sent to the Crimea at the outset to ensure that the Russian government be recognised as the protector of the Ottoman Empire's Orthodox subjects. This led to a breakdown of negotiations with Turkey and the beginning of the Crimean War. He had hugely underestimated his enemy and in one briefing, referred to their enemy as "sailors dressed into military uniform". He changed his tune following their defeat. The British infantry, he said, "fought like red devils". He also referred to the bear-skinned Brigade of Guards as "fighting like hairy devils". Also, no one had warned him about the Highlanders, being "soldiers in petticoats".

Jacques Leroy de Saint-Arnaud

At 56 years of age, Jacques Leroy de Saint-Arnaud, was the youngest commander in the war.

He had a chequered military career and domestic life which once saw him banished as a Captain in the French Foreign Legion. He later rose to become the Marshal of France and served as French Minister for War until the Crimean War when he became Commander-in-Chief.

Saint Arnaud fought through the war with stomach cancer, from which he died on board a ship just over a week after the Battle of the Alma had been won.

The British Divisions

The British Army was divided into four divisions. Already referred to was the 2nd Division with Lieutenant-General Sir de Lacy Evans, the same commander who had commanded Luke's uncle, Dr John Gannon, at the first Carlist War.

Luke carried his uncle's sword into the battle of the Alma, this same sword which had been carried into battle by his uncle. Ironically, Sir De Lacy Evans was to command at both.

The other Divisions were led by The Duke of Cambridge (1st Division), Lieutenant-General Sir Richard England, (3rd Division) and the 4th Division led by Major-General Sir George Cathcart.

Luke's 23rd Welsh Fusiliers were within this 4th Division so, with all respect to the other 3 Divisions, this story will be centred more so, on Luke's 4th Division which, purely for the record, comprised the following:

One field battery of Royal Artillery.

Seventh Brigade under **Brigadier-General Torrens**
20th Regiment, 21st Royal Scots Fusiliers and the 68th Regiment

Eighth Brigade: 46th Regiment and the 57th Regiment, which did not land until after the battle.

Light Division: **Lieutenant-General Sir George Brown**
Royal Horse Artillery, one field battery of Royal Artillery plus the 2nd battalion of the Rifle Brigade.

First Brigade (known as the Fusilier Brigade): **Major-General Codrington**
7th Royal Fusiliers, **23rd Royal Welsh Fusiliers (Luke's own)** 33rd Regiment.

Second Brigade: **Major-General Buller**
19th Regiment, 77th Regiment and the 88th Regiment

Luke's 4th Division

In command of the 4th Division was **The Honourable Sir George Cathcart.**, the youngest of the four Divisional Commanders. He surfaced little during the Crimean war. When only 15, his father purchased his first promotion for him in the Lifeguards. By a succession of purchases and exchanges, he became a lieutenant-colonel in the 7th Hussars in 1826. He was described by many as 'an unfortunate choice'.

Sir George Brown was, perhaps, the most unpopular infantry officer in the Army, and was hated by his subordinates and superiors alike. He was often referred to by his young officers as "He blusters and bullies everybody" and "he dares and damns and swears at everything an inch high". Also, "An old imbecile bully".

He was a traditionalist, for example, he was a firm believer in the leather stock that soldiers still wore, constricting their throats like a garrotter, and flogging. He vehemently rejected the necessity of all suggestions about Army reforms, so much so, that it was as a protest against some minor administrative reforms which led him to retire. However, he was known to be a brave and resolute soldier, and he was given command of the Light Division, though many believed that he should have been appointed Lord Raglan's second in command.

Sir George was wounded at the Battle of Inkerman but recovered, and eventually, was given tactical control of the failed, first attack on the Redan fortress at Sebastopol. At the end of June 1855, he was invalided home. Despite Brown's harsh discipline and strict adherence to dress regulations leaving him deeply unpopular, it was Sir George who gave his support for Luke's nomination for his Victoria Cross.

Brigadier General Sir Arthur Wellesley Torrens had been a career colonial administrator. Educated at Sandhurst and commissioned as an ensign in the Grenadier Guards, he was appointed brigade major at Quebec on the staff of Major-general Sir James Macdonell. He commanded a brigade in Canada and on his return to England in 1840, he was promoted to lieutenant-colonel.

Torrens transferred to the 23rd Royal Welsh and obtained its command on 15 October 1841. He again saw service in Canada. He took command of the first battalion, from Quebec to the West Indies. For two and a half years, he commanded the troops in St Lucia and administered the civil government of the island. Although offered, he declined the appointment of the lieutenant-governorship of Saint Lucia. The battalion returned to England in September 1848, and he was stationed at Winchester, which was where Luke was first stationed in the July of 1849.

Brigadier General, Torrens commanded the infantry brigade. He joined them at Varna and in addition to being the head of his brigade at Alma, led them at the Battles of Balaklava and Inkermann where, following the receipt of a serious bullet wound, he was invalided home. He died in August 1855.

General Sir William John Codrington

Codrington first entered the Army as an ensign in the Coldstream Guards in 1821. He had risen to colonel by 1846 but had never seen active service. Promoted to major general in June 1854, he was requested by Lord Raglan to take command of the 1st Brigade of the Light Division, which had become vacant owing to the promotion of Brigadier General Airey.

With no experience of conflict, his very first battle was at Alma. Some reports suggested that on crossing the river and seeing that his men were in danger of being slaughtered by the Russian guns, he boldly charged towards them. They escaped fairly unscathed and his bravery in this battle showed that he deserved his command.

As a Liberal Party candidate, he contested Westminster in 1874, and Lewes in 1880. He died in his 80th year on 6th August 1884.

General Sir George Buller was the third son of General Frederick William Buller of Cornwall. The first twenty-five years of his career in the army were spent in a time of peace, and his marriage with Henrietta, daughter of General Sir John Macdonald, Adjutant General is said to have helped his rapid promotion. He became a lieutenant-colonel in August 1835; and colonel in November 1841.

Sir George saw much action in South Africa and in 1847, he was honoured with a CB and then served under Sir Harry Smith in the war against Pretorius. He eventually succeeded Somerset in the command of his division in August 1852.

His conduct at the Battle of the Alma was criticised at the time, but was approved by military writers when reflecting on his actions, after the war had ended. Being severely wounded at the Battle of Inkerman and promoted to Major General in December 1854, he was returned home in March 1855 and knighted in the same year.

ONWARDS TO THE CRIMEA

So, having sketched over the causes of the war, and its main participants, prior to homing in on Luke's involvement, it will be beneficial to look at the backcloth; in particular, the geography of the area and its significance to Russia and Europe.

It should also be recognised that a landing was not possible until mid-October and so it would be essential to get it all over with before winter took its grip. It was a long voyage with the alliance carrying little or no land transport or other equipment. Food and water would be scarce.

The map below, is a closeup view of the Bosphorus, also known as 'The Strait of Istanbul'. It not only divides the continents of Asia and Europe, but also divides Turkey, including the city of Istanbul itself.

Its location emphasises the international significance of this world's narrowest strait because it connects the Black Sea with the Sea of Marmara and, by extension via the Dardanelles, the Aegean and on to the Mediterranean Sea.

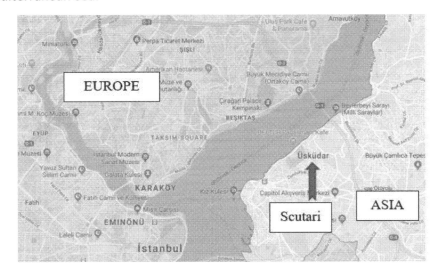

The city of Istanbul was, of course, at that time, named Constantinople. Its location is at the bottom left of centre of the map. Luke's camp at Scutari (now called Uskudar) was in that part of the city located on the Asian side.

The 2nd map below, is of a smaller scale, providing a wider view. It demonstrates the significance of the Bosphorus Strait, providing access to the Black Sea and the Crimean Peninsula. It also shows the locations of the Russian and Alliance Fleets at Sevastopol and Varna respectively.

Luke's regiment had moved from Plymouth, to Portsmouth, and on 4th April 1854, they sailed from Southampton, for Turkey on board RMS Trent. This was a Royal Mail paddle steamer weighing 1,856 gross tons and could carry 60 passengers. She had been serving the transatlantic passenger route until she was requisitioned by the British Government as a troopship on the outbreak of the war. She returned to her former civilian service after the conclusion of the war, in 1856.

RMS Trent was just one ship of a huge fleet of vessels which were ultimately to be joined by the French fleet on their way to Turkey. The British / French alliance comprised 54,000 Infantry and 1,000 Cavalry which were added to by 7,000 Turkish Infantry. This must have been a huge logistical exercise, especially at embarkation and disembarkation times.

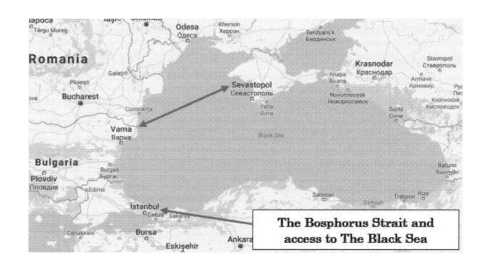

The Bosphorus Strait and access to The Black Sea

It had taken them just over 3 weeks to reach Constantinople. (Istanbul) In his autobiography, Luke describes how the vessel was overcrowded and without any of the present-day comforts. He had probably forgotten the dreadful conditions he and his family had endured during their passage to Canada when he was a small child.

With no recent wars being fought, this was the first time that he and most of the young soldiers with him, would be setting foot in anger on foreign soil. They were to camp at Scutari, Turkish barracks which, although Luke described them as 'filthy', their condition, he says, was compensated by the magnificent sights of the Bosphorus.

They remained there for almost a month until, on 29th May 1854, when they boarded the S.S. Victoria which took them to another place described by Luke as *'This Miserable Place'*. This was 'Varna', on the Black Sea, Bulgaria, where the Anglo-French alliance based its headquarters and became the principal port for its fleet. His description of Varna had probably resulted from the cholera which caused more deaths than those lost through enemy actions.

Even prior to their first battle, the Royal Welsh lost an officer and 36 other ranks to that dreadful disease. Luke recounted that his company lost men every day, and that a man died in his own tent overnight. His survival must surely have been represented by one of those proverbial cat's 'nine lives' that he had been blessed with.

In 2011, a monument to British cholera victims was opened at Devnya near Varna. It was erected near to the mass grave where the unlucky ones were interred. In addition to the cholera, the men had to suffer inadequate amounts of food and what they received, was of atrocious quality.

The quality of the food was later described in a book, *'The Crimean War from First to Last'* written by Major, Daniel Lysons, who was to become Luke's close friend in later years. He wrote: - *'the food is very bad and insufficient. A lump of bad beef without any fat, boiled in water, and a bit of sour bread is not sufficient to keep men in good condition. We can get no vegetables whatever, and the people here, will not sell anything'.*

Following several marches during which soldiers and their wives were dying of cholera, Luke and his disheartened colleagues returned to their Varna camp.

The Disembarkation

It was those long marches, the cholera deaths, and the great heat, which had turned Varna, into being by comparison, quite a pleasant place. Soon however, they were to once again, embark the vessel, 'Victoria' where several men, including their Captain Sutton, died on board.

Luke arrived in the Crimea on September 14th. when he describes what he saw as his first realities of war. The Bosphorus and then the Black Sea, must have been full of British and French vessels, not to speak of the Russian Fleet operating from the port at Sevastopol.

The Russians were now in occupation of the Crimea. They had been there for the past 70 years and, in effect, were on their 'home turf'. The troops of the alliance, were very much aware that they were on enemy soil. It had been such a long time since the Russian's had annexed the Crimea and so, to most of the local population, the landing of the Alliance's troops appeared to them as being an invasion. They were too few to be hostile to such a large incursion, but they weren't going to be friendly or helpful either.

There are many facets of the disembarkation worthy of comment. It hadn't been too long after the Napoleonic Wars and the French / British relationship hadn't been particularly friendly for some considerable time. Indeed, they hotly disputed the fact that the British were first to land at Kalamita

Bay, about 13 miles south of Eupretoria. (Sometimes referred to as 'Old Fort') What wasn't so widely reported, was the fact that almost 1,000 alliance troops were immediately re-embarked and taken back to Varna as they had contracted cholera during their passage to the peninsula. Could this situation be any worse?

The sheer number of vessels carrying so many troops and equipment, meant that their landing continued for many days and in appalling weather. Thankfully, although they were aware that the Russians were watching their every move, they didn't interfere at all. That must have presented an ideal time to attack and it is wondered why they didn't.

This situation resulted in a beachhead of troops, stretching inland, for about 4 miles. However, being the first to disembark, wasn't the wisest choice. It rained hard and continuously overnight and the troops, who had landed without tents or shelter of any sort, were drenched to the skin.

Waiting for the British

The disembarkation of the armies had taken so long that it was thought impractical to commence the march south until 5 days after the first troops landed. Heaven knows what would have happened if the Russians had attacked them during that operation. Here again there was discord between the English and the French who allegedly, were ready days before the English.

Luke asserted in his memoires, *"The next day the French landed, lit large fires, and went foraging, while we were forbidden to touch a thing"*. This is an indication that the French would have taken longer to disembark? However, the French allege the opposite and blamed the British for taking their time. Many letters written home by the French mention this aspect The following, written by the French Commander, Saint-Arnaud to his wife, expresses his frustration at the apparent lack of urgency displayed by the British.

> **17th September 1854**
>
> *"Two notes very quick, my sweet love. The English are not ready, they keep me here, I'm furious. Their disembarkation will finish this evening, mine is finished since yesterday evening. Tomorrow, I will march on the Bulganeck, and on the 19th hopefully beat the Russians; I will push forward as quickly as possible……."*

It was not just Saint-Arnaud who was frustrated by the slowness of the British.

Lieutenant Cullet acidly remarked: -

"The 16th, 17th and 18th of September were passed in a state of inactivity. It was not difficult for us to see that the English were the cause of the delay. This might be disastrous as it allowed the enemy time to strengthen his position."

Finally, an exasperated Saint-Arnaud wrote to Lord Raglan on 18th September informing him that he had waited long enough and that he would be marching early in the morning.

The march to Sevastopol finally began the following morning but Lord Raglan kept him waiting from 6 am until 9 am. Saint-Arnaud joked to his personal physician, "Either these allies or this campaign will kill me". (*Recalling he was suffering with cancer*)

It was also a fact that compared to the French equipment and sustenance supplies off loaded, the British commissariat had short-changed its Army in not only equipment and transport, but also in supplies of food. Although the British undoubtedly made sorties inland to take what they could find from the locals, orders had been given that they should refrain from foraging and plundering. However, the French who had brought more sustenance of all types, looted as much as they possibly could with the blessing of their officers. Unlike the French, the British had landed with only a few essentials rolled into their greatcoats. In so far as nourishment was concerned, their kegs contained only 3 pints of water and in addition, each was given one pound of pork, 10 biscuits, tea, and sugar. Many of the letters sent by the French made mention of the British visiting their camps to beg what food they could. If true, this couldn't have been good for the alliance's welfare and morale.

The March South to the Alma

The alliance set off on the 19th, September. Transport was scarce and although horses were brought, the French were better equipped with load carrying carts. It was blistering hot and during the march, two or three Russian guns opened fire. Cossacks were seen hovering in the distance and they were charged by The Earl of Cardigan's men. They retreated till the British cavalry were sucked into the range of Russian fire. This led to four dragoons being killed and six wounded, the first who fell at this battle.

The Alliance's troops spread along a four mile line from the sea. The French, Turks and Sardinians were nearest the sea, facing the highest ground. The British, being the furthermost inland, were on the other, eastern end, of the flank, roughly in line with the lower inclines and the valley through which, the road to Sevastopol ran. The River Alma with its small bridge at the village of Burliuk needed to be crossed on route to Sevastopol. The last of the three photographs below, provides an indication of how the one bank of the river, rises far steeper than the other.

The 19th September closed with more rain and the armies camped on the banks of the narrow river Bulganak, the first of the rivers needing to be crossed. The French had encountered some Russian sharpshooters earlier and exchanges of fire were made. However, it had been an uncomfortable march on a very hot day with little or no water.

The mouth of the River Alma and the high ground south of it
faced the French, Turkish and Sardinian troops ahead of them
on the western flank of the alliance's line.

A more 'inland' view of the heights facing the Alliance's right flank.
They were occupied by two Battalions of the Russian forces.

Showing how the slope from the Alma rises so steeply on the Russian side of it.

The troops were exhausted and so it was decided to spend the night rested, which would also facilitate an opportunity for the Generals in command, to meet and come up with a final plan of attack to ensure their crossing of the River Alma, i/n order to reach their intended destination of Sevastopol. This River Bulganak was a welcomed sight to exhausted and thirsty men, some of whom were dying for the want of a drop of water. The River Alma would be, the next river to be crossed during the very next day.

Sevastopol was about 40 miles to the south of Kalamita Bay, (quickly nicknamed 'Calamity Bay') where they had disembarked. The below map provides a useful scale and thus an appreciation where the rivers flow to the west coast from the higher mountains.

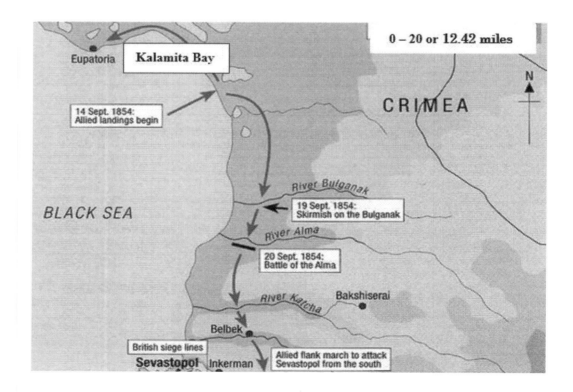

They rose in the morning with the River Alma and the heights beyond, were now only a matter of 4 or 5 miles away and they could guarantee that the route to Sevastopol would be heavily defended. Although they now outnumbered their enemy, it was they, who had to march to meet and attack their foe, who would have already made their defences from superior positions on the heights which overlooked the bridge, which would have been the most ideal method of crossing the river. As the Alliance drew closer, the Alma and the hills beyond it, could be plainly seen.

The Russians were confident that their enemy would not breach the natural defences nearer to the sea because of the sheer 350 feet high, steep gradient which extended from the sea, inland for about 2-3 miles. The route to take for Sevastopol, therefore, would be further inland where the slopes were not so steep until it met a difficult steep hill, known as 'Telegraph Hill'. This was so named because a telegraph station had been in the process of being erected on top of it. It also marked the extreme left flank of the French army, where it met the right flank of the British, where Luke was positioned.

The Alliance was located on the north side of the river they needed to cross. Some small villages including Burliuk (*sometimes Bourliuk*) situated near to the bridge and the vineyards also lay on the British side of it. Unbeknown to the Alliance forces, the houses and buildings of the villages had been stuffed with straw so that at the appropriate tactical time, they could be set alight so that dense smoke would blind the advancing troops. This was, indeed, to happen when they were about a mile from the high ground.

And so, not only was the alliance going to have the vineyards, their walls and the river to cross, they had the fires and smoke to contend with. The rough sketch below, indicates the geography of the area and the location of the participant armies which were to go into battle.

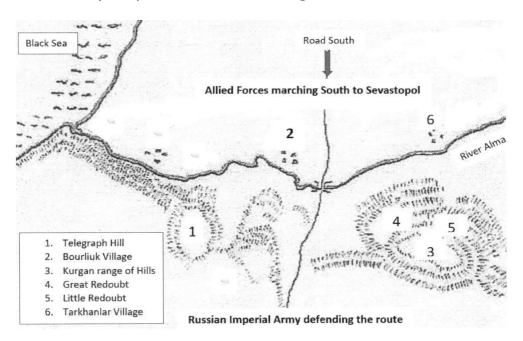

Black Sea

Road South

Allied Forces marching South to Sevastopol

River Alma

2

6

1

4

5

3

1. Telegraph Hill
2. Bourliuk Village
3. Kurgan range of Hills
4. Great Redoubt
5. Little Redoubt
6. Tarkhanlar Village

Russian Imperial Army defending the route

On approach to the Alma, the alliance forces first bivouacked on the northern side of it, where the ground sloped gently down to the river. Running along the Russian, southern bank of the river, were those higher steeper hills, as described earlier. They had tapered down as they stretched from the coast, to the narrow bridge over the Alma, located near to the village of Burliuk.

The road and bridge lay in a valley between these hills and to the east of the road, was Kurgan Hill, (*sometimes Kourgane Hill*) a natural strongpoint with fields of fire covering most approaches. Two redoubts (fortifications) had been constructed to protect Kurgan Hill from infantry assault; the 'Lesser' or 'little' Redoubt on the eastern slope and the Greater Redoubt on the west. (*See sketch plan above at numbers 4 and 5*)

The bridge and the road to Sevastopol ran between the 'Telegraph' and 'Kurgan' Hills, and was covered by a massive 33 battalions of Russian infantry plus a large force of cavalry. Some earthworks on these hills had been constructed for protection. On both sides of the road and 600 yards from the river, was a battery of 16 guns. (*In the Great Redoubt*) In addition, 12 guns had been positioned on a spur of the Kurgan on the east side. (*Little Redoubt*) These could fire down onto the river at a range of 400 yards and across the road to about 800 yards.

It wasn't that the river was tremendously wide or deep, but the small bridge was insufficient for this huge body of men and their equipment, to cross at speed. Also, the banks on the Russian side were far steeper as is portrayed above, in this photograph by Colonel Klembovsky. In any event, the bridge lay in a valley between two of the overlooking higher mounds. The Russians would have known that this would be the natural crossing point for their enemy to take. It would obviously be heavily defended.

In a short space of time, the 20th September, was to witness a bloody 'human slaughter' in which many men from all participating countries were never to see another night fall. As many were 'virgin' soldiers, one wonders what they had on their minds. Was it those that they had left at home? Was it their lives to be saved or simply, that they must, at all costs, defeat their enemy? I guess that all three occupied many minds but 'fear' would surely have been among them.

So, it had been just over 23 weeks since Luke and his regiment had left Southampton bound for Istanbul. He had not shot a round nor faced the enemy until now. They had trained for such situations but training and the killing of the enemy in training situations must have seemed miles apart from the reality they now faced.

As mentioned earlier, Luke had been given a fine sword by his guardian, Dr. John Gannon. It was an 1822 officers' pattern with a brass scabbard as shown below.

The author is indebted to Dr Kevin Mason of the Royal Welsh Fusiliers Museum, Caernarfon for supplying this photograph and for allowing it to be handled when he made a visit to the museum. Luke was to carry this sword into this battle and he would have been so proud to do so. Varying accounts have been written about what exactly happened on 20th September 1854. Luke's modesty is suspected to be a factor in the absence of much description, though maybe it was editorial pressure, that could have been the cause of him reducing his own account to only 673 words.

Unlike the Russians, who had as much time as they needed to prepare for the attack, the Allied armies had just arrived with all of the problems concerning the weather and the lack of resources as described, not to mention what was in front of them. Their foes' advantage was terrifying and every one of them, being raw to the catastrophe that battles of war, might bring, would surely have wished they were elsewhere.

It was eventually discovered that the Russians had done very little on the hills to physically reinforce their defences. They had relied more on their advantaged positions and the natural geographical defences of them. It was as if they were so confident of success that the high ground and their heavy guns pointing towards the enemy and their troops armed with muskets and grape shot, would be sufficient to repel any attack. However, it would be impossible to negotiate the valley whilst the Russians held them and the two redoubts on them. There is little doubt they needed to be taken.

It appears that they hadn't taken into consideration, the strong will of the alliance's troops, to overpower their enemy, come hell or high water, even whilst many of them, suffered with dysentery and cholera and weren't at all, 'battle hardened'.

What with their poor physical condition, the lack of food and fresh water, the rain and the heat, a victory would be no mean feat. Whilst skirmishes with the enemy were experienced en route, it was at the River Alma that the Russians decided to stand their ground and put a halt to their enemy's march to Sevastopol. With all the above taken into consideration, the Imperial Russian Army should have started as firm favourites for victory, but it was a goal they weren't to achieve.

In his memoire, Luke comments that they were able to see the enemy on the high ground early in the morning and that he had been unaware until then, that he would be selected as 'Centre Sergeant' of the colour party which would become the 'Battalion of Direction'. It seems remarkable that these decisions weren't made much earlier.

This is an appropriate time to explain the significance of these regimental colours. What are they and why was it so important to carry and protect them in the fields of battle?

THE REGIMENTAL COLOURS

Luke's appointment to form part of the colour party, came to him as something of a surprise, not only to Luke himself, but also to his captain, who at first, declined the adjutant's direction on the matter, insisting that he was required where he was. One thing is for sure, and that is, there would be no point in appointing troops to the colour party unless they were courageous because being of such a significant importance, the colour party would obviously attract the early attention of the enemy's marksmen.

It wasn't until the adjutant returned with a directive from the colonel insisting that Luke should be released to the colour party, that he was, indeed, so released. That, in itself, is surely an indication that his senior officers had already identified him with leadership ability. In his autobiography, he expresses being delighted by the order of events. On joining the colour party, he was to discover that it was a Lieutenant Joseph Henry Butler who would be carrying the Regimental Colour and a Lieutenant Harry Anstruther who had been carrying the Queen's colour.

The role Luke was to play as the centre sergeant, was to be positioned between these two, colour bearing lieutenants. His description indicates that at first, he positioned himself at the regulation six paces in front of them, until he was directed to fall back to the colours as they approached within firing distance of the enemy. How proud must he have been, as guardian of those colours.

It would be disastrous to have the colours captured by the enemy or otherwise lost and that the bravery and direction of the bearers, should act as an example to the following troops. Simply put, any colour party should comprise of those who were '**born to lead**'. The 'colours' were the symbol of any regiment.

ALMA

REGIMENTAL COLOURS.

THE ROYAL WELSH FUSILIERS. 1ST Battalion.

Two examples of the Royal Welch's colours with Welsh spelt in both traditional and modern ways.

New Regimental Colours are presented from time to time, normally by the monarchy, when the need arises or following victorious battles.

As at The Alma, they would be carried together with the Union Flag of the United Kingdom. (The Union Jack)

The regimental colours carried at Alma were peppered with holes from gun shot and although they were present at Farm Street Church on the occasion of the 50th Anniversary of Luke's death, and although they have been sought by many since then, it appears that their present location is unknown.

ORGANISATION AND STRUCTURE OF THE BATTLE

Whilst concentrating on Luke and his regiment's role in the Crimea, in order to capture the correct path of events, it is sometimes necessary to describe the roles and activities of the other units comprising the alliance, in order to gain a broader picture of how the events unfolded. This applies to the commencement of the battle and involves the French army in line to the right of the British, and therefore, closer to the sea.

Whilst all of the generals met during the previous evening, it is remarkable, that apparently, no firm plan was conceived. The French had been keen to attack on that day, but Raglan wanted to wait and see what transpired. He would guarantee nothing other than to cover the French's left inland flank which was abutting his extreme right flank.

At about 11 am the allied armies advanced, the whole front covered by a chain of light infantry. French troops with some Sardinians and Turks were on the extreme right, nearest the sea with the British to their left. The steeper faces of the higher ground running from the sea inland meant that the French were to encounter the more difficult terrain.

However, so far as the numbers of defending Russians were concerned, there were far less of them in front of this right flank because the majority of them were concentrated on the lower ground around the area of the river bridge, which lay more in the path of the British.

The crests of the hills ran for about six miles inland from the sea and for the first mile or so, Prince Menshikov had considered that the cliffs were so steep a gradient, that he need only protect them with a token force.

It was the French who started to advance first but due to mistakes made by staff, the British moved much later, but were then halted by the constant fire from Russian canons. Doubtless due to the terrain and Russian fire power, the French were finding it difficult to proceed and constantly called for Raglan on their left, to engage the Russian right flank which would take the pressure off them. Raglan was reluctant to do this until around 3 pm when he ordered the Light Division, in company with the 2nd Division to advance in line with the other 1st and 3rd Divisions in support.

Luke's 4th Division under the command of Sir George Cathcart and the Light Cavalry were to provide protection for the flank. As can be seen by the plan below, apart from the cavalry which were on the extreme left flank, they were positioned much as a reserve, but being to the rear of the Highland Brigade, they were immediately in front of the two redoubts on Kurgan Hill, whilst providing cover to their colleagues on their right.

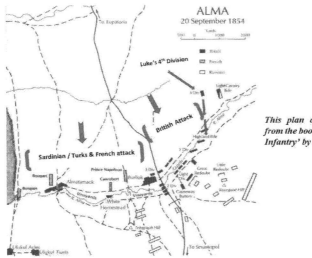

This plan of attack reproduced from the book 'That Astonishing Infantry' by Michael Glover

According to Luke's memoirs, it would have been around this time, before the advance, that he was appointed as the centre sergeant with the colour party.

The two forward divisions (*2nd and Light Divisions*) had deployed all their six Battalions in a single 'two-deep' line and one battalion of the Rifles Brigade were deployed to screen the whole front. This drew much criticism as no one had ever before seen 12 battalions deployed in that way. Luke and the colour party were now on the march but had not reached the vineyards. At that point, he had taken the regulation 6 paces ahead of the colours but on reaching the Russian's heavy fire General Cathcart called him back.

No doubt the bridge was used by some of the allied forces to cross the river, but with so many men and equipment needed for a rapid attack, it was obvious that most would need to wade across. It was also obvious that Prince Menshikov would have heavily defended that route on the plain and on the gentler slopes overlooking the road. A lower ridge of hills ran across the amphitheatre, and at various points, batteries of field-artillery were posted, commanding the river and its approaches.

Numerous Russian riflemen were scattered among the gardens of the villages and in the vineyards spread along the banks. The Russian right was protected by large bodies of cavalry, which constantly threatened the British left, though held in check by the cavalry under Lord Lucan. On the Black sea, to the right of the Alliance where, as close in shore as they could get, was a fleet of steamers throwing shot and shell onto the heights occupied by the Russians.

Many accounts relate to the French being the first to actually attack this heavily defended Russian line on the south side of the river. That fact is not in dispute, however, whether this was part of a tactical plan to draw Russian troops away from the heavily defended area in front of the British line, to bolster up their weaker defence of the higher ground now under attack by the French, is in dispute.

Such a tactical plan could well have been operated, because it was bound to do just that, i.e. draw at least some of the Russians away from the area where it was most likely that the Alliance would cross the Alma.

The French troops which advanced earlier than the British, nearly succeeded because they had taken the enemy totally by surprise. However, having realised their predicament, they brought forward vast masses of troops against them and forced them back. It cannot be denied, that this French's decision to attack early, may have been an accident, or done through sheer frustration, having to wait for a decision to be made as to what to do next, especially in the light of their earlier patience being tested when they had been waiting for the British to disembark.

We should remind ourselves that at this time, Luke, as a very junior soldier, had not been part of the meeting held by the generals during the previous evening. His position might have meant, therefore, that he was unaware of the earlier French attack of the high ground.

These possibilities are mentioned because such a plan is discussed in Anthony Dawson's book, 'The Siege of Sevastopol 1854 – 1855'. He describes the meeting as including all commanders, not only of both French and British armies but including Admiral Hamelin, the Admiral of the French Fleet which was to shadow the approach of the troops on shore, and to provide a mobile artillery reserve.

Marshal Saint-Arnaud wrote in his journal: -

> *The fleet should protect.......the right; General Bosquet (* 2nd Division*) will attack the enemy to turn his flank, who is far from expecting a surprise such as this. The three other Divisions will attack the centre. Whilst the English, on the extreme left, will make a flanking movement to turn the enemy and converge, to fully envelope the enemy, who will be engaged in the centre on a cross-fire.......the arc of the circle which is to be executed by the*

English is very long but so too is that of the Division of Bosquet.....the Cavalry will be provided by the English.

General Francois Canrobert, the Commander of the French 1st Division wrote: -

The plan of the battle for the following day was well conceived. Relying on our superiority of numbers, we would profit from this and turn the enemy.

General Bosquet's 2nd Division along with the Turkish Division, were to cross the Alma by the sea, scale the cliffs which dominate the river and debouche onto the plateau attacking and putting into disorder, the Russian left flank. At the same time Bosquet arrives on the heights, Prince Napoleon's 3rd Division and the rest of the army will cross the river and attack at the front. The Marshall proposed to Lord Raglan that the English would make the same movement but by inversion. Bosquet's Division was to leave camp at 5 am and the others at 7 am. No one objected to this plan.

Dawson's book includes other quotes which generally agree that the planned frontal attack of the French and English should commence at 7 am other than General Bosquet's 2nd Division with the Turks, who would have commenced at 5 am to scale the cliff heights close to the sea.

Whatever had been agreed, Raglan did not order his army to commence the attack with the French so early. Having received repeated requests, he kept responding by saying that his troops were not yet ready.

A Colonel Trochu later wrote a furious letter to the state newspaper, 'Le Moniteur', concerning the fact that he repeatedly sent staff riders to British lines to enquire why they were not moving. In a fit of pique, at 7 am he rode over to Lord Raglan who told him that they would not be ready to move for a further two hours.

Of course, the French fleet were not told of this delay, nor were the advancing French Divisions who had started their central attack. An attempt was made to halt the troops and the fleet but it was too late. This was the first indication that the plan had intended Luke's 4th Division and the Cavalry, to turn the Russians by marching around their right flank and attacking them from the rear. A successful attack by Bosquet on the cliffs nearer the sea, would have had the Russians torn apart, especially due to their belief that no such attack would be made via the highest and steepest of the cliffs.

However, if the accounts provided by the French were only half true, it appears that Lord Raglan had scuppered them and he would now take the Russian position 'head on', attacking the batteries and redoubts that Saint-Arnaud had been eager to avoid tackling in front. This was due to the urgency of the situation and was now unavoidable as the French troops were being severely massacred.

The book 'That Astonishing Infantry' by Michael Glover and Jonathan Rile does not, of course, dwell on this start of the battle for long or in much depth. Nor does it make mention of the 'plan of action' meeting held during the previous evening. They do, however, state……..

"the French started to advance at an early hour, the British, largely due to bad staff work, moving forward much later to the last ridge before the Alma where they halted under damaging canon fire. Meanwhile the French were finding progress difficult and repeatedly called on the British to support them by engaging the Russian right. This Raglan was unwilling to do until 3 pm when he decided to seize the hills to his front and sent orders for the 2nd and Light Divisions to advance in line with the 3rd and 1st in support, flank protection being provided by 4th Division and Light Cavalry.

The two leading British divisions comprising the Light and the 2nd Division, aligned themselves with the French columns in lines of only two deep. As hinted above, they had been ordered to wait and lie down, presenting as small a target as possible, until any further developments ensued with the initial French attack. Lord Raglan's lack of action was severely criticized during 'post war' revues.

The Russian riflemen now opened fire, and the village burst into flames, no doubt caused by their heavy guns and the enemy soldiers among the villages who were there to set fire to the straw in the houses.

Descriptions of the men clambering over stone walls and negotiating the mass of grape vines prior to wading the river, are constant. Many grapes were thankfully plucked as they passed, for they had little food or fresh, non-disease bearing water. A huge number of the casualties were killed or injured as they tried to negotiate the cultivated vineyards and wade the river.

Such obstacles were naturally to be expected, but the major impediment of all, was the Russians who were there before them and had taken the high ground many of them, within their redoubts. Their guns were aiming below them, they were most definitely, in the best commanding position and for all intents and purposes, without knowing the end result, one would have imagined that the alliance would be totally wiped out.

It would have been about this juncture, when Lord Raglan and his immediate staff, crossed the river towards the end of his right flank and where it met up with the French Tirailleurs (*Recruited from the French colonies*) to take up a position on the very top of Telegraph Hill, miraculously without any hindrance from the enemy. Amazingly, this was at a position, actually behind many of the enemy.

Some reports describe Lord Raglan advancing fearlessly, others describe this action as 'foolhardy'. How he was to efficiently command his army from a distance, is unknown though reports indicate that he was required to send riders to gallop back to the troops with the commands he had set. The consequences seem unthinkable.

On the positive side, however, in double quick time, his men managed to haul two nine pounder guns to the top of that hill and it was from there, that they later managed to hit an ammunition wagon in the causeway battery. The huge explosion undoubtedly caused the surviving enemy to withdraw from the redoubt. They were now under the belief that they were being overpowered by a superior army. This allowed the 2nd Division to continue their advance with the guns on the hill continuing to blitz the Great Redoubt with a similar result.

From what we now know, Luke would have been at the head of the advancing party and Lord Raglan would have been some distance away, on the hill overlooking the action. All this, I suspect to be part of what became a confusing scenario. Luke describes the situation as thus: -

> *On nearing the first vineyard, the order came to charge; we dashed over the wall and rushed through the vines, I plucking at the grapes as I went to quench my thirst, for the day was oppressively hot. We pushed through the river, which was deep in some places and took me up to my knees; here the men began to drop very fast. After crossing, Lieutenant Anstruther, carrying the Queen's colour, said to me: "The regimental colour and Lieutenant Butler are missing". I replied, "The closer we get to the enemy, sir, the safer we shall be".*

Sadly, most accounts of this charge, ordered by Raglan, hint that the situation grew into chaos, a 'shambles' and a 'free for all. All these descriptions have been quoted, which never did get to bring their actions into anything like an effective and efficient fighting force, at the time when it was most needed. Sadly, this occurred at a time when many of the commanding officers had been killed, which was probably the most poignant cause of the so called shambolic actions of the fighting forces.

The accounts recorded following the battle, also hint at an element of surprise that the Russians didn't put up such a strong defence as might have been expected. They suffered fewer losses and appeared to retreat quickly, presumably in order to assist in what was perceived as the weak defences of Sevastopol.

However, returning to that scenario, we know that many of the alliance fighting forces were killed during the crossing of the River Alma. We know that whilst the guns ordered up by Raglan had a great effect, those on foot were being picked off and peppered with musket fire and grape shot. Some accounts record, that had it not been for Raglan's disappearance, casualties might well have been reduced with a more efficient means of communication and overall leadership.

In comparison with previous wars, this battle had been witnessed by an improved media machine. However, no photographs or other evidence is available now, which might give credence or otherwise, to that which has been previously described as a 'shamble' of organisation. It would only be those survivors who could have painted a clearer, honest picture of what actually occurred at the time.

However, the cruel vision still remains of a 65-year-old Commander in Chief, with short sightedness, being hard of hearing and with one arm, sitting on his horse some distance away, attempting to direct the advance of his forward approaching armies and their regiments. He had also, not played the 'team game' by ignoring the plan involving a march around the Russian's right flank to turn them into a 'crossfire situation'. The spontaneous frontal attack had worked, but at what cost? One presumes that he commanded an excellent view of the battle but whether or not he could effectively communicate with his officers, is open to question.

Some commentators were supportive in their comments, possibly because of the outcome, however, others were not so gracious in their criticism. The following is, but one example: -

'There was no standard battle drill, each regiment's conduct depending on the individual approach of the commanding officer. Some regiments felt it necessary to form line and advance methodically, while others rushed up to the Great Battery as quickly as they could, without forming up after crossing the Alma River.

There seems to have been little control at brigade or divisional level. There was no co-ordination between infantry and artillery, the guns being left to come up and open fire, as and where their officers thought best.

Due to his curious expedition behind the Russian lines, the commander in chief, Lord Raglan, lost control of his army. Hamley makes the comment: "It was fortunate in the circumstances, that the divisional commanders had so plain a task before them." It is apparent that, however plain their tasks may have been, it was necessary for some control to be exercised.

The mention of regiments rushing up to the great battery as opposed to forming up after crossing the river, may well have applied to Luke and his colour party, because that is where the colours should have been.

It is clear that this confusion reigned prior to the Russians fleeing, but what isn't clear in research, was where Lord Raglan was towards the end of the battle. Surely, he wouldn't have remained at his distant vantage point when the 'business of the day' was coming to an end? The colours of direction would have been nowhere near him. What did help him, however, was that he only had to make one command, though, as previously stated, there were instances when he apparently, sent orders via horsemen attached to his party.

Luke mentions that Sir George Brown was now in command of the 4th Division as opposed to him previously only commanding the Light Brigade. The Division now consisted of 2 Brigades, Sir William Codrington was commanding Luke's Light Brigade, consisting of the 7th, 23rd and 33rd Fusiliers. The 95th and the Rifles, were also another part of the Light Division. The other Brigade was commanded by Brigadier General Buller with the 19th, 77th and 88th. Perhaps they were unaware at this time, that it would be themselves who would lead the attack of the great redoubt and would face the most of what the Russians were to throw at them.

The unattributed painting below, is what is suspected to depict Lord Raglan on the high ground of Telegraph Hill overlooking proceedings from slightly behind the enemy lines. Regimental colours can be seen being carried but they are unlikely to have been the Royal Welsh's, because Luke was with them at the head of the main frontal attack.

It is now that we can place Luke somewhere near to the head of the advancing forces. The two leading divisions advanced towards the enemy, General Codrington's brigade leading straight for the Russian entrenched battery. We know that General Codrington was Luke's commander and thus placing him, with the colours, at the head. It was also Codrington's earlier order that Luke should pull back from his regulation six paces ahead of the colours. So, it may have been, that the 23rd's regimental colours were the order of direction of General Codrington's Brigade and not, with the Commander in Chief as may have been suggested.

The light division, Luke included, under Sir George Brown, became somewhat tangled up with the vineyards, walls and inequalities of the rough ground. Those who had negotiated the vineyards and the river were fortunate to be alive but facing them now, was a steep slope up to 12 feet high and then an unsheltered plain of up to 800 yards from the base of the redoubts.

The situation was worsened for the fusiliers because on their right flank was the 2nd Division who had come under severe fire from the Causeway Battery and on their left flank, the brigade of the Light Division, having crossed the river with slight loss, were stopped from advancing by Brigadier Buller who was convinced that they were threatened by the enemy's cavalry. This made him call in his narrow, two lines to form a traditional square.

Could this unknown painting be depicting Lord Ragland's position on the high ground?

The first sketch plan, shows more clearly, the order of battle. It should assist in picturing the overall spread of the fighting forces. However, when viewing the next sketch plan, it must be remembered that it is displayed in the reverse direction with The Black Sea, now on the right, with the allied forces attacking towards the South. However, finally, Codrington bit the bullet and shouted, "Fix bayonets, get up the bank and attack!"

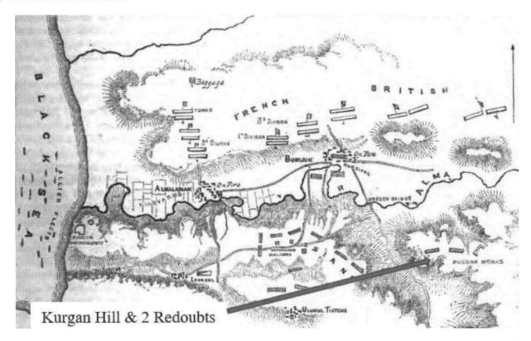

Kurgan Hill & 2 Redoubts

What a responsibility that was. He must have known that in ordering that command, he would have been sending many, if not all of his men, including himself, to their deaths, or was this for Queen and country? Such are the responsibilities of those who declare war and those who are commanded to carry out the actions deemed necessary to win them, or at least, to fight them.

THE ATTACK

They sprang from their limited cover, firing as they rushed towards their foe. General Codrington's Light Brigade comprising Luke's 23rd with the 33rd Regiments, and 7th Fusiliers, with the 19th on their left and the 95th on their right, were now in direct line, and in full view of the great Russian battery. General Codrington was mounted and to the head of the advancing soldiers.

In his memoire, Luke mentions the confusion which ensued. It must be remembered that many of the commanding officers had been killed and Lord Raglan was assumedly, sitting on his mount at an observation point, some distance away. He recounts that the standard was riddled with shot but as he had intimated to Lieutenant Anstruther, getting to the base of the hill would actually provide shelter from the overhead shots.

Regiments became mixed up and the lack of 'on the ground' command, must have contributed to the loss of life. Without their leaders, the men themselves, were shouting commands which generated even more confusion. Luke says that he heard cries such as "Look out for Cavalry", Some bugles were also sounding the retreat. This caused Colonel Chester, who was at that time, commanding the regiment, to gallop up in an attempt to stop the retreat. He was shouting, "No! No! No! At that very moment, Luke describes how, in an instant, he saw him fall dead, being shot off his horse.

It is very difficult to adequately describe the mayhem that must have occurred. Bodies and fresh blood would have been scattered all along the lines of attack. And yet, more blood was to flow as 'hand to hand' conflict was bound to follow. But this would only be, if they survived to get that far. Although adrenalin would have filled their veins, these young boys must have been terrified and perhaps they only continued as a means of self-preservation, but only if their enemy were defeated by them taking the lives of those in front of them who were trying to do likewise.

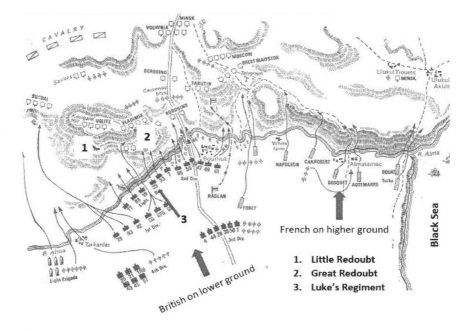

French on higher ground

British on lower ground

1. **Little Redoubt**
2. **Great Redoubt**
3. **Luke's Regiment**

By now, the 19th (Green Howards) had ignored Buller's command to form square, and so they came up to the 23rd's left flank. In all the confusion, it is sometimes difficult to place the activities described from various sources, into any sequential order. It is now, perhaps fitting, to revert to Luke's own account in that having the responsibility for the safety of the colours, he alleges that he suggested to Anstruther, *"The closer we get to the enemy, sir, the safer we shall be".*

It must have been close to that time, that Luke, together with Lieutenant Anstruther, paused a while and discussed their situation. His memoirs reflect that he suggested to Anstruther that if they stayed where they were, the colours could be taken because they had forged further ahead than the rest of the men. This confirms the suggestion that troops were very much working on their own initiative. It also confirms that despite any fears they possessed, they had found themselves leading from the front, even though, ideally, they were too far away from those they were leading.

It was then that among others, Luke describes the shooting dead of his officer, Sir William Young. The below is an account of his death, discovered in The Essex Standard of 3rd November 1854, and surprisingly, in a newspaper from Sydney Australia.

Because of poor reproduction qualities, the end of the letter, which was only printed in the Australian newspaper, has been transcribed above, beneath the newspaper clipping. As can be seen, it identifies the author of the letter as Sir William's brother.

This account is included because it may be remembered that in Luke's autobiography, he mentioned Sir William Young when he described the boarding of the vessel, the S.S. Trent at Southampton Docks on departing for the Crimea. That small section is repeated here, as a reminder: -

> *"On April 4th (1854) we embarked at Southampton on the S.S. Trent for Turkey. I saw sad scenes on leaving, especially the parting of Sir William Young, of ours, from his young, newly married wife. The poor lady was so overcome, she was carried off the ship insensible".*

So, one can well imagine how his new wife, would have received the terrible news of his death from his brother whose account provides far more detail than contained in Luke's memoire. In particular, in suggesting that a column of the enemy was mistaken for being part of the Alliance's troops, it confirms the many accounts of the chaos involved, and in this instance, the loss of many lives because of it. Seven other soldiers surrounding Sir William, were killed at the same time.

DEATH OF SIR WILLIAM YOUNG, AT ALMA.—The following account of the death of Sir William Young, Bart., of the 23rd Fusiliers (nephew of the Rev. H. T. Young, Vicar of Munden), written by his brother, differs from the accounts before published, and confirms the statement of the *Morning Chronicle's* correspondent, that the fearful slaughter of the 23rd was occasioned by a mistake of a column of the enemy for our allies :—" Thank God, he died most nobly, while trying to rally his men in front of a Russian battery. The 23rd were awfully cut up, having eight officers killed and five wounded in the space of about five minutes. The Light Division went up and succeeded in driving back the troops opposed to them, especially the 23rd, who behaved most gallantly. After they had driven back their adversaries a large column of the Imperial Guards came down on their right flank, whom they mistook for the French. It was a fatal error, for when the 23rd ceased firing the Russians poured in such a terrible fire that the men turned and retreated. The officers sprang to the front, to bring them on once more, and were instantly shot down. The colonel (Chester), two captains, and five subalterns (among them poor William) were killed on the spot. I saw ——— to-day, who brought me William's shoulder-belt, sash, &c., &c.; his sword was smashed to pieces by the shot, and he told me that William was the first who fell. When I saw him he was hit in five places—one bullet in his mouth, a second in his neck, and a third in his right breast; a fourth was right through the left hand, and the fifth through the left leg, below the knee. When the regiment retreated he spoke to Captain Bell, and said, " It is all up with me," and when they came up again a minute afterwards he was perfectly dead. It is a comfort to know that he did not suffer any pain. We buried to-day the nine officers of the 23rd in one grave; the chaplain of the light division read the service over the grave, and it was a great consolation to be able to hear the words of St. Paul, ' Not to sorrow as men without hope;' and again, ' To trust in a sure and certain hope of a joyful resurrection.' Nevertheless, when standing by the grave, I could not but wish to God that he had taken me instead of William; still, ' not my will, but Thine be done.' "

I put his cloak over him, which some of the others had not, and at any rate he died a true soldier's death and met a fitting grave. If it be God's will that I should survive this turn, I trust to live to erect a stone over their common grave someday. I cut off two locks of hair from my brother before he was buried – one for myself and one for some of you: but no more tears until I make my mark on these same Imperial guards, which I trust to do before this reaches you. I have got his pistol as he loaded it, and that is not fired until we storm Sebastopol. Today for revenge – tomorrow for mourning.

Sir William Young was the last of five baronets named William Young and sadly, his younger brother, the author of the above letter was killed during the siege of Sevastopol. How sad was that? It seems that he, personally, was never to avenge his brother's death. No doubt his colleagues put that right.

The question was discussed, 'should they carry on or should they retreat a little to rejoin their men'? There would have been no time for debate, this would have taken a split second and Luke says that he reasoned that to carry on, might cause them to be sheltered from enemy fire because the shots would go over their heads. Currently, they were about 80 yards from the base of the redoubt.

It is this period, of which Luke's and the many other descriptions of it, are slightly at variance. Fundamentally, the variations concern the fact that whilst Luke suggests that they were about 80 yards from the redoubt, there are others which suggest that when Anstruther was shot dead, he had already planted the butt of the colour in the base of the redoubt. Also, Luke makes no mention of other soldiers picking up the colour before he took charge of it and ran to the redoubt and planted it himself. As being the guard of the colour and, as a Sergeant outranking any other who may have retrieved it, it would have been the natural course of action for him to have claimed it off others.

However, at that very moment, Luke took a shot in the chest which broke two ribs. (*Other descriptions indicate it was a shoulder injury*). The force of the impact also dropped him to the ground. Harry Anstruther fell with the colour now draped across his body. If others had retrieved it before Luke, the focus of opinion was that it was a Private William Evans who handed it to a Corporal. Some accounts suggest that this was Corporal Luby, others suggest a Corporal Southey or Soulbey.

Whoever it was, Luke's version was that he was helped to his feet, whereupon, and no doubt in furtherance of his theory that he would be safer closer to the base of the redoubt, he snatched the Queen's colour and amid a shower of bullets, he made a dash for the base of the hill which gave shelter to both redoubts.

Unbeknown to him at that time, Lieutenant Butler, who had been carrying the Regimental colours, had been one of the first of those killed whilst crossing the river. Thankfully, the original colour being carried by Lieutenant Butler, among many other of the Regiment's colours, is on display at the Royal Welsh Fusiliers Museum.

Luke continues, that he planted the colour on the redoubt whilst encouraging the men behind him to continue their attack as depicted in the painting below.

Whilst reading this, it may well be perceived that in rushing to the base of the hill, he was, as described by himself, only preserving his own life by seeking the shelter from the bullets above. However, the commanders and men who were left alive, principally Sir George Brown of the Light Division and General Codrington, had actually seen what Luke had done, and how he did what he could, to encourage the men behind him to continue their attack and in defiance of the enemy's fire.

The General and Sir George were under no doubt that his actions were not only valiant, but his encouragement had urged on the troops behind him; such actions which played a major part in the taking of the two redoubts. They were in no doubt and he was promoted to colour sergeant on the spot.

In the book, 'The Regimental Records of the R.W.F. Vol. II' by Cary and McCance, the following unattributed quote is recorded : -

> *'Where all behaved so well, it would be difficult to mention the name of any one man as more gallant than another. The conduct of Sergeant Luke O'Connor, Corporal Luby and Corporal Chadwick, however, was conspicuous.'*

Amid all this, the battle roared on and the whole British line to the left of the French, now opened a continuous fire. The enemy were seen to be turning. Our artillery were marching forwards on their left flank and Codrington's brigade were streaming up the centre, firing as they rushed up the slope.

The original of the painting below, by Louis William Desanges (1822 -1905), the famous painter of Victoria Cross winners, is lodged in archives of the Royal Welsh Fusiliers. The author is also proud to display a copy of it in his home.

Having studied many accounts of this battle in action, what happened next was more than remarkable. The Russians had suffered far less casualties than the Alliance's forces. They had commanded the high ground and their batteries made fearful havoc in the British and French lines leaving a wide street of dead and wounded from the river upwards. Though many of our troops fell, the enemy could no longer maintain their ground, but fled as a rabble. They had killed many, but had been outnumbered. The battle hadn't hardly lasted for half a day.

Luke's colleagues of the centre regiments, breathless, decimated, and broken, dashed over the intrenchment and into the great battery in time to capture two guns. It has been said that the enemy's fear of their guns being captured, may well have contributed to the reason why the Russians fled so soon. More on that, a little later.

One other reason for the victory, lies in the Russian's doubt that their left flank next to the sea, would be too difficult to attack and hence, why just a token defence of it was provided. The following is an extract of an account by Captain Henri Brincourt a 31-year-old Company Commander of the 3rd Regiment of the Zouaves. (*Mainly regiments of French North Africans*) : -

> **The action began at 5 am. The newspapers will undoubtedly tell you what happens, I can only speak for my Division, and even my regiment. Our mission seemed most difficult. We had to cross the river near its mouth and climb the steepest slope. We crossed the river at 10 minutes past 12. Naturally, the Zouaves were in the lead. Climbing up like cats the steepest heights, they were scattered at first, but were soon on the plateau. The few hundred Russian infantrymen were so surprised at the speed of the Zouaves arrival in the ravine, they discharged their weapons and ran away in disorder.**

> **The action began at 5 am. The newspapers will undoubtedly tell you what happens, I can only speak for my Division, and even my regiment. Our mission seemed most difficult. We had to cross the river near its mouth and climb the steepest slope. We crossed the river at 10 minutes past 12. Naturally, the Zouaves were in the lead. Climbing up like cats the steepest heights, they were scattered at first, but were soon on the plateau. The few hundred Russian infantrymen were so surprised at the speed of the Zouaves arrival in the ravine, they discharged their weapons and ran away in disorder.**

The Russian Infantrymen were soon supported by three Russian artillery battalions rushing to their aid with heavy weapons, but their move from whence they came, quite obviously weakened that area. This was exactly what had been planned; maybe fate was on their side in its encouragement for the British weren't ready to advance with their French colleagues, as planned.

At one time, the enemy's reserves, seeing how depleted they were, and in such a shamble, with many of their officers killed, made a last ditch fight and it seemed for a while, that until the alliance's units received the support of the three regiments of Guards, victory might not have been gained. This would have been when fierce 'hand to hand' fighting would be required. From the accounts previously included, concerning Sir George's disposition, he does not appear to be a man who would describe such actions as heroic and fearless, should that not be true.

Sergeant Luke O'Connor's VC action at the Battle of the Alma

Luke had been urged to relinquish the Queen's Colour, which by now, had been peppered with 42 shots (*anything from 22 to 76 holes have been quoted*) and to retire to the rear so that his wounds could be treated. He refused to relinquish the colour until the victory had been won and only then, did he retreat when he felt faint due to his loss of blood. Not only was he praised at the time by Sir George Brown and General Codrington on the field, but he was immediately promised a commission.

As if to confirm their presence at the head of the battle, it was soon conformed that the 23rd suffered the most casualties of all. It has been written that:

> **"In this fight the Royal Welsh Fusiliers especially distinguished themselves by their heroic valour and no less than 211 officers and men, upwards of a quarter of their number, were killed or wounded during the battle. (8 officers and 44 men killed. 5 officers and 154 men wounded)**

Luke states that both officers rode up to him and thanked him and although they demanded that he retired to the rear to have his wounds attended, they reluctantly agreed to his request that he continue to carry the colour until the fighting ceased.

With Luke eventually retired to the rear, it became necessary for a Captain Bevell Granville to be promoted to colour-sergeant on the spot and it was he, who carried the Queen's colour from then on. The regimental colours were initially retrieved and carried by Colonel Chester following Lieutenant Butler's death. However, he too, was later shot. It was Captain Edward William Derrington Bell who finally held them at the victory. Luke specifically mentions how amazed he was, that the Russian's didn't offer more resistance, since had they done so, he felt that the Alliance may have lost that battle.

It appears that the Russians, having realised that they had failed to stop the Alliance from proceeding onwards to Sebastopol, may have decided to suddenly withdraw their armaments to protect Sevastopol, rather than failing to defend their River Alma positions, without that option. The capture of a team of horses with a canon attached, may well have contributed to the reason why they 'threw in the towel' so early.

Following many of his senior officers being killed, Captain Edward William Derrington Bell took over command of the 23rd when they recovered from the scene of the battle. It was his gallant actions which led to the capture of the team of horses pulling a canon in retreat. However, before that, and having read many different accounts of Luke's actions, one of the most explicit of them, was written by Alexander William Kinglake and had been included in 'Kinglake's History of the Crimean War'. Whereas most newspapers appear to be mere duplications of others, Kinglake's version is said to have been commissioned by Lord Raglan's widow who, following his death in 1856, gave him her husband's papers to write the complete history of the Crimean War. This seems to have taken almost the rest of his life and involved his interviewing and corresponding with many of the participants.

The papers are now under restricted access at Cambridge University Library but this 'Alma Battle' section was reproduced on the 10th July 1896 within the 'South Wales Daily Post' newspaper. Unfortunately, the English is far from modern and in parts, almost illegible. It has therefore been transcribed below and only obvious mistakes such as spelling errors and line duplication etc. have been adjusted. Sentences which might not make sense, have been left untouched for the reader to unravel.

The only adverse comment which seems very apparent is that it would have undoubtedly upset the Welsh because on every occasion when describing the soldiers, he calls them 'the English'! It is fairly long, but it provides a vivid description of what these soldiers went through.

How the welsh fusiliers won the great redoubt at alma-

The column descending from the eastern flank of the redoubt marched against that part of our line which was formed by Lawrence's Rifles, by the 19th Regiment, and by the 23rd Royal Welsh Fusiliers. Already this right- hand Kazan column had advanced some way down the slope before any great number of the English had clambered up to the top of the bank and our soldiers, it would seem, at that time might have been forced back into the channel of the river by a continued and resolute advance of the descending force, but when, one by one in knots and groups, our men gained the top of the bank, when they saw the ground above spreading smooth and open before them, and the huge grey square-built mass gliding down to where they were, then, happily for England and for where the measure the common weal seems to rest - it came to be seen that now, after near forty years of peace, our soldiers were still gifted with the priceless quality which hinders them from feeling, in the way that foreigners feel it, the weight of a column of infantry.

In their English way, half sportive, half surly, our young soldiers seemed to measure their task and then—many of them still holding betwixt their teeth the tempting clusters of grapes they had gathered in the vineyards below—they began shooting easy shots into the big, solid mass of infantry which was solemnly marching against them. The column besides at this time was moving under a fire directed against its right flank by some of Norcott's Riflemen (then ensconced some way off in a farmstead) and yet. as seen by our people, it did not appear unsteady. It was perhaps an over drilled body of men unskilfully or weakly handled. At all events, the mass failed to make its weight and strength tell against clusters of English lads who stood facing it merrily, and teasing it with rifle- balls. The column before long was ordered or suffered to yield and, because falling, back in a hollow, it lapsed nearly or quite out of sight. Then, having thus ridded themselves of the infantry force in their front, Colonel Lawrence's Riflemen, and the 19th Regiment, and the Royal Welsh began, as they advanced, to bend towards their right, and thenceforth became a part of the force we shall presently see engaged in the storming of the Great Redoubt.

And now, whilst the assailing force was rent from front to rear with grape and canister poured down from the heavy guns above, another and a not less deadly arm was brought to bear against it; for the enemy marched a body of infantry into the rear of the breast - work and his helmeted soldiers, kneeling behind the parapet at the intervals between the, embrasures, watched, ready with their muskets on the earthworks, till they thought our people were near enough, and then fired into the crowd. Moreover, the troops on either flank of the redoubt began to fire obliquely into the assailing mass. Then, for such of our men who were new to war, it became time to learn that the ear is a false guide in the computation of passing shot; and that amid notes sounding like a torrent of balls, the greater part of even a crowded force may remain unhurt. The storm of rifle and musket balls, grape and canister, came in blasts, and although there were pauses, yet whilst a blast was sweeping through, it seemed to any young soldier, guided by the sound of the rushing missiles, that nowhere betwixt them, however closely he might draw his limbs, could there be room for him to stand unscathed. But no man shrank. Our soldiers, still panting with the violence of their labour in crossing the river and scaling the bank, scarcely fired a shot, and they did not speak; but they, every one, went forward. The truth is. that the weak-hearted men had been left behind in the gardens and buildings, of the village; the dross was below, and the force on the hillside was pure metal. Our men were so intent on their purpose that not one of them, it is said, at this time was seen to cast a look towards the ground whence support might be coming. The assailants were nearing the breastwork when, after a lull of a few moments, its ordnance all thundered at once, or at least so nearly at the last moment that the pathway of their blast was a broad one, and there were many who fell, but the onset of our soldiers was becoming a rush. Codrington, riding in front of the men, gaily cheered them on, and all who were not struck down by shot pressed on towards the long bank of smoke which lay dimly enfolding the redoubt. But already—though none of the soldiers engaged then knew who wrought the spell—a bar stress had been put upon the enemy. For a while, indeed, the white bank of smoke, lit through here and there with the slender flashes of musketry, stood fast in the front of the parapet, and still all but shrouded the helmets and the glittering bayonets within, but it grew more thin; it began to rise and, rising, it disclosed a grave change in the counsels of the Russian Generals. Some Englishmen—or many, perhaps, at the same moment—looking keen through the smoke, saw teams of artillery horses moving, and there was a sound of ordnance wheels. Our panting soldiers broke from their silence. 'By all that is holy, he is limbering up'! He is carrying off his guns'! Stole away! Stole away! Stole away! The glacis of the Great Redoubt had come to sound more joyous than the covert's side in England.

The embrasures were empty, and in the rear of the work, long artillery teams—eight-horse and ten-horse teams were rapidly dragging off the guns.

Then a small child-like youth ran forward before the throng, carrying a colour. This was young Anstruther. He carried the Queen's colours of the Royal Welsh. Fresh from the games of English school life, he ran fast; for heading all who strove to keep up with him, he gained the redoubt, and dug the butt end of the flagstaff into the parapet, and there for a moment he stood, holding it tight, and taking breath. Then he was shot dead, but his small hands, still grasping the flagstaff, drew it down along with him, and the crimson silk lay covering the boy with its folds. His successor in charge of the colour, namely, centre Sergeant Luke O'Connor, was brought down at nearly that moment by a shot which struck his breast; but William Evans. a swift-footed soldier, ran forward, and caught up the fallen standard, when O'Connor (finding strength enough to be able to rise) made haste to assert his right, and then proudly upholding the colour, he laid claim to the Great Redoubt on behalf of the Royal Welsh. The colour floating high into the air, and seen by our people far and near, kindled in them a raging love for the ground where it stood. Breathless men found speed. General Codrington, still in the front uncovered, saluting the crisis waved his cap for a sign to his people, and then riding straight at one of the embracers, kept his grey Arab into the breastwork. There were some eager and fast footed soldiers who sprung the parapet nearly at the same moment. More followed. Fire opening then on our people from a battery higher up the hillside, both Lawrence and his adjutant Ross were unhorsed by a blast of grape shot, but the ground that received Lawrence falling was indeed, the very goal he had sought, for he rolled at the foot of the breastwork. At each flank of the work, no less than among its whole front, agile men were now fast bounding in.

The enemy's still lingering skirmishers began to fall back and descended—some of them slowly—into the dip where their battalions were. The bulk of our soldiery were up, and they flooded in over the parapet, hurrahing, jumping over, hurrahing - a joyful English crowd.

The cheer had not yet died away on the hillside, when from the enemy's battalions standing massed in the hollow there rose up, as though it had been wrung from the very hearts of brave men defeated, a long, sorrowful, wailing sound. This was the bitter and wholesome grief of valiant, soldiers not content to yield. For men who so grieve there is hope. The redoubt had been seized by our people; it was not yet lost to the Czar.

At the sight of the brass howitzer which was found in the work, a characteristic desire to assert the claims of private or corporate ownership began to seize upon the crowd and more than one man— so they say—scratched his mark upon the piece that he might make it the peculiar trophy of himself or his regiment. But there was a better prize within the reach of a nimble soldier for the guns moving off towards the rear there was one which, dragged by only three horses, had scarcely yet gained the rear of the redoubt. Captain Bell, of the Royal Welsh, ran up, overtook it. and, pointing his cap less pistol at the head of the driver, ordered him, or rather signed to him, to stop instantly and dismount. The driver sprang from his saddle and fled. Bell seized the bridle of the near horse, and he had already turned the gun round, when Sir George Brown riding up angry, and ordering him to go to his company. He of course obeyed, yet not until he had effectually started the horses in the right direction, for they drew the gun down the hill, and the capture became complete.

Of the men who had moved forward from the top of the river's bank, many now lay upon the hillside dead or wounded, and the Royal Fusiliers, with fragments of other regiments, were still engaged with the enemy's infantry but the greater portion of five battalions were now upon the ground which the enemy had made his stronghold.

Thus the assaulting force had carried the great field work which guarded the key of the enemy's position on the Alma; and if at this time the supporting division had been halfway up the hill, or even if it had been beginning to crown the banks of the river on the Russian side, the toils and perils of the day would perhaps, have been over. But our men were only a crowd; and they all of them, wise and simple, now began to learn in the great school of action that the most brilliant achievement by disordered mass of soldiers requires the speedy support of formed troops.

Then—and then, as it said, for the first time —the men cast back a look towards the quarter from which they might hope to see supports advancing; but when they carried their eyes down the slopes strewn thick with the wounded and the dead, they saw that, from the ground where they stood down home to the top of the river's bank, there were no succours coming.

As can be seen below, it was just after Luke's death that an unattributed account of Luke's valour appeared in the Montreal Gazette published on 27th February 1815. It will be noticed from the content, that the author, either directly or third hand, would have had access to the papers that Lady Raglan had given to Kinglake because the clipping mentions that a note within them, contained a punctilio (*order of process*) concerning the matter.

This appears to infer that the colours should have been handed along the line, to the most senior ranked soldier present and with Luke being a Sergeant in the colour party, he would have been the one to pass them to.

Common sense also tends to suggest that having been felled by a bullet in the breast, breaking two ribs, Luke wasn't likely to have jumped to his feet and snatched the colours, as has frequently been described. He most certainly wouldn't have hung around, but at least, he would have steadied himself, which would likely be when Evans gave the corporal the staff and it was handed to Luke. There can be no problem with this, as mentioned elsewhere, Luke would have ensured that the butt of it was planted at some stage and in any event, Sir George Brown and General Codrington had witnessed his actions, so much so, that they were content to have him promoted on the spot and given a commission.

> Kinglake says that it was William Evans, a private of the Welsh Fusiliers, not O'Connor, who took the color from the dead hand of young Anstruther. There is, he explains in a note, a punctilio which governs such matters in the service. Evans, therefore, had to give up the flag to his next superior, Corporal Soulbey, and the latter promptly handed it to Sergeant Luke O'Connor.

The Montreal Gazette 27th February 1915

If the version of the planting of the colours described here, is correct, Luke's brevity, as his autobiography indicates, was possibly responsible for him omitting the fact that private William Evans and maybe others had recovered the Queens colour from where it lay on the ground before he gathered himself, having been shot. His gallant actions would have been recognised from what he did with it thereafter which was to parade it to those behind them to encourage the attack and not to part with it until it was necessary for him to do so. In that respect, no argument can be found with Kinglake's version.

Captain Edward William Derrington Bell

The below photographs of the captured gun and of its captor, Captain Bell VC, were both taken from the aforementioned book by W. Alister Williams.

The Russian troops had been instructed by their Czar, that under no circumstances, were they to allow their enemy to capture any of their weapons. It was important to them to make haste to Sevastopol with all of their weaponry before the Alliance got there.

This order had been drilled into the heads of all ranks some time prior to the battle commencing. The voices of their commanders may have rung in their ears far louder than their thought of the necessity to defend their positions.

As contained within the above account, it was Captain Edward William Derrington Bell, of Luke's regiment, who dashed forward and with the help of a private, managed to gather the reins of one of the horses about to pull away this heavy gun and with his pistol held to the driver's head, captured the gun.

The Russian Gun captured by Captain Edward Bell

Captain Edward Bell VC – courtesy Diana Bailey

It is ironic that Bell was castigated for leaving his duty, to perform this gallant act, but in others' minds, he and Luke were both regarded as gallant heroes. Both were to receive the Victoria Cross for the actions they performed on that day.

Captain Bell's family home was in the Village of Kempsey, Worcestershire, not a stone's throw from the village of Crowle where the author resides. Indeed, when launching his research, he was to pay a visit to an elderly Bell family member in Pershore, a neighbouring town. The lady in question, Mrs Diana Bailey, was accompanied by a 'military historian' friend and an enjoyable afternoon was had chatting over Luke's and Bell's actions at Alma.

Among the topics discussed was the statement made in the above book, that when Bell was asked to endorse his support for Luke's Victoria Cross, he was alleged to have done so, but only if Luke would similarly endorse a proposal for his own VC.

Photographs of Bell himself, his Kempsey residences and indeed, the gun seized which is currently at the RWF's museum within Caernarfon Castle, are contained within the book, 'Heart of a Dragon' The VCs of Wales and the Welsh Regiments 1854 – 1902, which was written by W. Alister Williams.

Whatever the reality, Luke and Edward Bell justifiably received their Victoria Crosses, though because the deed performed by Luke occurred prior to that performed by Bell, Luke's claim to be the first soldier to win the VC, would be true. It was only a couple of weeks prior to the intention to seek a further meeting with Diana Bailey, that her death was discovered to have occurred on 22nd May 2019, not long before the completion of the manuscript for this book.

POST ALMA BLUES

The numbers killed and injured have always been disputed but it is believed that the Russians casualties were 5,709 killed, wounded and captured. The official French return claimed casualties of 1,340. The British belief is that this return was incorrect. Lord Raglan set French casualties at 560. Three French officers were certainly killed.

British casualties were set at 2,002 killed, wounded, and missing. Of these, 86 officers from most of the regiments involved, were killed. The rest were described as 'men'. The distinction between officers and men would probably not be made in these more enlightened, modern days.

Luke's Royal Welsh Fusiliers were to lose 13 officers and 198 men. This total of 211 was only surpassed by the 33rd Regiment of Foot (The Duke of Wellington's Regiment) who fought alongside of Luke's 23rd, which lost 239 officers and men. They too, were in the 4th Division and being a part of the Light Division under the command of Sir George Brown, were among those being at the head of the attack up the slopes towards the enemy.

Formations and tactics were little changed from the Napoleonic wars but the development of firearms had seen the retirement of the old 'Brown Bess' musket and as the Crimean War broke out, the British Army's infantry was being equipped with the new French Minié Rifle, a muzzle loading rifle fired by a cap. Unfortunately, Luke's 4th Division was the only division who had not then been supplied with this weapon.

This couldn't have been more unfortunate because it was the troops of the 4th Division who headed the attack of the Great Redoubt and who had suffered the most casualties, but many historians claim that much to do with their victory, was the fact that the British troops out skilled their enemy when it came to rifleman ship. Attacking from a lower position than the enemy, the odds were stacked against them, yet they were victorious and had 'sent them running'.

In that respect, the question has been asked by many, "Why didn't the Alliance chase down the fleeing Russians"?

There have been many answers, the most popular of which are: -

1.   They became disorganised owing to many of their senior officers being killed.
2.   The survivors were exhausted and their dead required burials.
3.   The Russians were more equipped to run, than the Alliance forces were, to chase.

The P. & O's Colombo

So, no doubt earmarked as a hero, due to his actions and the wounds he received, Luke spent the night, all bandaged up on the field of battle. Although he wished to remain with his regiment, on the following day, 21st September 1854, the surgeon attending him, ordered him on board the troop carrier, 'Colombo', so that, with other injured soldiers, he could receive treatment at the Scutari hospital.

Among many others, nine ships belonging to the shipping company, P & O were requisitioned by the government as transport ships during the Crimean War. Colombo, was one of these.

One of her uses was the carrying of Christmas mail and provisions and the picture here, is said to show dead rabbits and birds hanging from her sail spreaders. Presumably that without any form of refrigeration, this was an attempt to keep them fresh. It was due to the nature of most of her voyages in delivering food and mail to the soldiers, that she was affectionately known by them as 'Santa Claus'. However, on this occasion, she was to carry many of the soldiers injured at the Alma, across the Black Sea and down the Bosphorus strait, to the hospital at Scutari.

Luke describes how many of the injured were without food or medical care and when they died, they were thrown overboard. Fortunately for him, he could get about the ship, helping where he could.

The vessel was equipped with both steam and sail but nevertheless, the voyage lasted five days and they landed at Scutari, six days after the battle, on 26th September 1854.

Scutari with Florence Nightingale

Luke was treated at the Scutari hospital until his discharge on 20th October. (24 days). Unfortunately, he contracted a fever on board and was landed at Balaklava (*sometimes Balaclava*) hospital to be sent back again to Scutari where he was treated by Florence Nightingale and her 'Sisters of Charity'. She had arrived in Constantinople (Istanbul) on 3rd November.

Born to a wealthy, well connected Catholic family in Florence, the city after which her parents named her, the family moved back to England where, she was raised from about one year of age in Hampshire and Derbyshire.

Florence had inherited her parents' liberal-humanitarian outlook and it was no surprise that with the family's prominence and wealth, she became something of a 'Social Reformer'. She came to prominence in the Crimean war while serving as a manager and trainer of nurses which she organised in their care for wounded soldiers. She became an icon of Victorian culture, especially in the persona of 'The Lady with the Lamp' as she made her rounds of wounded soldiers at night.

In Luke's autobiography he makes the point that although he was anxious to rejoin his regiment, as his health was improving, he was appointed an acting sergeant-major to take charge of invalided British soldiers on board a Turkish man-of-war.

This was the very thing he had been doing when he was first shipped to Scutari on board the Colombo. It didn't go unnoticed that he had made a very good job of what he had voluntarily been doing. Maybe his health had improved to such an extent, that this would act as further recuperation until he could return to the battlefields.

Whatever, all this meant, of course, was that he was not involved at all, with the next battles of the Crimea which, were at Balaklava (25 Oct. 1854) and Inkerman (5 Nov. 1854). It is clear that at least until the February of 1855, Luke had not yet re-joined his regiment, because he says,

> *"Meanwhile in February, (1855) I received the good news I had been promoted to an ensign's commission in the Royal Welsh Fusiliers, and this was subsequently antedated to November 5th 1854".*

It must always be kept uppermost in our minds that Luke had been an enlisted soldier who had taken the Queen's shilling. He had not received a military education whereas, in general terms, officers who were commissioned into a regiment, were normally fast tracked through military academies to almost automatically becoming officers and in general terms, they were the ones who, by tradition, attained higher levels of command.

So, in acknowledging Luke's promotion from Colour Sergeant to an ensign's commission, although ensign is of a junior rank, we must regard Luke's promotion as being of something special. The promise of such a promotion made by his general on the field of battle, had indeed, come to fruition.

The doors of higher rank had appeared to be just pushed slightly ajar and most important of all, not one penny had been expended in opening them.

The other fact to be remembered, is that all this had happened whilst he had been away from his regiment since 21st September, the day following the Battle of the Alma. This signifies that it was his heroic actions at that battle, which had led to his commission. Maybe it was pre-dated to the 5th November 1854, following the commission being approved.

Meanwhile, Luke's 23rd Regiment of the Royal Welsh, had marched on from those heights overlooking the Alma which they had so gloriously seized from the Russians.

They had marched on, victoriously at Balaklava and Inkerman in Luke's absence, to play their part in the initial stages of the Siege of Sevastopol.

Luke must have been delighted to find that on his return to his regiment, he was received with warmth by Major Daniel Lysons, the same man who Luke had previously described as *'a very active and intelligent officer'*. Not only had Lysons been promoted to Colonel, he was now the commander of Luke's Regiment and, as such, they were in close contact with one another. He was later to become one of Luke's closest friends. Indeed, Lysons had also, endorsed Luke's recommendation for the Victoria Cross. It is no wonder that Luke says, that he received:

> *"the kindest welcome from Colonel Lysons, now in command of the regiment, and all the officers. Of my new colonel I cannot speak too highly; he did everything he could for the men."*

SEVASTOPOL – THE REDAN AND THE MALAKOFF

The siege of Sevastopol lasted from 17th October 1854 to 11th September 1855. The only clue available to discover when Luke re-joined his regiment, is his mention of: -

> *"In the same month, February, promotion was then so rapid, I became a lieutenant. The weather was dreadful; cholera and other diseases pestered us, and the work in the trenches was continuous. Our troops suffered from want of clothes and food, and words can hardly describe our suffering during that winter".*

Luke describes his night-time activities being almost wholly within the trenches. It seems that he slept when it was light and fought when it wasn't. He also mentioned that his activities in the forward trenches were volunteered, because when he was able to take 'off-duty' time, he could obtain a 12-hour period. (*Presumably, this was longer than the day shift's time off?*)

He mentions that the Russians made several sorties and that during the early stages of their attempted taking of the Redan, he happened to be in the quarries during one such surprise attack. Several of his men and officers were killed whilst driving them back and his efforts at that time, were included in the citations for his honours.

We must not, of course, forget that the main objective of the Alliance, was to capture the strategically positioned Sevastopol port from the Russians who had been strengthening its defences for some considerable time. The location and navigability of the city's harbour made Sevastopol a strategically important port and naval base. Indeed, it continues to be so.

The Redan was one of the large fortifications that ringed the city. It is the French word for 'tooth' and maybe that's how it got its name, because it is shaped in the form of a tooth. To some, it became the centre of the Allied troops' attack and so, if it fell, it became thennn symbol of the city being captured.

However, to others, the similar fortification named the Malakoff fort, was a more important capture and would have achieved the same objective.

On 18th June 1855, there had been an attempt by the French to take the Malakoff. This attack was recorded as a near-miss because although they had operated a surprise attack, and had managed to push the Russians out of the fort, the Russian troops had been quickly reinforced with reserve regiments and almost immediately, they were able to launch a counter attack which regained it very quickly.

Luke makes the point that had the first attempt to take the Redan been co-ordinated with the French attack on the Malakoff, then it might have been more successful. This is what Luke mentions about it : -

"On June 18th we made our first attempt to take the Redan. I volunteered with others for the storming party, but at the last moment, a newly arrived regiment – the 34th replaced us. We were all repulsed with great loss, and our colonel was wounded. No doubt, if we had assaulted at the same time as the French, who attacked the Malakoff we should have had a better chance but our allies had already been badly defeated.
That same evening, I went back to the trenches where Guards and Highlanders had been sent on duty for the first time. As they were new to the work, there was a false alarm followed by panic, during which they fired into my men holding the advanced works, wounding two of them. A guardsman charged at me in the dark with a fixed bayonet; it slightly wounded me but had I not struck it partly aside with my sword my leg would have been pierced through."

The more successful attack on the Malakoff was launched by the French on 8th September 1855. The way this was achieved was described in an article published in the 'Illustrated London News' dated 13th October 1855 and much of the facts reported, were confirmed in many private letters sent home by the French who took part in it. The letters contained details of the sacrifice of British troops at the Great Redan. These were troops who were acting to divert the Russian enemy, whilst the French were capturing the Malakoff.

It was said that the bravery of English soldiers who took part in the capturing of Sevastopol on 8th September 1855 owed as much to the resistance of their soldiers at the Redan, as to the troops employed directly in the taking of the Malakoff.

The overall plan was said to have been hatched between the French General, Pelissier and his British counterpart, General Simpson, who had by now, replaced Lord Raglan. In short, Pelissier would take a leaf from the tactics employed by Napoleon Bonaparte in sacrificing one part of his army for the gain of another part. Except that on this occasion, Pelissier would not be asking for the sacrifice of many men, since all that he wanted was for the enemy to be engaged for long enough to allow his troops, not only to force the Russians out of the Malakoff, but to fortify it with the necessary reserves and artillery, so that they would be able to retain it.

The situation was that the French had pushed forward to only 25 yards from the Malakoff. Its guns had been virtually silenced, and its walls levelled in parts. Whereas the British, attacking the Great Redan, were about 200 yards from it and under severe pressure from the Russians to advance much further.

The French were therefore sufficiently close enough to take the Malakoff but Pelissier knew that whilst he could easily force the Russians out of it, it would be difficult to retain it for long enough to bring his reserves and artillery into it, to defend a counter attack, as had happened on 18th June. The intention was to learn from that earlier failed attempt.

Pelissier therefore asked General Simpson for just one hour of a diversion at the Great Redan even in the knowledge that it would be highly unlikely that they would be able to take it. He said that he could guarantee that the hour would be sufficient for him to accomplish his taking and arranging the defence of the Malakoff, so that the Russians would be unable to regain it.

The contents of many private letters sent from Sevastopol confirm this pact had been agreed between the two Generals. Pelissier believed that the taking of the Malakoff would be the key to the taking of Sevastopol and the riddance of the Russian fleet from its port.

The pact was agreed and as it happened, Simpson gave Pelissier, almost twice the time that he had asked for. He gave the Great Redan, such a pounding, that as soon as the Russians had fled from the Malakoff, instead of forming another defence of it, most rushed to the Redan in support of their comrades who were being attacked by Simpson's comparatively small number of troops. It would be doubtfull whether the generals had appreciated such a move and it makes one wonder whether Simpson's attack on the Redan was so well accomplished, that their success there, in the early stages, had caused a greater fight than they would have wanted.

Having studied this magnificent plan quite deeply, doubt remains whether Luke and his men had known of the pact. On the one hand, he played a pivotal part in that it was he, who actually led the storming party in which half of his men were killed before reaching their goal. This was to be another occasion when he used up yet another of those nine cats' lives, that are pet pussies are said to be blessed with. This is said, because sadly, most of the men attacking the Redan who were not killed, were severely wounded. The wounding of both legs was all that he could remember. He was shot down from the parapet and fell into a ditch. He could remember no more.

It is these, deaths and injuries, indeed, Luke getting on top of the parapet and being shot off it, which makes one believe that, perhaps they weren't aware that this was just a distraction, to keep the Russian's busy. On the other hand, if they didn't put up a good fight, their lack of effort, may not have held their attention sufficiently enough to prevent, at least, some of the Russians from dashing off to help their comrades at the Malakoff. Other historians have proffered their theories on both sides, so the jury remains out.

Thankfully, those lives that were lost, were not lost in vain, because the plan had, in the end, achieved what it set out to do. The Russians were ejected, and Simpson's attack gave Pelissier sufficient time to put his reserves into position and retain possession of the Malakoff. It became universally accepted that had not the Russians been over engaged by those brave British at the Redan, for such a long period of time, the French holding onto the Malakoff would not have been successful. Here is Luke's account but when you read it, try and gauge whether Luke had been made aware of the plan.

On September 8th, we made our second attempt at the Redan; again, we allowed the French to go first at the Malakoff, and as the Russians, when driven back, immediately reinforced their comrades at the place we were to attack, our difficulties were doubled. I volunteered to command a storming party; we had to run 180 yards in the open under a terrific fire of shot, shell and musketry. I gave orders to our men not to draw a trigger until they reached the parapet, and then to use bayonet or ball as much as they pleased, but half of them fell before they got there. I arrived safely at the top of the work, cheering on the rest, when, I was shot through both legs, and, fortunately for me, fell back into the ditch. I remembered no more until I came to myself in camp some hours later, still grasping my broken sword. Seven of our officers were killed, including our gallant adjutant who was called 'Soldier Dynley' and five others wounded in this affair. Being young and strong, I escaped amputation, which at one time was thought necessary.

Luke's account suggests that maybe he did not, after all, know that their efforts to take the Redan on that 2nd attempt, were merely to provide the French with a diversion. If that was true, then it would have been tremendously hard for those involved and who survived, because they would have instantly realised that their colleague's lives had been wasted for the victory. That, supposedly, was war!

Luke himself, was so injured that he was almost immediately shipped home to receive treatment at the Haslar hospital in Portsmouth, as was Colonel Lysons himself. The 23rd lost more than any of the other regiments involved in that attack. The taking of the Redan was such a hopeless task. With so many men falling, others abandoned the cause and deserted. The taking of the Malakoff as a result, however, culminated in the fall of Sevastopol and the end of the Crimean war. The regiment lost 754 lives of whom, 530 died of disease. Luke re-joined his regiment at Aldershot, a year later.

Only three days following the taking of the Malakoff Redoubt, the Russians blew up the forts, sank their ships, and evacuated Sevastopol. Although the end of the war was signified by their accepting preliminary peace terms on 1st February 1856, for all intents and purposes, the taking of the Malakoff and the Redan, saw the end of the war.

The loss of Russia's base, at Sevastopol, the Black Sea and a potential gateway to the Mediterranean, meant that she could not sustain her presence there. They had also expected Austria to join them in the war, but instead, Austria threatened to join the Alliance. This must have been the final turning of the tide and Russia formally accepted defeat on 30th March 1856, when they signed 'The Treaty of Paris'.

Although one of the shortest engagements, the battle of the Alma had been hailed as one of The Royal Welsh's greatest. If the alliance had been defeated there, they may never have reached Sevastopol and goodness knows how the pages of history would then have been written.

THE VICTORIA CROSS PRESENTATIONS

The first VC presentations were made in Hyde Park on Friday, 26th June 1857. The medal's institution stemmed from questions being asked in parliament by a back-bench MP, Royal Navy Captain, Thomas Scobell on December 19th, 1854. This, of course, was actually during the war and only three months following the battle at the Alma. No other suitable medal was then in existence.

Luke and Edward Bell's actions were acclaimed the spark which ignited the formalities necessary to introduce the medal and for it to include retrospective actions since the start of the Crimean War. Having undergone various amendments, it now includes most acts of bravery and valour. So, what was Luke O'Connor's relationship with it, in the context of the presentation of it to him?

Countless books, magazines, articles and internet mentions of every description, have made claims that Luke was the first winner of the Victoria Cross, or that he was the first to receive the Victoria Cross or that he was the first **soldier** to win or receive it. Which of these statements are true?

It is a little ironic that although great emphasis was made, that the medal would be aimed at all ranks, when it came to the presentations, rank after all, had its privileges. Being the senior service, the 14 members of the Navy and Royal Marines were presented with their VCs first and **in rank order**. So, with the list of the order of presentations now in front of us, we can look to answer those questions posed above.

This will be discussed following the below cutting and roll of honour taken from the London Standard newspaper dated 27th July 1857: -

THE DISTRIBUTION OF THE VICTORIA CROSS.

The first distribution of the new order of the Victoria Cross by her Majesty to the officers and men who distinguished themselves in the field during the late war, took place yesterday morning in Hyde Park, with the greatest *éclat*. The creation of the new order of valour, as it is called, took its origin from the exigencies of the late Crimean war, during which so many acts of individual bravery on the part of both officers and men forced themselves upon the attention of the authorities that it was thought advisable to institute some distinction which should mark in a suitable manner the estimation in which those exertions were held by the country. The Crimean medal was too general in its distribution to confer any special honour on those who e individual actions so frequently set a brilliant example to the army, being given alike to all who saw active service. The various degrees of the Order of the Bath were equally inapplicable to such cases, being too exclusively conferred upon officers of standing in the service. A distinction was accordingly instituted which may be considered as a medium between the war medal and the Order of the Bath, and yet which, from its peculiar constitution as an order of merit, to which neither routine services nor interest could possibly entitle, may be considered to rank above both. The order itself is a simple Maltese cross of bronze, cast from the Russian cannon taken at Sebastopol. The front is surmounted by a lion and crown, under which is placed the inscription " For Valour." On the back of the clasp is engraved the name of the holder and the date of the action for which the distinction is conferred. It is suspended by a scarlet ribbon for the army, and a blue one for the navy. So far the insignia is plain and unostentatious in the extreme ; but the most material fact connected with the order is yet to be mentioned—viz., that in all cases it entitles the holder to a life pension of 10*l*. a year. The selection which has been made of officers and men from the army and navy to enjoy the distinction has by no means been so numerous as to render the order common, and almost in every case the services for which it has been given have been known and appreciated, not merely by the army, but by the country at large. In this respect the Victoria Cross forms a strong contrast to the majority of the honours which have been of late conferred for so-called military achievements. From a very early hour in the morning that peculiar race called the London sight-seers, probably on account of their being the only people who never get a sight of popular spectacles at all, mustered in strong force in the neighbourhood of the park. Thousands of them crowded through the park gates in one continuous stream for some hours, and took up the positions which were allotted to them by the police with an avidity which plainly showed that they entertained an infatuated opinion that for once they were to be spectators, if not partakers, in the interesting ceremony. But they were doomed to disappointment, if any such sensation could be felt, at not receiving that which they ought never to have expected. Nothing whatever could be seen except by those who were the happy possessors of seats on the platforms. The would-be sight-seers of London will not learn, though experience reminds them of the fact every day, that a popular spectacle always means a spectacle which the populace are rigorously excluded from witnessing.

The preparations in Hyde Park were on a scale commensurate with the occasion, though the arrangements were not completed until a late hour on Wednesday evening. Nearly the whole of the large space of open ground, extending from Hyde Park-corner to the Marble Arch, and fronting Park-lane, was enclosed for the purpose of holding the ceremonial. On the Park-lane side of the enclosure, and immediately fronting Grosvenor Gate, was erected the principal stand for the Royal family, the diplomatic corps, and the members of the legislature. To the right and left of the grand stand extended galleries, in all nearly a third of a mile in length, which afforded accommodation for about 10,000 persons. A long way beyond the ends of the two galleries were the spaces which were appropriated to the people, the nearest of whom were consequently about half a mile from where the proceedings were taking place. Though ultimately excluded from a view of the actual ceremony itself, yet they possessed a very good sight of the troops as they formed upon the ground, which all the ingenious arrangements of the authorities could not deprive them of. The troops as they arrived in the Park took up their position fronting Park-lane in the following order :—On the extreme left were drawn up a troop of Horse Artillery, and next to them came the two regiments of Life Guards, the 5th Dragoon Guards, and the 11th Hussars, drawn up in lines of contiguous columns. Next came the infantry, comprising a company of the Engineers, the 1st battalion of Grenadier Guards, the 1st of the Coldstreams, and the 3d of the Scots Fusiliers, a battalion of the Royal Marines, the 79th Highlanders, 800 men of the Rifle Brigade, the extreme right being occupied by two batteries of field artillery and a military train. The centre of the line was occupied by a detachment of 102 sailors, all Naval Brigade or Baltic men, who were selected from her Majesty's yacht the Osborne, and the Excellent. On their appearance on the ground the little detachment attracted the greatest possible attention, and was received with no little enthusiasm by the people ; but at the same time a very general feeling of disappointment seemed to prevail that the great naval power of England should be represented by a hundre f men. Though the assistance rendered by the fleet during the war, both active and moral, was of the most useful character, their absence would not have been so much noticed—the character of the spectacle being peculiarly military—could it have been forgotten what arduous military services in the trenches had been performed by the Naval Brigade, and to which so large a proportion of them fell victims. A detachment from the Chelsea pensioners in their long red coats, together with the whole of the boys belonging to the Duke of York's Military School formed in lines at each side of the principal stand. The morning was extremely hot; not a breath of wind was stirring. The latter circumstance was fortunate, as it eventually turned out, for the whole of the park was covered with a stratum of fine dust, which a very moderate gust of wind would certainly have converted into a perfect simoom. Ten o'clock was the hour fixed for her Majesty's arrival on the ground, and consequently the spectators anticipated to undergo the process of sun-drying for at least an hour beyond that time; but they were agreeably disappointed in that respect, for precisely as the clock struck ten a salute from the battery situated on the left of the line announced that the *cortège* had left Buckingham Palace. The order of procession was most correctly given in yesterday's *Standard*.

Her Majesty was attired in the uniform of a field marshal, and wore the usual military mourning band of crape on her left arm. The Prince of Wales and Prince Alfred rode behind her Majesty, and were dressed in the Highland costume. The Royal *cortège* having passed along the whole line of troops, took up a position, still mounted, facing the officers and men to whom the crosses were to be distributed. A short pause then ensued, during which the staff in attendance on her Majesty retired to one side, leaving the Queen in the same position, and only attended by Prince Albert, his Royal Highness the Duke of Cambridge, Prince Frederick William of Prussia, the Prince of Wales, Prince Alfred, Lord Alfred Paget, Lady Churchill, Viscount Gough, Field Marshal Viscount Combermere, and the officers in the suite of the Prince of Prussia. It was generally believed that her Majesty would dismount to distribute the crosses, and indeed a platform and a table, covered with scarlet cloth, were placed there for the purpose, and considerable disappointment was expressed when it became manifest that the Queen would not dismount. The ceremony would undoubtedly have been impressive had the distribution taken place from the dais, but as it was, the proceedings were as tame as can well be imagined. The officers and men passed rapidly in the undermentioned order before the Queen, who merely dropped the fastenings of the ribbon into the loop placed on the coats to receive them, being perfectly hidden from everybody the whole time by the horses of the mounted group by whom the Queen was surrounded. The officers and men belonging to the Naval Brigade, and who had served in the Baltic campaign, came first, in the following order, as printed in yesterday's *Standard*, but which we give again to-day, to render the account complete:—

There then follows the complete list (roll of honour) of all recipients: -

Name	Rank
THE NAVY	
Raby, H.J.	Commander
Bythesea, J.	Comander
Burgoyne, H.T.	Commander
Lucas, C.D.	Lieutenant
Hewett, W.N.W.	Lieutenant
Robarts, J.	Gunner
Kellaway, J.	Boatswain

Cooper, H.	Boatswain
Trewavas, J.	Seaman
Reeves, T.	Seaman
Curtis, H.	Boatswain's Mate
Ingouville, G.	Captain of Mast
THE ROYAL MARINES	
Dowell, G.D	Lieutenant
Wilkinson, T.	Bombadier

THE ARMY		
Grieve, J.	Sergeant-Major	2nd Dragoons
Parkes, S.	Private	4th Lt. Dragoons
Dunn, A.R.	Lieutenant	11th Hussars
Berryman, J.	Troop Sergt.-Major	17th Lancers
Dickson, C.	Colonel	Royal Artillery
Henry, A.	Captain	Royal Artillery
Davis, G.	Captain	Royal Artillery
Cambridge, D.	Sergeant	Royal Artillery
Arthur, T.	Gunner & Driver	Royal Artillery
Graham, G.	Lieutenant	Royal Engineers
Ross, J.	Corporal	Royal Engineers

Lendrim, W.J.	Corporal	Royal Engineer
Perie, J.	Sapper	Royal Engineers
Percy, Hon. H.H.M.	Colonel	Grenadier Guards
Russell, Sir. C. Bart.	Brevet-Major	Grenadier Guards
Ablett, A.	Sergeant	Grenadier Guards
Palmer, A.	Private	Grenadier Guards
Goodlake, G.L.	Brevet Major	Coldstream Guards
Conolly, J.A.	Brevet-Major	Coldstream Guards (late 49th Foot)
Strong, G.	Private	Coldstream Guards
Lindsay, R.J.	Brevet-Major	Scots Fusilier Guards
McKechnie, J.	Sergeant	Scots Fusilier Guards
Reynolds, W.	Private	Scots Fusilier Guards
Grady, T.	Private	4th Foot
Hope, W.	Lieutenant	7th Royal Fusiliers
Hale, T.E.	Assist. Surg.	7th Royal Fusiliers
Hughes, M.	Private	7th Royal Fusiliers
Norman, W.	Private	7th Royal Fusiliers
Moynihan, A.	Ensign	8th Foot
Evans, S.	Private	19th Foot
Lyons, J.	Private	19th Foot
O'Connor, L.	Lieutenant	23rd Royal Welsh Fusiliers
Shields, R.	Corporal	23rd Royal Welsh Fusiliers
Coffey, W.	Private	34th Foot
Sims, J.J.	Private	34th Foot
McWheeney, W.	Sergeant	44th Foot
Walters, G.	Sergeant	49th Foot
Owens, J.	Corporal	49th Foot
Lumley, C.H.	Brevet-Major	97th Foot
Coleman, J.	Sergeant	97th Foot
Clifford, Hon. H.H.	Brevet-Major	Rifle Brigade
Wheatley, F.	Private	Rifle Brigade
Cunninghame, W.J.M.	Captain	Rifle brigade

Knox, J.S.	Lieutenant	Rifle Brigade (Late Serg.Scots Fus. Guards)
McGregor, R.	Private	Rifle Brigade
Humpston, R.	Private	Rifle Brigade
Bradshaw, J.	Private	Rifle Brigade
Bourchier, C.T.	Brevet-Major	Rifle Brigade

It can be seen that Luke was never the first to be presented with it. Quite clearly, that was Commander Henry James Raby who was the first of 62, to receive the medal which was pinned to his breast by Queen Victoria herself. *(As were they all)*

The first deed of valour attracting a Victoria Cross, was performed by 'Mate' Charles Davis Lucas who, when in the Baltic on board HMS Hecla on 21st June 1854, witnessed a live Russian shell landing on the deck, with its fuse burning. Whilst most others fled, he picked it up and threw it into the sea. It exploded before it hit the water, saving many lives. His captain promoted him to lieutenant on the spot. Two other naval officers won the next two, again in the Baltic. Apart from Luke, five more were won at the battle of the Alma.

So far as the Army was concerned, their presentations were to be the last 48 of the 62 medals presented at this first ceremony. There were 23 regiments represented. The first soldier to be presented with it was Sergeant Major J. Grieve of the 2nd Dragoons. It will be seen that Luke was the 32nd soldier to be presented out of the 48 from the army and so, including the Navy and the Marines, he would have been 46th out of the 62 recipients to receive the VC on that first presentation of them. The deed he performed on 20th September, made him the first soldier to win the VC. Not the first person to win it, nor the first to be presented with it.

What at first sight seemed to be an omission, was the name of Captain Edward William Derrington Bell, whose capture of the team of horses pulling a canon at Alma would have been accomplished on the same day and not many minutes after Luke's brave action.

Luke had, of course, been held back at Aldershot following his recovery from his leg wounds and he was afterwards required to catch up with his regiment who were on their way to China before they were diverted to the Indian Mutiny. Captain Bell, then Colonel and commander of the 3rd Division, had embarked to China, on 23rd May. He was therefore unable to be spared to attend. His investiture occurred on the 2nd August 1858 at Southsea Common, Hampshire.

And so, it becomes very clear that Luke's deed wasn't the first to earn a VC, nor was he the first to receive one. The only relationship left would concern him being the first soldier in the British Army, to win a VC. And that was on 20th September, 1854.

It is hard to believe that others have made a counter claim in that Luke's citation for his VC mentions his valour at the Alma and also, his gallantry on 8th September 1855 at the attack on the Redan. This counter suggestion made by a minority, was that because Luke's action at the Redan was also mentioned in the citation, maybe he wouldn't have received it just for what he did at the Alma because the action hadn't concluded until the fighting at the Redan had terminated.

That was a suggestion which never gained any momentum at all. Indeed, some say that he should have received a bar on his Alma VC for his heroics he performed at the Redan.

THE ALMA'S LEGACY AND THE INDIAN MUTINY 1857.

With the Crimean war well and truly over and Luke now having been presented with his Victoria Cross, he was, of course, to live for another 58 years. One can imagine that as pleased as he would have been in the immediate years that followed, he would not, in a million years, have imagined the acclaim and pleasant consequences that indeed, were to follow in his lifetime.

It is easy to forget that this new found era of honour which had been unwittingly bestowed upon him, had come after he had been orphaned as a young boy, who had only known life as a member of a struggling Irish farming family. He was now only 24 years of age, so what was his future to hold?

One of the first indications of his fame, was the sitting for his portrait painted by one of the famous portrait painters of the day, Mr Louis William Desanges, the product of a French 'noble' famil, long since settled in England. He had hit on the idea of including in his portfolio, the portraits of the heroes of the Crimean war and the Indian Mutiny, actually in the act of winning their VCs.

Luke would have sat for his portrait in late 1860 or 1861. As his portrait portrays, all of the figures in them, were very definitely of the winners themselves. The acts of winning them were painted from descriptions given to him by his subjects and their colleagues, as they sat.

The unveiling of Luke's portrait was reported in the national press on 2nd April 1861. Many were exhibited at the Egyptian Gallery in Piccadilly, and 47 of the paintings were exhibited at the Crystal Palace, Sydenham in 1862. Most were acquired by Lord Wantage in 1900 and hung in the Victoria Cross Gallery. Many, including Luke's, were later dispersed to the various regiments represented. The Royal Welsh later donated Luke's to Wrexham archives. Of his portraits, Desanges commented : -

> *"I am very sensible that in a work of this magnitude, at which I am compelled to labour single handed, there must be many shortcomings; but as I have painted each scene from the description given to me by my gallant sitters themselves, assisted by their friends and companions-in-arms, eye witnesses, many of them, of the several actions depicted, the pictures, whatever may be their demerit as pictures, have the positive value attached to national records of events that must live forever in the history of our country's glories".*

Whatever was thought by Desanges, Luke and all those that were acquainted with the painting could not have foreseen the accolades that were to follow, with his painting being replicated on the signs of the many public houses given the name 'Alma Inn' in honour of that battle in the Crimea.

He would have almost instantly taken on the mantle of a celebrity. He would soon be shaking hands with the Prince of Wales and the future King of England. The St James's Palace would almost become his second home and he would be introduced to all of the aristocrats in London and Ireland. For Luke, this was a life changing experience. But wait, there's still some battles to be won!

Having been relocated to Aldershot and attending the VC medal presentations, as mentioned above in the context of the now Colonel Bell's absence at those presentations, the colonel and the regiment had earlier set sail for China. But Luke had received a telegram that he was required to remain at Aldershot in order to attend the medal presentations. This news obviously meant that he was unable to have joined the regiment's embarkation for China.

His autobiography continues: -

> *The Royal Welsh were ordered to China in 1857, but owing to the Sepoy revolt landed instead at Calcutta. Here I joined them overland, having been detained to receive the Victoria Cross from the Queen in Hyde Park in June of that year. The decoration was not instituted until after the Crimean War, and it was my old Colonel, Daniel Lysons, himself the bravest of the brave, who recommended me for this honour, as well as for the Sardinia Order, the latter because I had served longer in the trenches than any other officer of the regiment.* (This was the reference to his night time activities in the trenches)

It was obvious when reading Luke's memoirs, and later when mapping the career paths of Colonel Lysons and himself, that even including the fact that in retirement, they lived a stone's throw apart, they were obviously good mates. It was not surprising to learn from Luke's autobiography, that it was Daniel Lysons who also supported him for the receipt of the Victoria Cross.

The three Divisions of the Regiment had embarked for China on three vessels; the 2nd Division on H.M.S. Cleopatra on 16th May, the 1st Division on H.M.S. Adventure on 20th May and the 3rd Division, under the command of Colonel Bell, on H.M.S. Melville on 23rd. May.

However, trouble had been brewing in India, and on the 10th May, Indian Sepoy soldiers had shot their British officers. The bubble of discontent had finally burst, causing the deployment of the regiment to India. Meanwhile, HMS *Cleopatra* had been delayed for two days at Madeira and a further five days at Ascension through coaling necessities, but she arrived at Table Bay on 5th August, where they were directed to proceed immediately to Calcutta.

Luke being left high and dry in London, was probably aware of the revolt before the ships had been located and diverted, and he was shipped directly to Calcutta, where he met H.M.S. Cleopatra as she arrived on 18th September. He was again, united with his colleagues.

Due to adverse weather, Colonel Bell on H.M.S. Melville didn't arrive in Calcutta until 18th November.

For the record, it was also in 1857 that the King of Sardinia conferred the Sardinian War Medal on Luke together with Colonel Dan Lysons, C.B., Major F. E. Drewe, Captain S.C. Millett, Corporal E. Luby and Corporal T. Symonds.

Also, in March, the Sultan of Turkey awarded the Imperial Order of the Medjidie, in approbation of their distinguished services before the enemy in the Crimea, to Luke and the following officers-

Colonel Daniel Lysons C.B., Lieutenant-Colonel H. W. Bunbury, Lieutenant-Colonel A.J. Herbert, Brev. Lieutenant-Colonel E.W. Bell, VC, Brev. Major H. D. O. Torrens and Captains F. Sayer, F.F. Vane, S.C. Millett, T.S. Bigge and Surgeon W. G. Watt.

So, returning to events leading up to the Indian Mutiny, it is not the author's intention, nor is he qualified to review the 'whys and wherefores of British rule in India. In simple terms, although the people of India were Indian in blood and colour, by their nature, they were not, of course, of a British culture, even though maybe unwittingly, many of their British masters may have tried to manipulate them into so being. On reflection, how can we decry slavery yet celebrate our Colonialism and its excuse for 'using' or 'mistreating' members of the Indian nation in Colonial times?

Having researched the issues of the uprising, the majority view (with which I agree), was that liberties were taken and the Indians were being exploited to the extent that their traditional Indian culture was being threatened. In addition, we were forcing the commercialisation of farming, imposing taxation on communities and needlessly claiming estates when such taxations were not forthcoming. Hadn't we already tried this in Boston, America in 1770?

The British Army had taken on many Indian nationals to fight for us in wars around the world. These were largely from the South, Bengal soldiers, commonly known as 'Sepoys'. The disrespect held for these soldiers extended to a story, (true or otherwise) that was, in any event, spread among them, that the cartridges to be used in new issue Enfield rifles, were greased with a mixture of pork and beef fat, which, of course, was anathema to their Muslim and Hindu religions. They were expected to bite into the paper cartridges to load the gunpowder and ball.

Was it not foreseeable, therefore, that these soldiers might rebel? For rebel they certainly did in some scale and fashion. It was on such a scale that it became necessary for the British Government (through the crown) to eventually take over from their own Government's agents in India, the 'East India Company', in an attempt to rebuild the respect for Indian traditional values and their culture.

In the meantime, however, Sepoys had shot British Army officers and their white families and children which caused reprisal atrocities, by British soldiers on Indian families. The 'Great Rebellion' was well under way!

In Bengal and generally, in the south, where Britain had long established itself, there were no revolts. To be a soldier in the Bengal army was an occupation for them, which carried a privileged high status. However, in the north, Britain had more recently annexed the kingdom of Awadh where its ruler had been deposed and landowners had lost their estates. There was also a fear that the British would try to impose a Christian offensive at the expense of their Hinduism and Muslim traditions. It was their 'Sepoy' soldiers who eventually started the 1857 rebellion. Their dissatisfaction quickly spread and support gathered from princes and aristocrats, and for village and town people, to revolt alongside the soldiers.

Without mentioning any of his specific involvement, Luke merely indicates: -

In the Indian Mutiny I was present at the relief and capture of Lucknow, the defeat of the Gwalior contingent at Cawnpore, besides many other affairs, and escaped unscathed through the campaign, during which time I was promoted to Captain.

THE SIEGE AND RELIEF OF LUCKNOW AND CAWNPORE

Lucknow is in the north of India and in the centre of the city, was a group of buildings known as 'The Residency' or 'The British Residency' which served as the residence for the 'British Resident General'.

The first British Commissioner appointed to the newly acquired territory was Coverley Jackson. He was said to have behaved tactlessly and Sir Henry Lawrence, a very experienced administrator, succeeded him only six weeks before the rebellion broke out. Sir Henry began fortifying the Residency and laying contingency plans for a siege; large numbers of British civilians took cover there, having made their way from outlying districts.

On 30 May, Bengal troops at Lucknow broke into open rebellion. In addition to his locally recruited pensioners, Lawrence also had the bulk of the British 32nd Regiment of Foot available, and they were able to drive the rebels away from the city. Luke's 23rd Regiment had disembarked at Calcutta in mid-September and made its way north to Lucknow to assist with the residency's relief.

So far as Luke was concerned, his autobiography entitled, *'In the Days of my Youth'*, is intentionally ended with his presence there, during the rebellion. His description of events is therefore, not so detailed from hereon. After all, the title of his account pretty much dictates that it ends to coincide with the end of his 'youth'. He must have witnessed some atrocities in India, including some British actions of revenge, of which he wouldn't have been proud. So, reading between the lines, it is as if he wanted to end his memoire where he did, without going into much detail.

Rebellious incidents at Lucknow and Cawnpore had begun to rumble at around the same time (Lucknow on 30th May and Cawnpore on 5th June) way before the Royal Welsh had been diverted there. So, dealing with Lucknow first, with around 3000 British occupants, the 'Residency' had served as a refuge for the occupants, but it came under capture and then a siege situation between 1st July and 17 November 1857. During that period, it was virtually destroyed by the rebels.

The grounds remain the same today and contain the burial place of about 2,000 soldiers who perished during the conflict. Only about 1,000 of the inhabitants who had fled their homes to seek refuge there, had survived the attack and its later relief, by Sir Colin Campbell and his troops.

General Sir James Outram wrote soon after the Residency was recaptured: -

"I immediately ordered the advance and took possession of the Residency, with little opposition, the 23rd Fusiliers charging through the gateway, and driving the enemy before them, at the point of a bayonet......"

So, we can be sure, as he says in his account, that he was, at least present when the residency was relieved in the above 'muck and bullets' phase of it, which occurred in the March of 1858. Having arrived on 18th September, 1857, he had been there for around six months.

The regiment remained at the Residency and kept a reassuring presence until the beginning of 1859 when it took part in occasional forays with the remaining rebels.

The city of Cawnpore is now known as Kanpur and lies about 57 miles south east of Lucknow and it was host to another important incident in the Indian Rebellion. It was an important base for the British

Government's agents, The 'East India Company'. Although rebellion had been experienced in nearby areas, the fact that the Sepoys employed there were very loyal to the British, had allayed fears that they would join the rebellion.

This was a garrison town with troops under the command of General Hugh Wheeler who had been taken to the hearts of the Indian population, probably because he had married a local woman, adopted local customs and had learned the language. All this gave him the confidence that the Sepoys at Cawnpore, would remain loyal to him.

There was about 900 British people in Cawnpore and 300 of them were military men. Others were merchants, business owners, salesmen engineers and others. They also included around 300 women and children.

The so called 'entrenchment' in the south of the city consisted of two barracks surrounded by a mud wall. At the time of the siege, General Wheeler had chosen this entrenchment in which to take refuge instead of. what others had thought would be a safer place in the north of the city which was the 'magazine' which had a thick wall, ammunition and stores. It also hosted the local treasury. He having not expected a siege at all, was later criticised on his defence choice.

The attack on the British 'entrenchment' began almost within a week of the uprising of the Sepoys at the Lucknow residency. Evidence exists that Luke served at both places. Cawnpore was the place where, in the early stages of the uprising there, and having surrendered to the rebel leader, Nana Sahib, most of the men were killed after being promised a safe passage to Allahabad.

Their evacuation turned into a massacre and as rescue forces of the East India Company approached Cawnpore, about 120 British women and children were killed in what became known as the Bibighar Massacre. Their bodies were disposed of down a well in an attempt to hide the evidence of their killing. (More on this later)

There were four Indian Regiments at Cawnpore but despite the Sepoy members of them initially remaining loyal to the British Army, with the European population being uncertain as to what would happen in the short future, families began to drift into the entrenchment where General Hugh Wheeler and his Indian Sepoys were based. As tension heightened, the Sepoys were asked to collect their pay individually, so as to avoid an armed mob. Wheeler also began to fortify the entrenchment's defences. One can imagine that the loyal Sepoy soldiers could only be counting down the time when the inevitable rebellion would spread to them. And which side should they take?

Also, the night of the 2nd June 1857 witnessed what must have been a disastrous episode which acted to fuel to the already simmering fire.

A British Lieutenant Cox got himself drunk and fired at an Indian guard. Luckily, he missed but he was locked up for the night until his court martial the following morning when he was miraculously acquitted. This obviously enraged the Sepoys who had also heard a rumour that they were all to be summoned to a parade where they would all be massacred.

And so, the rebellion of what were, loyal Sepoys, began during the early hours of 5 June 1857, (two days following the acquittal of Lieutenant Cox) with three pistol shots from the rebel soldiers of the 2nd Bengal Cavalry. A junior commissioned officer, remaining loyal to the crown, refused to hand over the regimental colours, and he was cut down by his rebelling colleagues.

The shooting awoke other units and some loyal ones attempted to leave. Unfortunately, they were mistaken for rebels and the European artillery opened fire on them. Other loyal soldiers were caught in the crossfire. This was obviously a complete mess with Sepoys not knowing whether to remain loyal to the Crown or join the rebellion. The shooting of their colleagues obviously became an influential factor encouraging many of them to join the rebellion.

This left Wheeler with only around 150 Sepoys who retained their loyalty to him. Those who fled to join the rebellion had taken with them the regimental treasure and as much ammunition as they could carry. Those soldiers who had escaped the entrenchment to join the rebellion had come across the rebel leader Nana Sahib who, having been rebuked by Queen Victoria in his quest to become heir to the Peshwa (equivalent to Prime Minister) and had, for a time, remained loyal to the British, persuaded the soldiers to return to Cawnpore to help him defeat the British.

Although the men were reluctant, he promised to double their pay and reward them with gold if they were to destroy the British entrenchment.

The attack commenced a day later 6th June and within a week, as news of the attack spread, these rebel forces grew to around twelve to fifteen thousand Indian soldiers. At first, rumours that trenches had been filled with gunpowder that would explode as they got closer, caused a reluctance to enter the entrenchment. However, after about three weeks of defending, the occupants ran out of water and supplies and many also died from dysentery, cholera and smallpox.

On 25th June 1857, the day prior to Luke receiving his Victoria Cross, Nana Sahib sent an elderly female prisoner into the entrenchment with a note signed by himself to the effect that in return for surrender, he would allow safe passage to Allahabad via 40 boats which he had arranged to set sail on the River Ganges at Satichaura Ghat.

Despite the reluctance of about half of those inside, their surrender commenced on 27th June 1857 but as they were about to board the boats, they were shot and killed. It has never been decided, whether this slaughter was planned or whether it occurred through mismanagement which caused rogue shots being fired which then spread to the mass killing. The fact that many arrangements to facilitate the surrender, for example, the provision of 40 boats in which those fleeing, could travel to Allahabad, tends to support the notion that mismanagement of the situation had caused this tragic slaughter.

The women and children had been separately taken to Bibighar (*The house of the Ladies*) but as the vast number of British troops, who had been sent overseas to help, approached nearer to Nana Sahib and his rebels, on 15th July, a command was given to murder the women and children. Blood and gore lay strewn over the ground, walls and monuments. It must have been a terrible sight. They were simply hoarded into the town square and slaughtered.

The reason for this has never been clarified; some say it was due to reprisals for the British soldiers using violence in the villages as they progressed towards them, others blame the fear of and the defeat of the rebel forces as the reserves advanced.

Whatever the reason, whilst some soldiers say that they were coerced under pain of death to commit these atrocities, these massacres will never be forgotten. Whilst understanding that reprisals would ensue, one cannot forgive the British for behaving in similar fashion to the rebels. Some of the Indians caught, were made to lick the blood of their victims from the floor and walls where they were killed. Their women were raped and similarly slaughtered with their children.

Most of the prisoners were hanged within direct view of the well at the Bibighar and buried in shallow ditches by the roadside. Others were shot or bayonetted, while some were also tied across cannons that were then fired.

So far as Luke and his regiment was concerned, it becomes clearer that neither had been immediately present at the time these rebellions and the ensuing atrocities, had occurred. They were obviously boiling, ready for eruption and he had joined his regiment in time to take part in the relief of both strongholds at Lucknow and Cawnpore.

The below unattributed clipping published in M.A.P for week ending 29th September 1900, makes it clearer that Luke and his regiment had come across the atrocities at Cawnpore on their march to Lucknow and therefore it was unlikely that members of the regiment had taken part in the reprisals. It also confirms that the siege at Lucknow had already taken place as that was their intended destination where they would assist in its final relief.

Luke's autobiography was published in the 6th October 1900 edition of M.A.P. (Mostly About People) magazine. However, the below clippings were published on 29th September 1900, one week prior to the edition which carried Luke's autobiography.

These advertisements had triggered several letters which were then published before the autobiography was printed. Although the authors of the clippings are unknown, (The one below right was probably written by Sir Howard Vincent) their content suggests that they must have been with Luke at that time. This one immediately below left, clearly demonstrates the type of person Luke was.

Luke's Clemency

"Some months later, the time came when we were strong enough to capture Lucknow, that before had only been relieved and abandoned, and O'Connor found himself fighting through its narrow streets; a fairly tough job, when you remember that from every flat roof and trellised windows came puffs of smoke and hissing bullets. Suddenly a grizzled old Sepoy subahadar dashed from a house, and falling at the British officer's feet, surrendered his sword, and cried, 'Aman! Aman!!' (mercy). Picking up the weapon, still kept as a souvenir, O'Connor called to his men, only too eager to thrust their bayonets into such tempting prey, to 'fall back and give the old chap a chance'! To be able to restrain excited troops, engaged with fury in a bloody task, speaks well not only for his gift of personal command, but for his merciful character. Despite a natural craving for excitement, 'Luke' was ever level-headed in a row. To those who in these days visit the site at Cawnpore, where so many innocent creatures were treacherously slain, it only presents the aspect of a beautiful and perfumed garden. On the sealed mouth of the awful pit stands a white figure of noble proportions, against a cool, green background of deep Oriental foliage. It is no sculptured presentiment of Glory or Revenge that stands above these sad relics of a never-to-be-forgotten past, but a fitter emblem of true national greatness — a marble statue of the Angel of Mercy!"

The Baton in the Knapsack

"The story of General Luke O'Connor, V.C.," writes Sir Howard, "is one which cannot be told too often. For gallantry it has few equals. It should act as a powerful incentive for many a generation. It is a story of a poor friendless boy, who, by sheer courage, rose from private soldier to be a general in the British Army. It is another illustration of the services of Ireland and Irishmen in the service of the British Empire. It shows that the Napoleonic maxim of the Marshal's baton in the knapsack of the corporal applies to this country at the beginning of the twentieth century, as it did in France at the commencement of the nineteenth. Hector MacDonald is a later witness from Scotland. More than one private soldier has been promoted from the field of battle in South Africa. 'Sergeant —— to be Second Lieutenant,' we read in many a gazette. In 1925, or sooner—if war looks as promising everywhere as to-day—M. A. P. will tell the story of this and that general in his youth.

General O'Connor's Secret of Success.

"The old warrior's simple tale of the Alma fight and what it led to for him will tempt many a fine young fellow to place his foot on the lowest rung of the military ladder, and if he has self-confidence, there is no reason why he too should not mount up—but mark this, only after he has learnt the soldier's lesson of how to cheerfully obey. That was the real corner stone to O'Connor's character, and on this was built his fortunate career.

Whatever Luke did in India, must have been to the satisfaction of his various commanders for he was promoted to Captain with effect from 24th August 1858. The complete warrant is far too big to copy here. However, although the promotion took effect on 24th August 1858, it wasn't signed by command of Queen Victoria until 8th June 1862.

Following the relief at Lucknow, it became the duty of the 23rd (Royal Welsh) to act as part of the escort for the large convoy of non-combatants who were to be taken to Cawnpore, but on approaching it, it was discovered that it was under threat by the notorious Tantia (Tanya) Topi, one of the more fearsome of rebel commanders, who had formed a 14,000 strong army, mainly consisting of the rebel Sepoy soldiers, based at the Gwalior fortress. They were known as the 'Gwalior contingent'. Their presence caused the convoy to be diverted to Allahabad.

Topi's main objective was to recapture Cawnpore, and by 19th November, a 6,000-strong force of his army had taken control of all the routes west and north-west of it.

However, they were defeated by Government forces under Sir Colin Campbell in what was referred to as 'the second battle of Cawnpore' which, in effect, marked the end of the rebellion in the Cawnpore area. It can only be assumed that this action was that referred to by Luke in the last few lines of his account.

So far as Luke's regiment is concerned, these three events had taken place almost concurrently. There followed a huge 'mopping up' operation and the 23rd remained in India until 1869, a total of 12 years. However, as will be revealed below, some, including Luke, were to serve on Gibraltar and in West Africa, where he fought another war.

Luke had successfully emerged through his Indian Mutiny experience, thankfully unscathed, and with flying colours. His service there was to earn him his promotion to Captain as detailed above. It was now all happening at home and in March 1858, resulting in the government's perceived need to bolster up the army, the 2nd Battalion of the Royal Welsh had been formed, but Luke was not to join that for several years and, for the time being, he remained with the first battalion.

The Royal Welsh were among many other 'one battalion' regiments to form extra battalions, but this was never understood, because this was in a period of peacetime. As the Empire had spread its wings and many of our own troops were abroad, this may have been part of a contingency plan to fill the gaps caused by our troops engaged in serving in the Empire, but that is only conjecture.

The new 2nd Battalion of the Royal Welsh was raised at Newport, Monmouthshire in March of 1858, which would have coincided with the final relief of the residency at Lucknow. It's first commanding officer was none other than Lieutenant Colonel Edward Bell, the Captain who had won his VC with Luke on the same day at the Battle of the Alma.

This new battalion's first tours of duty were in Malta and then in Canada until October 1867 when it returned to Newport, Wales until June 1869, the same year as Luke's brother Patrick had died of typhus fever. It then moved to Aldershot. Colonel Bell had remained with it since the battalion was formed, right up until Luke was to take the reins in November 1881 when it transferred to Pembroke Dock.

This period which followed India, was, by coincidence, a period of lull for Luke who, perhaps thankfully, would not be engaged in any sort of conflict until the Ashanti War in 1873. This, of course, makes it a little more difficult to track him down in that interim period.

In November 1860, however, he was engaged at Chatham barracks where, on one occasion, he escorted several battalions of soldiers from his own and other regiments, to the barracks at Eastbourne for a training exercise. It appeared that he had been regarded as an ideal 'role model' for others to follow. He had been assisted by two Lieutenants from the other regiments involved.

It was shortly after this, that evidence of Luke visiting Ireland since the time when he visited Boyle to show off his sergeant's uniform, had surfaced. This was still in that period of lull, but he may well have visited before, or since that time, but no evidence of such a visit has indicated that possibility.

It is easy to forget that even as a Captain, the holder of a Victoria Cross medal would be regarded as someone with a huge celebrity status. We are pleased to hear or read about gallant actions these days which lead to such presentations but in Luke's days, he couldn't cough without it being recorded in a newspaper, and, of course, this attracted numerous invitations to events attended by the aristocracy and others in high society. The below article published in the Freeman's Jounal, Dublin on 27th February 1863, is a good example. Hundreds appeared on the guest list. These included the 'upper crust' of society as well as very high-ranking military personnel and members of 'the cloth'.

This event, a regular occurrence, was organised by the 7th Earl of Carlisle, George William Frederick Howard KG, KP, PC who, at that time, was also the Lord Lieutenant of Ireland., a title regarded in status as equivalent to the King of Ireland.

It will be seen in the heading that this gathering was referred to as the 2nd 'Drawing Room' of the season. The section below, contains just the 'Captains' present in which Luke is unmistakably included.

THE DRAWINGROOM LAST NIGHT.

His Excellency the Earl of Carlisle held his second drawingroom for the season at Dublin Castle last evening. His Excellency entered the Throne room shortly after nine o'clock, accompanied by the following officers and ladies of the household :—

The Private Secretary, John Hatchell, Esq.

Below shows just the Captains present, which includes Luke. There were hundreds of Others.

Captains.—Vivian Ryan, Tipperary Artillery; De Moleyns, R A; W B Smythe, Royal Dublin City Regt; Hodger, 10th Regt; R B Lloyd, 36th Regt; Webber, 45th Regt; W Lynam, 5th West York Regt; O H Minchin, Royal Perth Rifles; J G Mathew, Gold Coast Artillery; Saunders, R H A; Geoghegan Carr, 36th Regt; L O'Connor, Victoria Cross, 23rd Royal Welsh Fusiliers; P G Vigo , Brigade Major; J W Lynch, Galway Regt; Smyley, Londonderry Light Infantry; Montgomery, 5th Dragoon Guards Warren, 60th Rifles; Pim, Royal Tyrone Fusiliers; P M'Donald, Middlesex Rifles ;

Freemans Journal Dublin 27th February 1863 at Dublin Castle for Earl Carlisle's 2nd Drawing Room of Season

It will be seen later, that Luke had often been invited to attend the Queen's, (and later the King's) Levees. These lavish affairs were held in the main, at St James' Palace on regular, almost monthly occasions. The Prince of Wales, on behalf of his mother, Queen Victoria, normally hosted them.

The status of the guests, here at Dublin Castle, was almost identical to the Queen's Levees, and for all intents and purposes, this 'Drawing Room' gathering would appear to be an identical affair. I have described in more detail below, how a Levee' is defined.

So, apart from Luke's participation in the Ashanti War, which will be dealt with later, the bulk of his 'enemy facing' days were thankfully over. Apart from the injuries described above, he had, against short odds, escaped the Crimea and India, with at least, his life. He was most probably in the minority, and for all intents and purposes, he could look forward to his retirement and, who knows, further accolades and a celebrity status.

So far as Luke's communications with his 'American' siblings is concerned, this story has previously discussed the likelihood of him keeping in touch with at least some, if not, all of them, by letter. This must have been the case for the reasons already stated but it is strongly suspected that due to Daniel, being the youngest survivor, and Luke being the next youngest, those two had probably become the closest. In addition, they had both served as officers in the military, Daniel having distinguished service during the American Civil War.

As tempting as it is to launch into Daniels life here, that must be avoided so as to prevent the duplication of the story involving all the siblings who had remained in the USA which will be published in a book by the same author. We do, however, now approach the time, when the two at last, became united again.

A RETURN VISIT TO GROSSE ISLE

So, returning to Luke, his exploits in most of the wars that he fought in, being described earlier, it was roughly during the era of the American Civil War, that Luke served in Gibraltar with the 1st Battalion. This was between 1863 and 1866 until he was transferred to the 2nd Battalion in Canada where his commanding officer was his fellow Alma VC winner, Colonel Edward Bell.

In the knowledge of their 'tête-à-tête' over Bell suggesting that he would only support Luke's citation for his VC at Alma, in exchange for him supporting his own VC citation, it is doubtful whether there was an air of 'entente cordiale' as there would have been with his old Colonel, Daniel Lysons. However, having got to understand Luke's character and manner through much research, it would be surprising if he hadn't treated his Colonel with the utmost respect and courtesies expected of him.

Luke's last trip to Canada proved to be a remarkable coincidence, because of all the Islands in the oceans of this world, his service with his regiment had taken him back to Grosse Isle, the very island where, around 27 years previously, his father, having already been buried at sea during that dreadful voyage, his mother and baby brother died.

No matter how young he was, he was surely to have vivid memories of his voyage and his time there. He mentions very little in his memoire, though that what he wrote, indicates that it hadn't escaped his memory. It was the newspaper clipping below, taken from the Hampshire Telegraph and Naval Chronicle dated Saturday, 2nd November 1867, which drew attention to the fact that Luke had also spent some time in Canada.

The content of this snippet takes some calculating, but from what can be understood, the 2nd Battalion had arrived in Montreal on 13th July 1866 and returned to Portsmouth on 29th October 1867, a period of 15 months. The difficulty in plotting Luke's service in Canada was eased when further newspaper articles, later threw more light on the subject.

The fact that Colonel Bell was in command was mentioned in the Montreal Gazette of 2nd August 1905, concerning the death of Captain Burden, a well-known Canadian Journalist who, like Luke, had joined the Royal Welsh Fusiliers as a non-commissioned soldier. It is remarkable that even after all those years, Grosse Isle was still being used as a Quarantine Island and Luke was having to spend several days there in quarantine, as he did all those years ago when people were dropping dead around him with typhoid and cholera. This makes one wonder if he was then able to trace any records of his parents and young baby brother's deaths. Luke was one of six Captains aboard, as can be seen in the clipping below.

It is, of course, possible that Luke may have returned to Ireland since his visit to Boyle as a Sergeant and on other occasions prior to being entertained in Dublin Castle by the Earl of Carlisle. His visits there, certainly increase, to such an extent that he became a regular visitor and even stationed there!

There is also evidence that his countrymen were now very much aware of his gallant, heroic exploits. They had been publicised around the world in newspapers and various military reports in magazines. Much like the celebrities of today, anyone who even had the slightest relationship or contact with him, would be keen to associate themselves with his name.

ARRIVAL OF THE "HIMALAYA."—Her Majesty's screw troopship *Himalaya*, Capt. S. B. Piers, arrived at Spithead at 6 a.m. on Tuesday, from Quebec, with the 2nd battalion of the 23rd Royal Welsh Fusileers on board. The regiment has arrived in the following strength:—Majors Hon. S. Mostyn and Charles G. C. Norton; Capts. Sydney C. Millett, George P. Prevost, Luke O'Connor, V.C., Jas. D. V. Tupper, Annesley Cary, James H. Welwyn; Lieuts. Gerald George Liddell, Charles Morgan, I.O.M., G. W. Adolphus Fitzgeorge (Adjt.), Edwin Stanley Creek, Robt. F. Williamson, A. F. Ramsbottom; Ensigns George C. E. Rowley, Charles John Gilbert, Robert T. Webber, Walter F. J. Cowan, Sydney B. Blyth, Edward C. T. Stone, W. A. Johnston; Surgeon Benjamin Tydd and family; Assist.-Surg. T. F. Barrow, M.D.; Paymaster George Knox Leet; Quartermaster George Burdon, Mrs. Burdon, and child; Mrs. Prevost, Mrs. Rowley, 676 non-commissioned officers and men, 57 women, and 81 children. The following were on the general passenger list from Quebec:—Lieut.-Gen. Sir John Michell, K.C.B., Lady Michell and family; Capt. the Hon. R. H. de Montmorency, 32nd Regiment, aide-de-camp to Sir John Michell; Lieut.-Col. Alexander M'Kinstry, 2nd battalion 17th Regiment; Major Francis G. Blood, 69th Regiment, and Mrs. Blood; Lieut. F. G. Bell, 53rd Regiment; Lieut. J. H. K. Fletcher, 15th Regiment; Assist.-Surg. Woodford, R.A.; Lieut. Stratford, 14th Regiment; Mr. Blood; 186 invalided soldiers, 37 women, and 60 children from various corps, and 19 naval invalids. The *Himalaya* left Ports-

month on her outward voyage in the latter end of August last, for the Mediterranean and Canada. She left Malta, on quitting the Mediterranean again, on the 5th of September, called in at Gibraltar five days afterwards, and arrived off the quarantine ground at Grosse Island on the 26th of September. From Grosse Island the *Himalaya* on the 27th proceeded on to Quebec, but returned the same day to the quarantine ground at the island, and landed some men there. She remained in quarantine until the 8th of October, when she was released, and proceeded again to Quebec. On the 16th ult. she embarked the 2nd battalion of the 23rd Regiment for conveyance to England, and sailed the following day, making a fine weather as well as a speedy passage homewards. The Royal Welsh Fusileers disembarked on Wednesday afternoon, according to official arrangements, alongside the dockyard, under the superintendence of the staff officers of Lieut.-Gen. Sir George Buller, K.C.B., the Lieutenant-Governor of Portsmouth and Military Commander-in-Chief of the South-west District. The head-quarters of the regiment, accompanied by the magnificent goat presented to the regiment some years since by her Majesty, left the dockyard by a special train at 6 p.m. for Newport and Cardiff. Four companies left the dockyard at 5 p.m. by a special train for Brecon. The invalided soldiers brought home with the 23rd in the *Himalaya* were transferred during the morning by the *Florence Nightingale*, hospital transport launch, to the Royal Victoria Military Hospital at Netley. The time-expired soldiers were forwarded by steamboat and rail to the depôts of their respective regiments. The *Himalaya* sailed on Thursday afternoon for Plymouth, to make good repairs.

However, very much unlike the celebrity worship of today, it would have been pride that would have been behind an announcement in the Roscommon and Leitrim Gazette dated 27th January 1872. This was at the time prior to Luke being promoted to major when he was 41 years of age and just prior to his fighting the Ashanti in West Africa. He was not, however, stationed in Ireland until some eight months later. The newspaper cutting in question, is very faint and so it has been transcribed below. It was written under the pseudonym 'A TOWNSMAN' -

> *We learn with pleasure from the following notice in the Army and Navy Gazette that our fellow townsman Captain Luke O'Connor, of world-wide celebrity for bravery in the field, is about obtaining a further step of well-earned promotion. Some of our readers were personal acquaintances of his during the earlier portion of his life and to them, his career has a double interest. The following is the paragraph we refer to – 'The Commander in Chief has been pleased to recommend Captain O'Connor VC, 23rd Royal Welsh Fusiliers, for promotion to a brevet majority. The gallant services of this officer in the Crimea and India are well known. For his conduct at the Alma, he was complimented on the field, and awarded the Victoria Cross, the latter honour being repeated for his behaviour at the attack on the Redan; thus he is the only officer in the Army who obtained the highest reward on two separate occasions. The case has remained so long in abeyance, in despite of the recommendations which support it, that we can but hope that it will at last receive the attention it deserves at the War Office.*

The phrase referencing Luke as '**Our Fellow Townsman**' might well indicate that he would have been acquainted with Roscommon friends in more recent times than all those years ago, dressed in his sergeant's uniform. Support for that theory is provided by yet another newspaper article within the 19th December 1872 issue of 'The Irish Times'. Again, the original is in such poor quality, that is transcribed here.

78

THE ROYAL WELSH FUSILIERS
(FROM OUR CORRESPONDENT)

A few evenings since, the dramatic amateurs of The Royal Welsh Fusiliers and the Roscommon Militia, gave an entertainment in Boyle, under the patronage of Captain Luke O'Connor, V.C., and the officers of the detachment and Auxiliary Forces. The elite of the inhabitants also honoured the performances by their presence. The drama selected was, 'The Charcoal Burner' or 'The Dropping Well of Knaresborough' and the play was entered into with a will to please which the most fastidious might consider sufficient to cover the inevitable faults of any amateurs. The scenery was specially painted for the occasion in the leisure hours of Private George McEvoy, Royal Welsh Fusiliers. The Afterpiece was the humorous farce of the Irish Tiger. The string band of the Roscommon Regiment provided the music in fine style. [sic]

He had been referred to as Captain Luke O'Connor VC in the above clip and because it was published in December 1872, this provides an insight into the fact that the 2nd Battalion had not arrived in Ireland until 16th September 1872, from Portsmouth.

This was also prior to the Ashanti War and before his promotion to major. He had, however, lost no time at all with re-acquainting himself with the barracks at Boyle and, no doubt, those old boys he had 'drilled' in the days of his youth. In those three months, it appears that he was already promoting this play (or was it a 'farce'), at Boyle.

The End of 'Purchase'

Another major chapter in Luke's life occurred just prior to his embarkation to West Africa to fight in the third Ashanti War. This concerned the changes which had been made by parliament in scrapping the traditional purchase of commissions which had been in existence since the mid-19th century and had caused considerable confusion. It had not existed in any other service.

Royal Commission after Royal Commission had hitherto sat to try and iron out various anomalies which existed. This particular episode had been arrived at, following the Cardwell Reforms which were introduced in November 1871. Until that time, officer promotions could only be filled either by purchase of a commission or by merit and the filling of dead men's boots.

The commissions purchased were in the form of bonds and when their holders wished to retire, they could be sold for quite a substantial profit which was regarded as a very good pension, enabling them to live comfortably during their retirement. The abolishing of this practice, also brought with it the end of the exchanging of officers' positions by, for example, volunteering to serve in foreign lands, which consequentially was to earn more pay than that to be earned in their homeland.

So, in Luke's case, because he had never purchased a commission, he obviously didn't have one to sell! He would be losing out considerably. Although he could receive a full pay pension, he would be unable to realise a lump sum. In addition, these changes also included mandatory retirements following five-year spells after being promoted to either Major or Lieutenant-Colonel.

Whilst this latter provision culled those who were too old to do the job and had been languishing in ranks for far too long, it conversely restricted those younger ones, including Luke, by not allowing them to progress even further along the ranks. The situation brought uproar within the officer ranks and it didn't take long before a 'Royal Commission' was set up to investigate the whole process of purchase and retirement. When it assembled in October 1873, Luke was one of the first witnesses to be heard. He wasn't only doing this to protect himself, but like his mentor, Daniel Lysons, he wanted to look after the youngsters, who themselves, would be caught in this trap.

Whichever way the commission moved, they were unable to announce any resolution which would be accepted by all, and indeed, they announced that the whole matter was so complex that it was impossible to mark out a general system of recompense which would be fair to everyone.

Luke was a Brevet Major (*Given the rank temporarily but without the pay and authority*) at the time but gave evidence that he looked forward to becoming a full Major and a Lieutenant-Colonel in the future when he could have retired with what had been the regulation payments including an 'over regulation' payment for serving abroad. This would be in the region of £7,000, a sum in 1873, which would have the spending power in 2020 of £766,125 which would have more than handsomely set him up for the rest of his life. Luke's actual response as quoted in the London Gazette was:

> " Since the abolition of purchase it has been decreed that my chance of obtaining that 7,000*l.* shall be swept away; but on the other hand, concurrently therewith, Parliament passes a vote granting money in compensation, and the amount of that money offered to me is 2,400*l.*; but I cannot receive that 2,400*l.* until I retire from the service, and with that condition attached I can never receive it at all, because I could not live on the interest of 2,400*l.* Therefore I have lost my 7,000*l.* which I entered the Army to obtain, or upon the chance of obtaining, and if I had not known that that was the goal which I was running for, I should never have entered at all. I have lost my (chance of) 7,000*l.*, and I cannot accept the 2,400*l.* for the reasons I have given, consequently I get nothing at all. I have to fall back upon my daily pay for life. I may certainly get full pay retirement, but full pay retirement means daily pay continued, minus work."

Another disadvantage caused by the new rules was that so long as a Major or Lieutenant-Colonel is on half pay retirement, his service would not count towards his 30 years' service, when he would be entitled to a full pay pension.

The full conclusions of the Royal Commissions are, even now in retrospect, difficult to understand because so many exceptions to the rules were drafted. Also, in some cases, longer service in the effected ranks were permitted in special cases. However, the payments received on retirement were in effect, accrued by the government, purchasing the commissions and not by individual junior officers. In other words, it got rid of the bartering that would have existed. Those such as Luke, would receive similar amounts in compensation. The government pledged that no serving officer would find themselves in a worse situation and this, answered most of the objections.

THE ASHANTI WAR 1873 – 74

The below announcement was taken from the Belfast News 18th November 1873. Luke's return from India meant that he could have enjoyed many years of continued peace, but for this war.

This really couldn't have come at a worse time, because in 1872, when it seemed like all his dreams would come true, he learned that his battalion was to be moved to Ireland. Nevertheless, he was a career soldier and he was soon promoted to major, the promotion being back dated to 5th July 1872, which wasn't long before he accompanied the 2nd battalion on their first action, to the Gold Coast (now Ghana) of West Africa.

The commanding officer of this expedition was Sir Garnet Wolseley, an Irishman who had fought with Luke in the Crimea and India. He, with other troops, had arrived much earlier to cut a road through the jungle to the River Prah, the boundary of the Ashanti territory in which was located the capital city of Kumasi, (sometimes Coomassie) which was their target

Having left Portsmouth on the troop ships Tamara and Himalaya on Friday 21st November 1873, the regiment finally landed on 5th January 1874. They had been held at sea because Wolseley was not ready to receive them and many were being taken ill and died of diseases and the heat. Local tribesmen, employed as carriers, had also deserted and even the goat mascot was to later die there.

It was not even two years later, when Luke received yet another promotion to Lieutenant Colonel, for the heroics he performed during the Ashanti War. That promotion took effect from 1st April 1874, just two weeks following the signing of a treaty which ended it.

Surely these meteoritic promotions speak volumes for the respect Luke must have received from his superiors during this war. The British Empire was, of course, still spreading its wings and since earlier days in 1823, the people of the Ashanti Kingdom were engaged in skirmishes and ultimately, two previous wars prior to this latest episode. Sadly, this latest one wasn't to be the last of them.

Their target, Kumasi was located inland about 130 miles from the coast. It was the Ashanti's continual incursions across their border, the River Pra, which had caused this string of wars to continue over many periods from 1824 to 1900, no doubt caused by the gold pickings of the coastal area and the sea ports, which were to prove too big a temptation for the Ashanti not to trespass across their river border.

Before it had any contact with Europeans, the Ashanti enjoyed a flourishing trade with other African states, mostly due to this gold wealth. They were therefore continually driven by their greed and their trespassing often involved overpowering weaker tribes and marching on towards the sea in pursuit of conquests and of the trade they knew was offered at the coast. Although a barbarous race, they were a powerful warlike people who did not to take 'No' for an answer.

Only 10 years earlier, they burned thirty villages. By early 1873, their army had grown to a 12,000 force. The Dutch were in possession of the Gold Coast from 1598 until 6th April 1872 when it became part of the British Empire. It is currently one of Ghana's 10 administrative regions but in those days, it was, of course, very much in our interest, to resist the incursions of the Ashanti.

This was the same position as it had been in the previous wars of 1824 and in 1863, when, despite victories being claimed in the first, by the Ashanti and in the second by the British, disease played its part with both sides losing more men to sickness than any other cause. This third war commenced in 1869 because of a European missionary family being taken to the capital, Kumasi. They were hospitably welcomed but were undoubtedly used as an excuse for this war in 1873. The Ashanti's invasion of the new British protectorate became the final straw and caused General Wolseley's expedition to be launched.

The Kingdom was then headed by 37-year-old King Kofi Karikari who was sometimes known as King Coffee Calculi. Was it any wonder, that his name was quickly reduced by the British to 'King Coffee'? He lived in his palace with several wives and should any Ashanti ever look at the unveiled head of any of his queens, then they would immediately lose theirs.

Ghana

**Major General
Sir Garnet Wolseley**

General Wolseley's mission was to stop King Coffee raiding and plundering settled tribes on the Gold Coast, which would be achieved by first taking its capital, Kumasi, but a major problem of the expedition, was that the area was a most inhospitable place constantly riddled with disease. The changeable temperatures and the frequent rains were almost unbearable.

Wolseley was known to be over cautious in his planning, so he took with him, no less than 70 doctors. The fact that only one officer and a small number of other ranks died, bares testament to that decision. The Royal Welsh had recently been issued with, what was to become an early version of the .303 Royal

Luke O'Connor

Sergeant, 23rd Royal Welch Fusiliers; The Alma, Crimea, 20 September 1854

Captain, 2nd Bn., 23rd Royal Welch Fusiliers; Ashanti, W. Africa, 1873-74

Enfield rifle which could be loaded whilst lying down. Also, as indicated below, their uniform had been designed to be more practical for warfare.

The newspapers of the day claimed that Wolseley had not been given sufficient military personnel to do this difficult job. King Coffee could raise at least 150,000 soldiers to defend their land and, they were acclimatised and knew their territory so well.

All Ashanti attempts at negotiations were disregarded. Wolseley finally led 2,500 British troops and several thousand West Indian and African troops to Kumasi. The capital was briefly occupied when the Ashanti had abandoned it after a bloody war. In accordance with their objective, the British destroyed it.

Wolseley's plans had included the training of fit young men from the many tribes who had suffered at the hands of the Ashanti, but he soon discovered that, no matter how well trained they became, most were generally too eager to turn their backs on the enemy and flee. However, in the end, the victorious final battle was at Amoaful which was fought on

31 January 1874, mainly involving the 42nd Regiment of Foot.

Even in defeat, tribute was paid to the Ashanti commander, the great 'Chief Amanquatia' who was killed at that battle. Admirable skill was shown in the position selected by Amanquatia, and the determination and general leadership he displayed in defence fully bore out his great reputation as an able tactician and gallant soldier.

> A DISTINGUISHED IRISH OFFICER.—Our valued old friend, Major Luke O'Connor, V.C., of the 23rd Fusiliers, has once more proved himself worthy of bearing the steel that he has already so frequently distinguished himself in the use of in so many lands. It appears his regiment is under orders for the Gold Coast, and he was offered promotion, with liberty to remain in England, if he thought fit, on the grounds of ill-health. He has bravely declined the promotion, as well as the privilege of remaining in England, and he will proceed with his battalion on foreign service, having been reported fit for duty by a medical board. This determination will not surprise his friends, and there can be no doubt but that his presence with the regiment on the African Coast will be most valuable to the expedition ; and no one will rejoice more at Major O'Connor's presence in Ashantee land than Sir Garnet Wolseley, who well knows the value of such men.

Although Luke's term in Africa was short, with some reports that he had returned early, suffering with a fever, he had impressed enough, to be promoted to Brevet Lieutenant-Colonel on 1st April 1874. To remind, the reader, the term 'Brevet' meant that it was an honorary promotion without the pay or authority carried by the rank. In effect, he remained a substantive Major, though carrying the badges of the rank of Lieutenant Colonel. Following a successful mission, the expedition returned to Portsmouth on 19 March 1874 when, 13 days later, Luke was promoted to the substantive rank of Lieutenant Colonel.

With so many years having passed since these historic events occurred, it is often the case that the less significant facts are exposed so that clues and assessments can be determined as to the personality and the character of the individuals under scrutiny.

In Luke's case, he had already proved that he was fearless and had been hailed a hero because of the great valour he had displayed. But what was it that drove him? What was in his heart and mind at the time? The below newspaper cutting taken from the Freeman's Journal, Dublin of 8th November 1873 just prior to his setting sail for West Africa, throws some light on the answers.

This article explains why his Brevet rank was soon converted into the full rank of Lieutenant Colonel and also, it serves to educate us about the existence of a hitherto unknown illness he was suffering prior to this war. An illness which could have so easily caused him to evade it. In addition, he was already aware that he was about to receive another promotion, without his even contemplating going to Africa to fight in what was to be an uncomfortable, messy war. He was also in Ireland, where he would have undoubtedly have loved to have stayed.

Above all, these were details which he didn't disclose himself, in his autobiography. With no family to worry about, this revelation is added evidence of him giving his heart and mind to his regiment. The regiment's return from Africa was around the time of their return to Wrexham, though it didn't fully occupy the barracks until 1877.

As a matter of interest, the Ashanti King signed a British treaty in July 1874 to end the war. Also, 22 years later, in January 1896, the British formally annexed the Ashanti Kingdom to the British Empire. Although he would not have been aware of it then, the end of the war in West Africa, was to be Luke's final involvement in a battle as an active soldier of the British Army.

TIMES OF PEACE

Whilst many books have been written about the conflicts in which Luke had been involved, the portrayal of them have been used purely to paint a picture of the man, rather than a detailed account of the battles themselves. Similarly, although additional emphasise has been given to the winning of his Victoria Cross at the River Alma and his gallant actions at Sevastopol, other of his actions involving less significant medals and honours received, have been given a less detailed account.

So perhaps with his sword tucked away in its scabbard, this is the time to reflect on those matters and what better way to start than with details of the nine medals which he so proudly and justifiably, wore on his breast.

Luke's own medal collection

This photograph, was taken at the Royal Welsh's museum at Caernarfon Castle, where there are many display cabinets full of fine memorabilia. However, they are housed in quite a dark place, behind sheets of sturdy plate glass which were illuminated by various spot lights.

Unfortunately, it was difficult to avoid the glass causing flash rebounds, even with the magnificent support provided by Keith Jones, of the museum's staff. This problem has caused the author to clip some of the below individual medals from other sources on the internet. An added short description of each, has been provided.

In the order of Luke's medals, from left to right, they are: -

1. Companion of the Bath (CB) Military Division

**An Ordinary Member of the Military Division
of the Third Class
Founded by King George I
on 18th May 1725**

**Awarded in the London Gazette
29TH June 1906**

And below, the most cherished

2. The Victoria Cross

'FOR VALOUR'

As fully explained in the above chapters on this subject.

Instituted by Queen Victoria, initially for the gallant deeds performed in the Crimean War.

3. Crimean Medal

Luke's medal as seen on his medal bar above, contained two clasps attached to the ribbon. Three were awarded in all but Luke missed the battles of Balaklava and Inkerman due to his recuperation at Scutari when he was treated by Florence Nightingale. The bottom clasp shown on Luke's medal was for Alma and the top one for the Siege of Sevastopol.

4. Indian Mutiny Medal

For those who were present at Lucknow, its defence and its relief.

5 clasps were issued but only 4 awarded. Luke's clasps were for Lucknow and its relief, not for its defence as pictured here.

He was being presented with his Victoria Cross during that time.

5. Ashanti Medal

British medal awarded to those forces who accompanied Major General Sir Garnet Wolseley on the campaign to oust King Kofi Karikari from the British territory in the Gold Coast (Ghana)

This was the 3rd Ashanti War 1873 - 74

6. Order of the Medjidie

Awarded by Sultan Abdülmecid of the Ottoman Empire (Turkish) as a reward for distinguished service to members of the British Army and Navy and the French Army who came to the aid of the Ottoman Empire during the Crimean War.

5th Class awarded on 2 March 1858

7. Sardinian Medal for Valour

A gallantry medal awarded by King Victor Emmanuel 11 of Sardinia for bravery during the Crimean War against the Russian Empire

8. The Turkish Crimean Medal

Issued by Sultan Abdülmecid 1 of the Ottoman Empire to allied military personnel involved in the Crimean War of 1854 – 1856.

It was only awarded to those who survived the war and not to next of kin.

9. Star of the Order of the Bath, Military, Knight Commander (KCB)

To be an Ordinary Member of the Military Division of Second Class, or Knight Commander of the said Most Honourable Order.

The London Gazette
3rd June 1913

At the time of the battle of the Alma, Luke was only 24. He would have been one of the youngest, if not the youngest of the Sergeants of that day. This pattern followed in years to come, when he would have been one of the youngest to receive the honours, he was later to receive. His youth would have also played a part in him eventually being the only surviving winner of those first 62 men who receive a VC during the first presentation.

So far as his physical appearance was concerned, apart from the many photographs of him obtained, which show him to be a handsome, upright gentleman with the bearing one might expect of a senior military officer, the only third party description obtained, was contained in the 6th October 1900 edition of M.A.P. , the same edition which carried his autobiography. Due to the poor quality of that copy, again, that has been transcribed below, which was compiled by the editor, his friend, T.P. O'Connor when Luke was approaching 60.

> *"Luke O'Connor was a sturdy and somewhat athletic man in his younger days, and carries his years well at the present moment. He stands somewhere between 5ft 10in. and 11in. in height. His countenance is stern and somewhat rugged, but often beams in a good-natured smile, and from it can flush fiercely or glean with friendly humour eyes of the purest Milesian blue. He is devoutly religious, and in politics has an idea that his countrymen ought to have a little more to say in the matter of ruling themselves, on the principle that some know so well where the shoe pinches as the actual wearers thereof. But it is difficult for his closest or most trusted friends to get him to talk on either religious or politics – military subjects are his favourite theme, and how best to benefit the British soldier.*

It is interesting to know that in 1873 (it was in 1875) *he was entertained at a public dinner given in his honour by the inhabitants of his native town at Boyle, when the gentlemen of his county presented him with a magnificent centre-piece in silver representing Ireland, Wales, England and Scotland. As he has never married, however, this superb gift has been intrinsically of but little use to him."*

His reputation obviously spread far and wide and as already mentioned, his VC had turned into something of a golden key which attracted many invitations, not only to military events, but other, very high society events such as the Royal Levees, garden parties and other esteemed gatherings.

The Royal Levees

These Levees were lavish, spectacular events, normally held in palaces, such as the Palace of St James and on other occasions, in the castles of Wales and Ireland. They were also held in other British Empire and Commonwealth countries and were only attended following strict invitation of the 'upper crust' such as the royal families of other nations, princes and princesses from every quarter, governors and other members of the home, commonwealth and foreign diplomatic corps and civil service members and members of parliament. Military personnel of the highest ranks of all services, and sometimes 'other ranks' were invited on the announcement of their promotions.

The following is included as an introduction to what they were, as apart from the present day 'Royal Tea Parties' held at Buckingham Palace, they have long since ceased. With literally hundreds of guests, they simply would not be justified currently, and, of course, we have no Empire to command. This statement is dated back in the age of our Empire: -

'Levee ceremonies were held by regal representatives of the British Empire, such as the Viceroy of India, the Lord Lieutenant of Ireland, Governors General and state / governors / provincial governors and lieutenant governors. The ceremonial event continues to be held in a number of Commonwealth countries. The New Year's levee is still held on New Year's Day in Canada, by the Governor General of Canada, the Lieutenant Governors, the Canadian Armed Forces, and various municipalities across the country.'

Countless newspaper clippings exist where editors have gone to great lengths to list every invitee. There are pages and pages of guests, including, on most occasions, Luke and a plethora of other VC holders being in attendance. The compilation of these lists much have been such a bore for those employed to compile them. But heaven help them if they accidentally missed one.

Luke had attended Levees prior to 1880 but one he attended at St James' Palace on 7th May 1880, was reported in America by the press wishing to associate Luke with the equally revered brother of his, Major Daniel O'Connor. This clipping below, was carried in Daniel's local newspaper, the Wilmington Morning Star on 9th June 1880. The Prince of Wales was hosting the Levee for his mother, Queen Victoria.

How spectacular that incident must have been to Luke and his siblings to realise that he had shaken hands with the future King Edward 7th and that he had recognised him from when he received the VC from his mother, Queen Victoria over 20 years previously. But couldn't that have been Albert Edward 'showing off' because he was, after all, the Commander in Chief of the Regiment, and had sat with Luke on many of the regiment's annual reunion dinners?

Another description of a levee worthy of comment above many others, appeared in the Burnley Express of the 8th June 1907. It was also accompanied by a sketch of Luke, but it was in too poor a condition to include here. With the sketch, was included the fact that he was the first wearer of the VC in India and that this had aroused great curiosity from his comrades.

A Pleasing Incident and a Flattering Compliment.

In the London *Court Journal* for May 22nd we find the following pleasant incident, which will be of interest to our readers when it is known that the Lieutenant Colonel O'Connor so flatteringly alluded to is a brother of Mr. Daniel O'Connor, of this city:

At the last levee an incident occurred illustrating the extraordinary faculty possessed by so many of the royal family of remembering faces, and, at the same time, the goodness of heart of the Prince. A number of officers of the 23rd Royal Welsh Fusiliers attended the levee, and among them Lieutenant Colonel O'Connor, V. C. By some mistake he was announced as Lieutenant O'Connor. The Prince said—"No, no; that is wrong; it is my friend Colonel O'Connor," and shook him heartily by the hand, and addressing the Colonel, said—"I remember quite well when I was a boy seeing my mother decorate you with the Victoria Cross, after your return from the Crimea, for your gallant conduct at the battle of the Alma. I am glad to see you, and hope you are quite well." The incident caused a considerable sensation among those who witnessed it, and it must have been extremely gratifying to the gallant Colonel to find that the Prince of Wales still remembered him and the occasion of his decoration after the lapse of nearly a quarter of a century.

In addition to his medals, he also received other commendations and honours including those by men who had held him in their highest esteem when under his own command, and those who were also of superior rank.

Apart from General Codrington and Sir George Brown, there appears no doubt that fellow Irishman, General Sir Daniel Lysons, both as Luke's senior officer in various ranks and later in retirement, as a close friend when they lived near to each other in Piccadilly, London. They held a tremendous amount of respect for each other. General Lysons died on 29th January 1898 and Luke attended his funeral.

Luke's meritorious activities in foreign lands, also hadn't escaped the notice of his brethren in Ireland, as will be discovered in the next chapter.

THE BOYLE PRESENTATION OF 1st JUNE 1875

Luke returned to Ireland with the 2nd Battalion in September 1872. He was now 44 years of age but no doubt, he would have cast his mind back over 30 years ago, when as a small boy, he had ogled over his hero soldiers at the Boyle barracks at those times when he emulating them by drilling his boyhood chums in the streets outside the barracks. Yet, here he now was, a hero soldier himself, being dined as the guest of honour of the town in which he had earlier been raised. He was now a son of Boyle and they were delighted to receive him with open arms.

The whole town had collected sufficient funds to commission, the renowned London silversmiths, Mappin & Webb, to make the magnificent centre piece pictured on pages below, which now stands on display at the Royal Welsh Fusiliers Museum within Caernarfon Castle.

The author is indebted to the Board of Trustees through the museum curatorial advisor, Dr Kevin Mason FMA, his staff, Keith Jones, (Visitors Serving Officer) and Shirley Williams, (Education Officer) who provided him with every assistance during his last visit. The photographs on the following pages are not of the best quality owing to being taken behind glass as the cup was deemed too precious to turn or even touch.

The presentation, as described in the newspaper, 'The Penny Illustrated', shown here, was made at the Royal hotel in Boyle on 1st June 1875, only two years, after his return from what was then, the Gold Coast of West Africa. Immediately below, is another cutting from the Naval and Military Gazette, 'The Broad Arrow' which was published on 19th June 1875. The same news item was also carried in many other newspapers including the Western Mail widely circulated in South Wales, since the people of Wales held a great passion for the Royal Welsh Fusiliers. Even as an Irishman, Luke was, of course, already a hero and any news of him was always interestingly received.

A GALLANT FUSILIER.

The career of Lieutenant-Colonel Luke O'Connor may be cited as one of the very few instances presented by the British Army of the promotion of a private soldier to a high rank as an officer. Luke O'Connor has literally fought his way upwards. He entered the Army, a valiant "Roscommon boy," twenty-five years ago. Step by step he rose, sword in hand he cleaved his way, earning the Victoria Cross by his bravery at the Alma, the Redan, and Sebastopol. Chivalrously he rushed to the rescue of his fellow-countrymen in deadly peril during the Indian Mutiny, serving during the relief and capture of Lucknow, at Cawnpore, &c.; and in our last little war Lieutenant-Colonel Luke O'Connor was one of the gallant officers who so well supported Sir Garnet Wolseley. Right nobly merited, therefore, was the handsome testimonial presented to this heroic soldier at the Royal Hotel, Boyle, Roscommon, on the 1st inst., when some friends and admirers gathered at a banquet to pay this substantial tribute to the distinguished Lieutenant-Colonel of the Royal Welsh Fusiliers.

The Penny Illustrated 26 June 1875

23RD (ROYAL WELSH FUSILIERS).—On the 1st June a public dinner was given to Lieutenant-Colonel O'Connor, V.C., at the Royal Hotel, Boyle, which was made the occasion of presenting that gallant officer with a silver cup in recognition of his brilliant military services and esteem for him as a friend. The chair was occupied by Captain E. R. King-Harman, while the vice-chair was filled by J. D. MacDermot, Esq. On the right side of the chairman sat the guest of the evening, and the Hon. Charles French, M.P., for Roscommon. On the left were—the Right Hon. the Earl of Kingston, and Colonel Chichester. The president said they had met to honour an esteemed friend and a tried old soldier, Colonel Luke O'Connor, who had the rare privilege of wearing on his breast the double Victoria Cross, besides medals and clasps bravely won in many a hard-fought battle. As a representative of an old Roscommon family he felt proud to belong to the army, and as long as men like Luke O'Connor fought and bled the country need not despair. It was a proud day when Colonel O'Connor instead of going in command of a detachment to Sligo, came as a subordinate to Boyle, to meet his old friends and acquaintances; the town was proud of him, the whole country was proud of him. He (the chairman) felt proud to be selected to present the testimonial to Colonel O'Connor,

and he would ask Captain Robertson to remove the covering from the cup, and he did not think the colonel would value it less because it was the work of an Irish firm. It was a gift intended to show the sincere esteem, friendship, and regard in which he was held, and Roscommon men thus conveyed their appreciation of the worth, and genuine honour of Luke O'Connor. He begged to propose the toast of Colonel Luke O'Connor. The toast was received with a perfect *furore* of applause, song, " For he's a right good fellow," and cheers three times three. Colonel O'Connor said it would require an O'Connell, or some other distinguished Irish orator rather than an old soldier to give utterances to the feelings of his heart, at the manner he was received that night by his kind, warm, and generous Roscommon friends. Eighteen years ago Her Majesty in the presence of thousands of her soldiers and thousands of her loyal subjects, pinned the Victoria Cross on his breast; but this

presentation he looked upon as a particular honour in itself—one which a soldier had no claim to. About a quarter of a century ago he went to London, where he enlisted, and was fortunate enough to join his present regiment, and fortunate again on being sent to active service. After the expiration of eighteen months he returned a sergeant; he was not a year in the Service when he was placed in command of thirty men of the Wiltshire Militia, and he was the youngest man of all. He had taken part in war after war and bore pains and troubles, but the grand reception he had now received was a solace and a comfort. But why was all this done? Was it to Luke O'Connor as a private or Luke O'Connor as a colonel decorated with medals? It was a recognition by Irishmen, by Roscommon men, that he had gained all his steps by himself. Before sitting down he once more thanked the chairman, Mr. MacDermot, and all his friends for the very handsome presentation they had made him.—The 1st Battalion will arrive in Ireland (says the *Irish Times*) about the first week in August.

Including the richly polished 'Bog Oak' base, the centre piece stands 3 feet high. Bog Oak is not a specific species of oak, but is a name given to oak that had been buried in a peat bog for a considerable time thus giving it a distinct dark brown, almost black colour.

Being partially fossilised timber formed over millennia, it is one of the rarest woods in the world and thus very expensive.

As can be seen, on each side of the base, are protrusions upon which stands an image of Luke in various aspects of his life.

On the right, he is a soldier standing at ease with his musket and on the left, he is a Sergeant carrying the Queen's colour.

The base also carries the two inscriptions; at the front is the original inscription of the presentation dated 1875 and the added one to its right is dated 1911, the year when, at the Regiment's annual dinner, Luke presented it to the Regiment. He was then, the only regimental survivor of the Alma Battle.

With the Regiment being based at Wrexham, the centre piece would have been transferred to the Wrexham museum following his death. The museum there, is part of the Royal Welsh Museum at Caernarfon.

The first inscription reads as follows: -

PRESENTED TO

Lieut. Col. Luke O'Connor VC &c &c &c

23rd. Royal Welsh Fusiliers

By numerous Fellow Countrymen of his in Roscommon and other friends

In Recognition of his Brilliant Military Career

Alma   Redan Sebastopol Quarries &c &c &c

Lucknow (Relief and Capture) Cawnpore &c &c Gold Coast

Note: &c = 'and so forth'. Today, it would be etc. etc.

The 2nd inscription reads: -

To the Officers of the Depot

The Royal Welsh Fusiliers

WREXHAM. FROM

Major General Luke O'Connor VC CB

Late Royal Welsh Fusiliers

June 1911

Although inscribed 'June 1911' Luke made the presentation on 30th May 1911 at the annual regimental dinner held at Prince's Restaurant, Piccadilly.

What a gesture it was for Luke to have presented this magnificent centre piece to his regiment, but on reflection, how sad was it to recognise that with no family of his own, in Luke's mind, he was indeed, presenting it to the regiment, which was, of course, 'his family'?

Returning to the images of Luke, on the very top of it, is another portrayal of him in his rank of Lt. Colonel which was the rank he carried of that day. His pose is typical of him as is evident in many photographs, with hand on sword and headdress of the day. The silversmith has done a magnificent job and has included his moustache and even his VC and other medals.

Billy Windsor's horns

The top of the cup

With an abundance of Prince of Wales feathers, leeks and battle scenes, the Dragon has centre place.

As indicated in the above, the artwork around the cup includes the head of a horned goat, depicting the regiment's mascot. 'Billy Windsor, the first of the mascot goats, which was presented by Queen Victoria in 1844. Since then, the British monarchy has presented an unbroken series of Kashmir goats to the Royal Welsh from the Crown's own royal herd.

As a matter of interest, the goat had an official army number, 25232301 and until 2006, during Billy's first overseas mission in Cyprus to celebrate the Queen's 80th Birthday, he held the rank of Lance Corporal. However, on that occasion and despite being ordered to keep in line, he refused to obey and failed to keep in step. He also tried to headbutt a drummer.

His behaviour resulted in Billy appearing on a disciplinary charge before his commanding officer, Lieutenant Colonel Huw James who sentenced him to be demoted to fusilier. This demotion meant that other fusiliers in the regiment no longer had to stand to attention when Billy walked past, as they were obliged to, in the rank of lance corporal. Billy finally regained his Lance Corporal rank three months later after behaving exceptionally well at the Alma Day parade.

Luke had apparently taken some leave of absence over the period of his presentation in Ireland, as indicated in Irish newspapers on 7th and 8th July 1875 when it was reported that he had sailed for Gibraltar to join headquarters, following a period of leave of absence.

On 3rd August 1879, the 2nd Battalion of the Royal Welsh were still in Gibraltar under the command of Lieutenant Colonel Sydney Millet who had served with Luke throughout the Crimean war and also with General Garnet Wolseley during the Ashanti campaign in West Africa. For his service there, on 1st April 1874, he too, was given the brevet rank of lieutenant-colonel and was awarded the Ashanti War medal with the clasp 'Coomassie'.

It was therefore, ironic that, at Gibraltar, aged only 42, Millet died of sunstroke on 3 August 1879, after only a few days illness and whilst in command of the 2nd Battalion. It is from a clipping from the 'Derby Daily Telegraph' dated 9th August 1879 which touches on what appears to be Luke's tour in Gibralter, when he went to assume Millet's command after his death.

The poor quality clipping is transcribed as follows: -

By a telegraph received from Gibraltar, I notice the death of Lieut.-Colonel Millet of the 23rd Welsh Fusiliers. This officer had seen good service in the Crimea and on the Gold Coast. His successor in command of the 2nd battalion of the regiment is the famous soldier Luke O'Connor, who has just started for the Rock. He served all through the Eastern campaign, concluding with the battle of the Alma, where, after being severely wounded, he carried the Queen's colours – Lieutenant Anstruther, who had previously borne it being killed – and planted it on the Russian redoubt, under a heavy fire, and stuck to it until the close of the action, when, on the field, he was thanked by General Codrington and Sir George Brown. At the siege of Sebastopol he distinguished himself again, and won the Victoria Cross. Thereafter, he went through the exciting times of the Indian mutiny, being present at the relief of Lucknow, and saw service also at Ashante.

On the 27th of August 1879, the Naval and Military Gazette, announcing Luke's promotion to Colonel. The actual entry is quite informative because it also carried the rank from which he was promoted to colonel. He had been Major and Brevet Lieutenant-Colonel.

As confirmed by his later promotion to the substantive rank of Lieutenant - Colonel, this promotion, would have been to properly formalise the promotion from major to the substantive rank of Lieutenant Colonel. These Lieutenant Colonels, (known today as half colonels) were often referred to as just 'Colonel'.

The authoritative record of promotions contained in the 'Hart's Index' indicates that Luke's promotion to substantive Lieutenant-Colonel was later, on 21st June 1880, which immediately followed Colonel Savage Mostyn's retirement. However, he would still have been addressed as 'Colonel' and from thence on, he was to assume command of the 2nd Battalion.

PRESENTATION OF NEW COLOURS

It was just a year ago when Luke was dispatched back to Gibraltar to command the 2nd Battalion of the Royal Welsh, and here he was now, on 16th August 1880, back in Portsmouth, as an honoured guest at the dockside celebration for the arrival of the Prince and Princess of Wales, and the presentation of new colours to the 1st Battalion, by the Prince of Wales (Albert Edward – Future King Edward 7th).

The 1st Battalion, under the command of Lieutenant Colonel Elgee, was to embark on the ship, *Malabar* for their voyage to India and so, with the Prince and Princess ariving at Portsmouth in the Royal Yacht 'Osborne', this was convenient for all.

Numerous digniatries were present and sat in a special V.I.P. enclosure. Thousands of excited members of the public were seated in an enclosure behind the V.I.Ps. Included below, is a clipping from a Hampshire newspaper, which provides a flavour of the scene and a 'Who's Who' of the honoured guests present.

The item describes in great detail, all Luke's exploits and the honours bestowed upon him. Of special interest in the proceedings was the mention of the process of casing up the 'old colours' and the sending of them to the rear of the formation. This was described as being done in the form of three sides of a square. All this was performed whilst the band played 'Auld Lang Syne' in slow time.

Both the new Regimental and Queen's colours were brought forward in their respective cases and were handed to the Prince of Wales, who then formally presented them individually to two Lieutenants of the Regiment who, as was the tradition, received them whilst on their knees.

The Prince wore the scarlet uniform of a field-marshal, and the Duke of Edinburgh the uniform of a rear-admiral, both having the sash and jewel of the Garter and the gold shoulder rope of personal A.D.C. to Her Majesty, while the Princess of Wales looked her loveliest in a bottle green satin dress spotted with gold, with bonnet to match. The Royal enclosure contained, in addition to the Prince and Princess of Wales and the Duke of Edinburgh : Prince and Princess Edward of Saxe-Weimar, Admiral Ryder, Rear-Admiral the Hon. and Mrs. Foley, Admiral A. W. A. Hood, Lord and Lady Cecilia Bingham, Admiral Sir Harry Keppel, Mr. and Mrs. Cornwallis West, Lieut.-Colonel Luke O'Connor, of the 2nd Battalion 23rd Regiment, General Crutchley, Colonel-in-Chief of the Regiment, Mr. Falbe, Danish Minister, Mr. H. Calcraft, Lord Henry Lennox, Commander Lord Charles Beresford, Captain Stephenson, General Sir Daniel Lysons (whose son proceeds to India with the battalion), General Connolly, Military Attaché at Paris, Lord Charles Scott, the Hon. Oliver Montagu, the Hon. A. F. Greville, Colonel Bray, Colonel Dormer, Captain Lord Albert Seymour, Captain the Hon. C. C. G. Byng, &c., &c.

Speeches were then made, first, by the Prince and in response, by Colonel Elgee. The Prince who was, of course, the eldest son of Queen Victoria and Albert, made mention that the old colours had been presented to the Regiment by his father, some 31 years previously. These, therefore were the very colours that were carried throughout Luke's tours of duty in the Crimea, the Queen's colour being the one that Luke had planted on the Russian redoubt, the deed which had won him his VC.

At the conclusion of the proceedings, the soldiers gave another royal salute before forming up into their companies to march off to board the *Malabar.* They were a total of 880 soldiers along with their senior officers and other staff. Their Royal Highnesses and their entourage boarded horse carriages which took them to the nearby dockyard where, prior to boarding the Royal Yacht Osborne, they gave a fine lunch to their V.I.P. digniatries, including Luke.

It was during this luncheon that the old and tattered colours, which were to be placed in Wrexham Parish Church, were, at the request of the Princess of Wales, taken on board *Osborne* and placed in the saloon. After all the battles that they had endured, they had now been reduced to mere shreds of silk but had a proud history of their own.

The Prince and Princess of Wales – The future King Edward 7th and his Queen Alexandra of Denmark

The report concludes that it was no wonder that the regiment was reluctant to part with them, so long as any officer who fought under them at Alma, remained alive. Their dilapidated state meant that they were prevented from being unfurled, but this was not caused through moths or wear but from the enemy fire during the taking of the Great Russian redoubt at the Alma. It was at the same time, that the colours were presented in 1849 by the Prince Consort, that the first royal goat mascot was also presented to the regiment.

The author, accompanied by the Reverend Bray, conducted a search of St Giles Church, Wrexham but failed to find these old colours. However, since then he has been informed by the Reverend that they are at Caernarfon Castle. Their condition, even in 1880, were too shredded to be unfurled, so although they are still to be uneathed for sure, it is possible that they will remain boxed, albeit in safe hands.

Following the luncheon, the whole party boarded the *Malabar* to join the regiment's soldiers by ostensibly, inspecting the vessel and the arrangements made for the comfort of the troops during their passage to India.

The carrying of, and the defence of the colours carried in battle, subsequently promoted discussion in parliament. The various distance ranges of munitions and the accuracy of the weapons firing them, were being developed and improved. This, coupled with the introduction of more modern methods of communications, negated their use as a symbol of direction and to identify the position of 'battle commanders'. After being debated in parliament, on 29th July 1881, the Secretary of State for War, Mr Childers decreed that the colours were no longer required for the purposes described.

This ended the long held tradition of carrying the colours into battle and Luke's deed, will have been one of the last of such occasions when so used.

They continue in use to this day, at ceremonial occasions.

LUKE'S PROMOTION TO LIEUTENANT COLONEL.

Luke received his promotion to Brevet Lieutenant Colonel on 19th August 1879 and as mentioned previously, his promotion to the substantive rank of Lieutenant Colonel occurred, less than a year later, on 21st June 1880. But sadly, in addition to having a promotion to celebrate, it sounded the death knell for Luke's Army career. The new regulations would now dictate that he could only serve for a further 5 years, yet he was only 49 and undoubtedly keen to continue his service.

Having returned from Africa, the regiment moved to their new barracks at Wrexham. The 1881 census was recorded on April 3rd and now records him as a Colonel, the commanding officer of the 2nd Battalion which was then based at 'The Citadel' in Portsmouth.

In November 1881, the battalion moved by train from Plymouth to Pembroke Dock, to what was known as the 'HUTS ENCAMPMENT, which was to be the battalion's new home. With the rank of Colonel, Luke was their commanding officer and his battalion consisted of 13 officers, 41 sergeants and 418 privates.

On 18th March 1882, Luke and other local dignitaries were to greet the Duke and Duchess of Edinburgh, when they arrived for the launching of HMS Edinburgh by the duchess, at Pembroke Dock. The Cardiff Times recorded that, **'The Royal Welsh Fusiliers were under the command of Colonel Luke O'Connor, V.C., a wonderful soldier, who has risen from the ranks and wears no less than 10 medals, and is loved and idolised by his men'……**

This type of description aimed to emphasise the respect held for him by the men under his command, is typical of many similar accolades.

HMS Edinburgh

The vessel being launched, was an 'ironclad' battleship specially protected by iron and steel against submarine attack. She was the 'state of the art' of British Navy battleships.

Below is a transcript of a cutting from the Western Mail dated 22nd September 1883, which describes another Alma anniversary.

The Royal Welsh on parade at 'Huts Encampment' Llanion Hill

PEMBROKE DOCK

ANNIVERSARY OF THE BATTLE OF THE ALMA – Thursday being the anniversary of the battle of the Alma, the Royal Welsh Fusiliers, who took part in that action, as well as their present gallant commander, Colonel Luke O'Connor, V.C., assembled on the parade ground, Huts Encampment, where the interesting ceremony of "trooping the colours" was gone through. One of the Cashmere goats recently presented to the regiment by Her Majesty the Queen, was present on parade for the first time.

As far as the goat was concerned, whilst this goat might well have appeared on parade for the first time, it was, of course, one of many goats that had been presented to the regiment following the first one donated by the Prince Consort, back in 1849.

Luke would have been so pleased to have ended his Army days following his last transfer with the regiment to Ireland, in November 1883, which will be touched upon later.

The effects of the 'Purchase Review'

Now that the purchase and selling of commissions had been banned, far more retirements and promotions ensued. No longer was the Army a home for elderly commanders or it being seen by them as providing a 'job for life'. In Luke's case as a bachelor, the Army was his life.

The royal commission and the changes proposed by the Cardwell Reforms, came into effect on 1st November 1871. The legislation was passed during Prime Minister William Ewart Gladstone's office. The views as expressed in the national press were mixed, but some suggested that the provisions had been ignored by some, or that maybe unwarranted exceptions had been made. Whatever, a whole host of impending retirements had been made, and very often, the names of those who would replace them were quoted.

One newspaper reported, *"Those officers commanding regiments or battalions who have so relentlessly remained on full pay since 1871, are at last to be forcibly ejected. Colonel Stanley has the warrant duly copied and signed by the Queen before leaving office. It gives only two months notice to the lingerers on the full page stage. But I believe that all of them would be provided with staff posts or those refuges of age or incapacity – brigade depots. This removal will give promotion in two cavalry regiments and in thirteen or fourteen infantry battalions"*

This was just a small part of a long article and unfortunately, the part containing details of the command of the Royal Welsh Regiment is lower down and unreadable. It has therefore, merely been added below, that part pertaining to Luke's retirement on half pay. This obviously confirms the fact that Luke's promotion ceased after he had served his five years in the rank.

Luke had been promoted to the substantive rank of Lieutenant Colonel on 21st June 1880 and now, with such promotions being only for 5 years, his retirement was compulsary. Yet, it appears blatantly obvious, that he had the wherewithal to reach a higher rank. The disappointment expressed in the article and the comments about him wouldn't have been unexpected. He could well have been given a grace and favour 'brevet' promotion to Colonel, following his full time retirement, but all that, and the circumstances of how he would acquire the rank of Major General, will be explained later.

These are good examples of how promotions were awarded in an 'honorary' capacity, sometimes as a 'thank you' for gallantry or other deserving conduct, as the regulations permitted. Ironically, promotions were awarded even after being retired. But why, oh why, did the Army make its rank structure so complicated?

So Luke had taken over command of the 2nd Battalion from Colonel Savage Mostyn in 1880. But what rank did he hold then? Thankfully, thanks to the discovery of the Hart's Army Lists 1882 to 1962, seen below, this can be explained. So here, it is revealed the date of Luke's promotion to substantive Lieutenant-Colonel, was on 21st June 1880. This would have been when he took command of the 2nd Battalion.

Hart's Army list provided just about every promotion and award of honours attained by every recipient during a period of 80 years.

Lieutenant-Colonels (with honorary rank of Major-General)—continued.					
NAME.	DATE OF BIRTH.	DATE OF FIRST COMMISSION.	DATE OF SUBSTANTIVE LIEUTENANT-COLONEL.	REGIMENT FROM WHICH RETIRED AND DATE OF RETIREMENT.	DATE OF HONORARY RANK.
Newbolt, Edward Dorrien	5 Mar 1838	2 Feb 1858	19 Nov 1881	Dorset R. 19 Nov 87	19 Nov 1887
Newman, Walter	18 Nov 1836	31 July 1855	15 Feb 1882	hp. R. Art. 15 Feb 87 Ret. Pay 15 Feb 87	15 Feb 1887
J.C.O'Connor, Luke [R]	21 Feb 1831	5 Nov 1854	21 Jun 1880	hp. late R. W. Fus. 21 Jun 85 Ret. Pay 9 Mar 87	9 Mar 1887

Luke's promotion to the substantive rank of Lieutenant-Colonels is indicated as 21st June 1880. It is also interesting to see that this Hart's list, known for its accuracy, records his date of birth as 21st

February 1831. One recalls in the first chapter of this book, how his date of birth was normally quoted as being one of two. Here is the reminder :-

20th	January	1831
21st	February	1832

Each element of the birthdate had been increased (or decreased) by one!

Well, here in comparison, we have a mixture of the elements taken from both. The 21st February is now taken from the 1832 date but used in the 1831 year. With Luke being on record stating that he was born in 1832, this definitely confirms suspicion that there was some jiggery-pokery going on and that he was most probably, the active participant.

But let's look at this document a little closer. For a start, its title is 'Lieutenant Colonels' followed by, in brackets (with honorary rank of Major General). So this was a retrospective document limiting those promoted to the substantive rank of Lieutenant Colonel, who went on to gain the honorary rank of Major General. In this case, it records Luke's retirement on the 5th anniversary, 21st June 1885. It is important to note that his retirement is preceded by the letters *'hp'* which indicates that his retirement was on 'half pay'.

The final column indicates that he was given the honorary rank of Major General on 9th March 1887, which was also the date of his retirement on a full pay pension.

What it records is very clear but it's what is missing, that is so important. There is no mention of Luke being promoted to the substantive rank of Colonel, even though he was always referred to as such. However, this only explains the fact that those possessing this Lt. Colonel rank were, in any event, always addressed as 'Colonel'. So did he ever indeed, receive that promotion? Although it appears from the above, that he did not, it was much later that it was discovered that, in fact, his appointment to be Colonel of the Regiment, did not occur until some 27 years after he had fully retired, when he was given the Honorary rank of Major General, in 1887, as disclosed below. Promotions given to him, long after his retirement on full pay! How complicated!

AN HONORARY MAJOR GENERAL

Luke's promotion to the honorary rank of Major General, resulted in his 1887 retirement on a full pay pension. However, the appointment of Colonel of the Regiment, was to come 27 years later, on the 2nd June 1914 upon the death of Major General, The Honorable Sir Savage Lloyd-Mostyn K.C.B.

It seems remarkable, that a retired Lieutenant Colonel in 1887, could, be given an honorary rank of Major General and then, 27 years later, be made a full Colonel, the head of the Regiment. No doubt he had been 'in line' for this honour, which could only be awarded on the death of the post holder. His elevation to Colonel of the Regiment in 1914, will be dealt with at the appropriate time. He would have undoubtedly regarded the Cardwell Reforms as the boot which kicked him prematurely out of the Army and had robbed him of the final years of the career that he would have yearned to have retained for a much longer period.

When giving evidence to the Royal Commission, he stated that he was aimimg for higher rank and we can be pretty sure that he would have reached his ambition. Yes, he was obviously grateful for his honorary rank of Major General, but the Army was his life and he would have given his right arm, to have continued in the service of the crown.

So having been in the Army for all his adult years, it will be interesting to learn about his life immediately post his half pay retirement during that one year and almost ten months of his life, after 1887, when he fully retired with his 'Major General' rank.

So far as his domestic circumstances were concerned when in service, he would possibly have been in 'quarters' and so, presumably, such accommodation would have ceased on his retirement. He was financially secure and eventually settled in London, at 34 Clarges Street, where he lived until his death. So let's examine what his circumstances were when he retired in June 1885 on half pay.

The presentation made to him in Boyle in 1875, was ten years before his retirement. He had, of course, been stationed there since September 1872 but his stay had been interupted by his involvement in the Ashanti War. He had already made his mark at Boyle, when he arranged the performance of a play by members of his battalion. He had also been to Ireland before, as a newly promoted sergeant and when he attended the Lord Lieutenant's 'Drawing Room' (Levee) at Dublin Castle in 1863.

I had often wondered how, in later life, the wounds he had suffered, had affected him. There was a hint of it when the presentation of new colours by the Prince of Wales was made in 1880. This event was also attended by John Griffith, Rector of Merthyr Tydfil who wrote a detailed account of the proceedings in the Western Mail newspaper, only two days later.

The Reverend gentleman admitted that (no doubt by using his 'dog collar' as an unchallengable invitation), he managed to 'weasle' his way into the VIP enclosure without being officially invited and that he had stood very close to Luke. He particularly commented on his appearance since he last saw him at Cardiff Castle only six years earlier, shortly after his Ashanti War experience. The below is a transcription of a section of this 1880 nepaper :-

> *"…….It was an Irishman, not a Welshman that did the gallant deed, and he today, Colonel of the 23rd. But oh, how changed from the last time I saw him at the ball at Cardiff Castle in the great temporary saloon erected for the purpose when Lord Bute came of age. He was then, a dashing young officer, dancing with every young lady that could get at him; but now, a dashing officer still, it is true, and nothing dashing is there that he would not do if called upon; but bowed in the back and looking more than 10 years older than he really is – he is only 51; the wounds in the breast have evidently told upon him."*

We can only assume that we get to look older as years fly by, though, such an obvious a statement that is to make, in Luke's case, his worth was to the young men who were to follow him, either on the battlefield or off it, at any age, the newspaper clipping on the next page, is testiment to the Army's loss.

The clipping was first published in the military newspaper, 'Broad Arrow' and then copied in many other newspapers across the nation in July 1885, just after Luke's retirement. He, and all those who had served under him, would have been justifiably proud of the content.

This was an excellent example of how he had wanted to encourage others to take the Queen's shilling. He obviously nurtured those he could see with potential and those who hadn't, he probably would have encouraged, at least to do their best.

Also, I suspect that to him, these youngsters were representing the sons he never had and his interest in them, was as a wise father of their regiment.

IRELAND AND THE MOVE TO RETIREMENT

Despite original beliefs to the contrary, Luke had indeed, visited Ireland when he was first promoted Sergeant and as a guest of Ireland's Lord Lieutenant and, of course, when he was posted there by the British Army in 1872.

The 2nd Battalion moved to Templemore, Ireland on 20th November, 1883 and it moved to Fermoy only a month after Luke's retirement on 5th June 1855. His base there, was undoubtedly the start of numerous ferry trips backwards and forwards to the mainland. It wouldn't have been surprising, had he chosen to retire to Ireland. However, during this time as a celebrated hero senior officer, the friend's he had made since, were mostly based in London.

O'CONNOR'S BOYS.—In commenting recently upon the retirement of Colonel Luke O'Connor, V.C., from the command of the Royal Welsh Fusiliers, we took occasion to point out the encouragement it must give to every recruit in the battalion to know that his commanding officer has himself risen from the ranks and takes a kindly yet discerning interest in his men. The excellent spirit pervading all ranks of the Royal Welsh Fusiliers is sufficient evidence of this fact. The interest taken by Colonel O'Connor in his regiment has resulted, as might have been expected, in the battalion having amongst its officers some who have, like their worthy commandant, "taken the Queen's shilling," and not a few of our crack infantry corps have on their roll of officers those who are familiarly known in the Service as "O'Connor's Boys." Two of the latest of these are Colour-Sergeant Wilcock and Sergeant-Instructor of Musketry Armitage. The former has been three years in the Fusiliers, and now goes to India to join his new regiment, whilst the latter has rendered good service in connection with the musketry instruction of the regiment. With so many examples of this kind before them, it is not surprising to learn that there are now in the battalion several gentlemen who have joined with a view of promotion, knowing the great interest Colonel O'Connor takes in such cases. We feel confident that though the gallant officer who has so long been at the head of the Fusiliers, has retired, the best traditions of the regiment will be continued by Colonel Williamson; and that the long list of "O'Connor's Boys" now serving in various parts of the world may rest assured that the good work carried on by their erstwhile chief has not been neglected by his successor.

For the record, the 2nd Battalion had also moved to Galway in September 1887 and The Currough in July 1890 from where it returned to Aldershot, England in September, 1892. Luke may have been lucky to spend the last two years of his service in the land he loved, but on the other hand, had they left him alone to continue for a while, he could have spent another seven years in Ireland. His gallant actions and bravery had robbed him of any domestic life, especially of homeland visits to Ireland.

We can be assured that he would have 'Made hay while the sun shone' in Ireland whilst he was there up until his retirement. It was no wonder, therefore, that many short newspaper notices to the effect that Luke was frequently transferring between England and Kingstown (Dunleary) Dublin from around the time of the 2nd Battalion's move there, were being published. One can well imagine that whenever he was in Ireland, he would have felt that he had returned home. As he said in his autobiography, he was **"Irish to the core".** It was so pleasing to have unearthed this below clip of 3rd January 1885, as it represented the first positive evidence of his return to Ireland.

CHRISTMAS DAY AT THE BRIGADE DEPOT.

Christmas Day was very pleasantly spent by the soldiers; the men's rooms presented more than the usual festive appearance of the season, and the good old custom of decorating the barrack room was kept up. Captain Evans and Lieutenant Walker (Companies A and B) dined together in No. 1 room, Wynnstay block, and Major Hutton and Lieutenant Gwyn (Companies C and D) in No. 3 room, Ellis's block. The entrance to the first was decorated with laurel and holly, and over the door in large letters was a "Welcome to all," whilst over the entrance door inside the room was placed crossed flags, surmounted with the letters "R.W.F." The shelves and window-sills along the room were ornamented with colored paper, which material was also largely employed in the way of festoons and window curtains. The honors of the 23rd were inscribed on the walls, as also the following inscriptions—"A Merry Christmas and a Happy New Year," "God Save our Gracious Queen," "Success to the Royal Welsh Fusiliers," "Long life and happiness to Captain Evans and Lieutenant Walker," "Success to Col. the Hon. S. Mostyn," "Prosperity to Quarter-Master Perris," "Long life and happiness to Color-Sergeants Phillips and Knightley." Over the fireplace at the extreme end of the room was a small picture of St. David, harp in hand, surrounded with evergreens, and underneath, the inscription "God Bless the Prince of Wales." Altogether the room presented a very neat appearance, and the decorations were highly creditable to all concerned. The decorations in No. 3 room, Ellis' Block, were very effectively carried out, and certainly carried off the palm in the way of artistic display. Over the entrance door was a pretty arch, formed of evergreens, and over the entrance door, inside the room, was a representation of the Prince of Wales' Plume, whilst on either side were the inscriptions "Health and good luck to our comrades in India, Col. Elgee and Officers, 1st Battalion," "Health and good luck to our comrades in Ireland, Col. Luke O'Connor and Officers, 2nd Battalion," "Health and prosperity to Capt. and Mrs Cowan." Over the mantlepiece, in the centre of the room, was a representation of the Prince of Wales' Plume, encircled with the regimental motto "Nec aspera terrent," and below were the words "A Merry Christmas to you all," the whole surrounded with the honors of the 23rd. Over the fireplace at the lower end of the room was a large picture of St. David, harp in hand, and underneath it "Success to our Colonel, the Hon. S. Mostyn, C.B.," and on either side "General Gordon, God bless him," "Success and long life to Major and Mrs Hutton and Lieut. Gwyn," "Good luck to our troops in Egypt." Around the walls at intervals were inscriptions such as "God save our Queen," "Good health to Deputy-Surgeon-General St. John Stanley," "Sir Watkin and family for ever," with the motto "Cymry am Byth," "Our best wishes to our Sergt.-Major," "Health and prosperity to Color-Sergeants Bennett and McGregor." The shelves and window sills were ornamented with colored paper, whilst the walls were decorated with evergreens and banners. Crossed rifles, chain pattern decorations of parti colored paper, hung from the ceiling to the side walls, the ceiling being decorated at intervals with circles of laurel leaves, whilst crossed hoops depended therefrom. Festoons of laurel and colored paper ran along the length of the room over the windows, and this had a nice effect. Indeed, this room presented a very attractive appearance, the adornment of which displayed a degree of taste and labor highly creditable. On Christmas morning the troops attended divine service, and were home in good time for their dinner, which was one o'clock. By the aid of the usual grant from the canteen fund and liberal

It was probably fortuitous that Luke had returned to his Irish base at Templemore, because, on the 3rd April of that same 1885 year, he attended a Queen's Levee at Dublin Castle. This, of course, was only two months before he retired on half pay on 21st June, 1885.

He had also attended a previous Queen's Levee at St James's Palace on 6th May. The mass of information about the guests, took up a double page in the Morning Post and so, suffice to say here, that the principal guests were the Dukes of York and Wellington.

So far as his actual retirement was concerned, the Army published the following 'farewell' order.

> *"Colonel L. O'Connor having completed his five years in command of the 2nd Battalion, Royal Welch Fusiliers, feels most keenly leaving the distinguished Regiment which he had the good fortune when quite a young man, to join.*
>
> *It will, however, always be with pride that he can look back, and know that he had the good luck to have shared in so many of its brilliant Campaigns and Battles, in different parts of the world, for which he was recommended and received many honours and decorations, and also for having attained the proud position of commanding a Battalion of the Royal Welch Fusiliers during the last five years of his service in it.*
>
> *Colonel O'Connor need hardly say that he will ever take the greatest interest in the welfare of the Regiment and wishes all in it every good fortune and happiness: he feels sure that the high discipline and esprit de corps which has distinguished the Royal Welch Fusiliers, since the formation of the Regiment, will always be maintained.*
>
> *In bidding farewell to all, he would wish to give a few parting words of advice to the Non-Commissioned Officers and Men of the Battalion, which at the moment is chiefly composed of such very young soldiers. That they must take interest in the service and particularly in the*

distinguished Regiment to which they belong, learning their drill and duties as quickly as possible. That they must always obey their superiors in everything, thus preventing much crime in the Battalion.

Lastly, they must remember that everything is done for their comfort and happiness, being fairly well paid, well clothed, fed and educated, and that by leading a steady life while in the service, they will not only be a credit to their Regiment, but also well fitted when discharged for civil employment".

His retirement on half pay is mentioned towards the end of the clipping on the next page, which first describes how some of the young boys under Luke's command, referred to as 'O'Connor Boys', had progressed and how they had joined the Army intending to follow Luke's example. It is so obvious that he had nurchered them.

The *Gazette* of Tuesday last announced the promotion of Serjeant W. A. B. Russwurm, Royal Welsh Fusiliers, to a Lieutenancy in the Lincolnshire Regiment. This makes the third of what are known as "O'Connor Boys" who have obtained commissions from the battalion of the old 23rd, lately commanded by that splendid old soldier, Colonel Luke O'Connor, in the last eighteen months. The three "boys" in question are all devoted soldiers, of good birth and education, who joined the ranks of the Royal Welsh, determined to follow as far as they could the example of its popular "chief." Colonel O'Connor soon found them out, and did what he could to push them on. It is surprising how the name of Luke O'Connor still lives among the rank and file of the Royal Welsh; it is even more surprising that one who has done so much in his time for his regiment and the service should have been entirely overlooked in the recent Bath selection. If ever a man deserved a C.B., Luke O'Connor did; and he has got nothing.

Army and Navy Gazette 5th June 1886

With all this publicity, and attendance at these Levees, it was no wonder that he was being tipped for an honour in the forthcoming June 1886, 'Birthday Honours'.

He hadn't yet fully retired and among further spasmodic visits to Ireland, comment was appearing in various newpapers about the prospects of Luke receiving a Companion of the Order of the Bath (CB). With his being omitted from the 1886 honours, the mood of many around the country was that the famous Luke O'Connor, should be honoured in the forthcoming Queen Victoria's 'Golden Jubilee Honours'.

Sad to say that despite his being heavily favoured again, to receive a CB, in preparation for a knighthood, his name had been completely missed from that list also. The subject was continually raised in national newspapers; as another example, quoted below from 'The People' dated 12th June 1887, suggests: -

It is to be hoped that in the forthcoming list of jubilee honours, the name may not be missed of Major General Luke O'Connor, V.C., who stands forward pre-emanently as the most truly representative soldier in the British Army. A man who has done for his country what Luke O'Connor has done – who has risen from the ranks to the command his regiment, and won his commission and the bronze cross 'For Valour' fighting against a European (not a nigger) enemy – possesses claims to recognition by his Sovereign which none can deny. Of Luke O'Connor, no one has had a bad word to say. His whole career has been an example of uprightedness and devotion to duty.

Unfortunately, another nine years had to elapse before he received any further honours and one wonders whether snobishness, had a hand to play. After all, he had only been a 'non-commissioned' officer! Many of the recipients were regarded as less deserving than Luke, indeed, most had not witnessed a bullet fired in anger, yet most, if not all, had received commissions.

It was at around this time, that some of the publicity surrounding Luke's retirement, had come to the notice of his brother, Thomas, in America. It must be remembered, that up until then, although no hard evidence had been forthcoming of any contact between Luke and his estranged siblings in America, circumstantial evidence tended to confirm that letter exchanges must have been made. The contact mentioned in the clipping below left, serves to corroborate such a distant affiliation existed with at least, his brother, Thomas. This clipping was taken from the Omaha Daily Bee dated 13th May 1887. Thomas, like his brothers, Daniel and Luke, was a respected citizen of his community.

A Soldier.

Thomas O'Connor, the veteran citizen and office holder in this community, has received information that his brother Luke, a distinguished officer in the service of England, has been retired with the rank of major general. Luke O'Connor was offered the governor generalship of Canada at one time, but refused it, preferring to be on active service. In speaking of him the London Times says:

"It is announced that the next Bath Gazette will include that gallant soldier, Luke O'Connor, who when sergeant at Alma, was one of the first recipients of the Victoria cross. He has recently retired from the service with the rank of major general."

The London *Gazette* of March 8th says Col. Luke O'Connor, V. C., of the British Army, has been placed on the retired list, with retired pay and with the honorary rank of Major General. The Col. O'Connor mentioned above, is an elder brother of Mr. D. O'Connor, of this city.

What is really amazing is that Thomas had apparently been informed by Luke that he had been asked at one time, to be the Governor General of Canada. Without knowing anything about this offer, it can only be presumed that it would have been made as a result of Luke's military posting to Canada, some years earlier. That vacancy was, indeed, filled on 23rd October, 1883 and presumed to have been the vacancy subject of the offer to him.

It was also revealing that 'The London Times' had announced that he would be included in the next 'Bath Gazette'. Brother Daniel would also have been aware of Luke's elevation to Major General – The below clipping was taken from the Wilmington Morning Star in North Carolina.

Distinguished Service Reward

The Army and Navy Gazette published on 18th December 1886, the announcement that Luke had been awarded a 'Distinguished Service' reward of £100 per annum.

Colonel Luke O'Connor, half-pay, late Royal Welsh Fusiliers, has been granted a Distinguished-Service Reward of £100 per annum. Colonel O'Connor entered the Army as a private, and raised himself, by his exemplary conduct, to a commission as Ensign November 5, 1854. He served in the Eastern Campaign of 1854-55 with the 23rd Fusiliers, including the battle of Alma, where, after being severely wounded, he carried the Queen's colour (Lieutenant Anstruther, who previously carried it, having been killed), and planted it on the Russian redoubt under a heavy fire, and carried it until the

$100 dollars in 1886, would have been a huge Christmas present for him and one wonders if it was made as compensation for loosing out financially, in his enforced early retirement. That, however, is just speculation.

FULL RETIREMENT

At age 56, and a bachelor, Luke voluntarily retired on 9th March, 1887 with an honorary rank of Major General and an annual pension of £420pa. The press considered that his honorary rank was probably a carot which softened the blow of his enforced retirement, a theory about which many would have agreed. However, using the CPI's inflation calculator, at 2020, his pension alone, would have provided him with a comparable income of £55,588 pa. In addition he was in receipt of his annual distinguished service reward and his Victoria Cross pension. He would have been more than comfortably off.

He was now taking to cruising on the best and most luxurious passenger liners available and was free to spend his time and money on enjoying himself. Whilst he has always appeared to be of the self effacing type and would have dearly loved to have continued his service in the Army, he certainly didn't appear to be of the complaining type. Indeed, his type and manner had endeared him to the community who were actively promoting him as a worthy candidate for a knightood.

The first evidence of his full retirement was published in Ireland, in the Belfast News Letter on 24th February 1887. The original is of poor quality and so, again, a small section of it has been transcribed below.

> *"I hear that Colonel Luke O'Connor, VC, late of Royal Welsh Fusiliers at Fermoy,* (he had not tranferred there) *and who is well known in Ireland, for he commanded the Battalion when at Templemore, has elected to be placed on the retired list, with the honorary rank of Major General. Luke O'Connor, as he is familiarly termed in the Fusiliers, who is one of the most popular officers in the Army, enlisted as a private, and his career has been very distinguished as a non-commissioned officer……"*

It may have been the case, of course, that the editor was unaware that Luke was actually born in Ireland. Indeed, having reviewed countless accounts of his daring deeds in numerous newspapers, they normally have started with his actions at the battle of the Alma. So far as can be recalled, his early life at Elphin, his Atlantic crossing, and his later life at Boyle Roscommon, when he was taken into the care of his uncle, have hardly been mentioned. This, despite his scant autobiography being printed in the not so well known M.A.P. magazine, overshadowed by his wartime exploits – and why not!

The first official announcement of Luke's retirement was made in 'The Times' on exactly the date of his retitrement, on 9th March 1887. It was followed on the day afterwards by many more across the world. The clipping below, mentions that Luke was the commander of his regiment until 1885. He was, of course, the commander of the 2nd Battalion and not the regiment. Even so, being a battalion commander was still a great honour. The commander of the regiment, was the full Colonel, Major General Sir Savage Lloyd-Mostyn. It wasn't until 27 years later when that honour was to be bestowed on Luke, but more on that at the appropriate time.

The press coverage afforded to Luke's retirement, had been carried in just about every county in Britain and in many abroad, especially within the Commonwealth / Empire. The clip on the left from the Hampshire and Naval Chronicle and the other, from the 'The Age' a newspaper published in Melbourne, Australia, are, but two of many.

FROM BRITAIN

The Army has lost the services of a gallant soldier in Colonel Luke O'Connor, V.C. Colonel O'Connor is already fifty-six years of age, and therefore had but two years to run, so he elected to retire on a pension of £420 and the rank of major-general. To the Royal Welsh Fusiliers the name of O'Connor will ever be dear as that of the man who, though severely wounded, saved the colours of the regiment at Alma, and, regardless of consequences to himself, carried them out of action. It was a noble act of heroism, fittingly rewarded by a commission and the Victoria Cross. Luke O'Connor lived to do what in our Army is quite exceptional—command the regiment, the ranks of which he entered as a private; and he vacated his command in June, 1885, carrying with him into retirement the admiration and kindly wishes of everybody who had ever known him during his long and honourable regimental career.

Colonel O'Connor, V.C., retires from the army with the rank of a major-general. The London *Dispatch* wonders if many of the present generation will recognise in this officer Private Luke O'Connor, of the Welsh Fusiliers, who not only won his cross and commission by his pluck at the Alma and at the Redan, but raised himself by valuable service to command, in his old age, the very regiment in which he enlisted when a youth. There is no finer or more soldierlike corps in the British army than the peppery Welsh Fusiliers, and Luke O'Connor has had no small share in making them what they are. Under his leadership, it used to be said, they would, if ordered, charge through a fiery furnace. General O'Connor's career is one of the few that redeem the British military system from the ignominy that has been cast on it by the homicidal incapacity of its aristocratic masters. His pension is one of the few that the people, from whose ranks he sprang, will not grudge. We think he is the only private soldier who has ever risen step by step in his regiment till he became its colonel—with the exception of the late General Macbain, who rose from being the drummer boy to be colonel of the 93rd Highlanders.

FROM AUSTRALIA

Despite Luke's feelings about his enforced retirement from the Army, he most certainly wouldn't have wanted to break all connections with it. This becomes immediately apparent because only three months into his retirement, we find evidence of his association with his old colleagues and the bands of military volunteers which, were springing up in number, all around the country.

He was fortunate because the Queen's Westminster Volunteer Corps was handily located not far from his home. Volunteer Corps had began to flourish in 1859 when England feared a French invasion. (Yes, only three years following the end of the Crimean War when our combined troops fought side by side!) The 'Queen's Westminsters was formed as a 'Rifle Corps' by the Duke of Westminster in 1860. It became the 13th Middlesex (Queen's Westminster) Volunteer Rifle Corps and was attached to the King's Royal Rifle Corps as a 'Volunteer Battalion'.

Being the largest of its kind in London in 1886, the battalion established its new headquarters at Buckingham Gate. This was a pleasant walk of around half a mile across Green Park from Luke's home in Clarges Street. He would have skirted Buckingham Palace to access Buckingham Gate, located behind it.

Little did he know then, that the very same regal lady, Queen Victoria, who had handed him, his Victoria Cross 54 years earlier, in 1857, and who had died on 22nd January 1901, would, herself, be honoured on 16th May 1911. This was when the unveiling of her memorial monument took place immediately outside the palace. At least, he was alive then and no doubt memories of her handing out his VC, would have flooded back to him when he passed it by, to attend meetings of this 'Volunteer Battalion'.

He must have been very pleased to have associated himself with this band of volunteers and equally, they would have been overjoyed at his association with them.

On 11th June 1887, the corps received its annual inspection at Wellington Barracks by the Hon. Colonel, the Duke of Westminster. There were about 800 volunteers who, following the Duke's inspection, marched to their new headquarters in James Street, Buckingham Gate. Their arrival coincided with the opening of a new block of buildings by the Duchess of Westminster who also presented prizes to various winners of competitions and farewell gifts to those retiring. This occasion was attended by a

108

number of V.I.P. guests, many of whom, were from the higher echelons of the regular army. But who should be among them besides Luke? His old friend, General Sir Daniel Lysons was also in attendance.

The proceedings of the day were reported upon in The Observer newspaper. The clearer clipping above is from the Sheffield and Rotheram Independent of 15th June 1887.

Just look at the 'top brass' present and the funds they had acquired. The fact that this event received national press attention on the following day, emphasises the point.

It has been fortunate that many of Luke's trips have captured him, when landing in Ireland, but unfortunately the media were less prolific when reporting his return to England. Although this trait had, more often than not, stalled an ability to capture his length of stays, the next trip captured was, indeed, a landing in England on 26th November 1887. He had been in Ireland for about 4 weeks. A similar return trip was reported a year later on 2nd October, 1889 when he arrived at Kingstown (Dublin) from England.

With nothing to constrain him, Luke was free to get around more and his visits to Ireland were developing into something of a pattern. Whilst it was impossible to capture all journeys, of those discovered, at least 14, ferry crossings between the date of his retirement in 1887, until the end of 1899, have been found.

With the dates of his visits to Ireland in mind, there are trips which, in themselves, provide an idea of the man himself. The first would be his visit captured by the clip on the following page, concerning his return from Ireland on 26th January 1893. This had been quite a long stay of just over 3 months.

It would appear from the opening paragraph that the meeting (nicely named, 'Falling in') took place in London as per the column heading "London Gossip" *"the other evening upon his return visit from the Emerald Isle"* and at the end of the column - Luke was *"staying in town for a few days on his way to the South of France"*.

With the item being published on the same day as Luke had arrived in England, then he couldn't have had the meeting with the author, on, as he says, 'the other evening' because Luke would have been in Ireland.

However, that taken at face value, it is the content that is bewildering, especially so, as it was recognised that Luke rarely spoke about politics or religion – *AND IT SHOUOD BE ADDED*, 'especially to journalists'. So, with all that taken into consideration, we learn that by conviction, Luke was a 'Home Ruler'. Yet as the author states, his declared views were not that of a 'Home Ruler'. He would not support a separate seat of parliament in Dublin, nor would he want the Irish members to leave Westminster. Surely this is anathema to the ideologies of 'Home Rule'? He also confirms that he had been approached during the previous year, to stand as a 'Nationalist Candidate' for a West coast constituancy.

We cull the following from the *World* of yesterday's date :—"Amongst Col. Howard Vincent's most recent recruits to the 'ranks' are Generals Sir 'Dan' Lysons, Henry Green, Paget, and Luke O'Connor, V.C. Never in the course of its history did that crack corps, the 'Queen's Westminster's,' present a more satisfactory appearance than it did on Saturday afternoon, when it was inspected by its honorary colonel, the Duke of Westminster. The Duchess afterwards distributed the prizes. The new headquarters in James street, Buckingham gate, are all that can be desired ; £10,000 have been expended on their erection ; and, in addition to the above-named gallant veterans, a great accession of new members is expected to mark the jubilee year.

The clipping is from the Dublin Daily Express of 26th January 1893, the same day as Luke had returned to England. The author does not reveal his identity other than under the column heading **London Gossip'**.

I had the pleasure of falling in with a gallant Irishman the other evening, upon his return from a visit to the Emerald Isle, who has views of his own on the Home Rule question. There is no more respected or more popular soldier in London than Major-General Luke O'Connor. V.C., late Colonel of the 23rd Royal Welsh Fusiliers. The General is a Home Ruler by conviction. but, as I think I mentioned on a previous occasion, he does not desire to see a separate Parliament at Dublin, and, in any case, he disapproves altogether of the Irish members being excluded from Westminster. He has discussed these matters on many occasions with his old friend Sir Charles Gavan Duffy, and with members of the Irish Nationalist Party, and he is not afraid to uphold and abide by his belief that a separate Parliament would be fatal to the peace, prosperity, and best interests of Ireland. But he would like to see a really wide and thorough measure of Local Government extended to Ireland. I have always understood, too, that the General is in favour of the office of Lord Lieutenant being abolished. He thinks that a member of the Royal Family ought to represent the Queen in Ireland. Despite these—for

a Home Ruler—somewhat heterodox views, he was, as I mentioned at the time, pressed to stand as the Nationalist candidate for a constituency in the West of Ireland last year. General O'Connor is staying in town for a few days on his way to the South of France.

It wasn't long after his full retirement that he commenced taking holidays in the South of France and Egypt, so it cannot be discounted that he may have been returning to London in connection with these holiday voyages to catch ferries from England. It is equally possible that he had just visited Ireland to reaquaint himself with his homeland and the friends he had made there, both in his youth and later, in his Army career. The below clip is also interesting.

This was the start of an extract from the Yorkshire Herald dated 15th September 1889. It wasn't surprising to find Luke involved in another Voluntary military unit.

His visits to Harrogate were also to form something of a pattern for a few years and it shouldn't have been surprising that if a town had a Volunteer Corps within it, then Luke was sure to find it. Here he is again, as indicated in the clipping below, offering his support to such a unit.

The article also mentions Major General Blacksley who had also been in India during the mutiny.

It may also not be a coincidence that when Blacksley retired, he wrote travel books, including guides and interesting routes to be taken, when visiting interesting places. This is just what Luke would shortly be doing.

For some 'fashionable' reason, the upper crust of society permitted (encouraged) their names registered in hotels, to be included in press reports.

Jump forward for just 12 months, to 1890, when we can find Luke at Harrogate again, in the late summer season. Inaddition, there is also a General Blakesley at the same place. Whether that is the same Major Blacksley who Luke was with at Harrogate at the Volunteers camp, during the previous year, must surely be beyond a coincidence. So here below, are both of those clips concerning his visits to Harrogate.

THE GRAND REUNION AT CARDIFF

Luke was a stickler for attending all the annual regimental dinners and all of the Queen's levees including those held in Dublin Castle by the Lord Lieutenant. It was the Lord Lieutenant who represented the Queen in Britain and also in Ireland but the position there, was also the title, according to the article quoting Luke above, that he suggested, should be abolished?

However, Luke's visit to Ireland on 4th October 1893, had caused him to miss the grandest of all reunion dinners. This was the *piece de resistance* of them all, and was held over the weekend of 25th / 26th of November. With him not returning until the 2nd December, he would need to apologise for his absence.

The event was organised at Park Hall, Cardiff where, not only veterans from the Royal Welsh would be present, but any veteran of any rank, from any other regiment who had survived the Crimean War and the quelling of the Indian mutiny. In total, 85 English and Welsh regiments were represented, making a total attendance of c350 people. It had been organised in conjunction with Cardiff City Council who were proud to host it. Bearing in mind that the battle of the Alma had occurred 39 years earlier, apart from a similar event held in Sheffield, this was the first in the Commonwealth held to ensure that these surviving veterans would not be forgotten.

It was a mammoth organisational feat requiring all participants to gather on the Saturday morning at the Cardiff Drill Hall where they were divided into six companies and marched through crowded streets of cheering onlookers, to reach the Park Hall in the afternoon for a grand banquet.

Lord Windsor was in the chair accompanied by other speakers including Lord Tredegar, the Mayor, Canon Thompson, Lt. General Sir Hugh Rowlands VC, Lt. General Sir James Hills-Johnes GCB, VC., Brigadier General Paton and many others.

Surely, there wouldn't have been anything in Ireland which would have kept Luke from missing this event but as it transpired, it was his presence there, that had caused him not to have received the invitation until it was too late. The content of the letter of apology read out by Canon Thompson, without him at first declaring who the author was, reveals what had happened. The clipping is of poor quality and so, it has again been transcribed, word for word as hereunder : -

> *"I have been away from England for some time and your kind letter only reached me yesterday. I regret very much I cannot have the pleasure and the honour of meeting at your banquet, comrades of mine, who fought so bravely in the Crimea and in India. It is, indeed, a kind and noble act on the part of the friends in Cardiff to think of banquetting their old soldiers. I am quite sure they will be most grateful for the honour paid them. I trust a good number of the old Royal Welsh and other regiments will be present at your banquet. A great number of the old Monmouthshire Militia joined the Royal Welsh when they were much wanted, and I know they fought bravely in the trenches. Will you kindly thank the committee for me for their great kindness in thinking of me, and also thank you for your nice kind letter and your kind remembrance of me. Kindly send me a paper."*

The clipping was continued in another column but in summary, Canon Thompson said that he would not disclose the name of the writer for a few minutes until after he recounted the action of the brave deed earned by the writer of the letter. On each occasion when the Canon mentioned the name of a regiment involved, it was followed by cheers from the audience. No doubt, as he began to tell the story, some would have guessed it, but right at the end of his reading the letter, Canon Thompson said,

"And now I would ask you to listen to the concluding words of this letter –

Yours sincerely, Luke O'Connor" (Loud Cheers)

This brought the house down. The newspaper column had bracketed the word (cheers) when referencing the cheers following the naming of the various regiments, but following Luke's name being disclosed, the brackets contained (loud cheers). Oh what a pity he had missed it!

Although Luke had returned to London on 2nd December 1893, it wasn't long before he was off on another trip. It is unknown when he left home for the South of France but the announcement of the arrival of passengers as contained in the newspaper, **'Homeward Mail from India, China and the East'** dated 18th May 1894, disclosed where he had been.

The Steam Ship 'Shropshire' had sailed from Rangoon, stopping at Colombo and Marseilles where passengers disembarked and embarked, before it reached London on 21st May. The list of passengers boarding and leaving at Rangoon, Colombo, Marseilles and London is long and it included Luke's particulars which were contained in the Marseilles to London passage. So, it was in the South of France, where he had been.

As if to make up for missing his grand reunion in Cardiff, Luke had been invited to Clarence House for a grand garden party on 2nd July 1894. This was to be given by His Royal Highness the Duke and her Royal and Imperial Highness the Duchess of Saxe-Coburg and Gotha.

The Duke was, in fact, Alfred Ernest Albert, the 4th child of Queen Victoria and her 2nd son. He had inherited this Dukedom and had married Maria Alexandrovna Romanova, of the Imperial Russian royal family. Perhaps no one had informed her about the defeat of the Russian Imperial Army in the Crimea, and if so, had she realised that one of the guests, Luke O'Connor had a big part to play in its defeat!

The Duke, had been posted as Admiral of the Royal Navy and although they lived in England, his wife neither adapted to the British court nor overcame her dislike for her adopted country.

GARDEN PARTY AT CLARENCE HOUSE.

His Royal Highness the Duke and her Royal and Imperial Highness the Duchess of Saxe-Coburg and Gotha gave a brilliant party yesterday afternoon in the grounds of Clarence House.

The Royal guests comprised their Royal Highnesses the Prince and Princess of Wales and the Princesses Victoria and Maud, their Royal Highnesses the Duke and Duchess of Connaught and the Princesses Margaret and Victoria of Connaught, their Royal Highnesses Prince and Princess Christian of Schleswig-Holstein and their Highnesses Prince Christian Victor, Prince Albert, and Princess Victoria of Schleswig-Holstein and Princess Aribert of Anhalt, her Royal Highness Princess Louise, Marchioness of Lorne and the Marquis of Lorne, their Royal Highnesses Prince and Princess Henry of Battenberg, her Royal Highness the Duchess of Albany, his Royal Highness the Duke of York, her Royal Highness Princess Louise, Duchess and the Duke of Fife, his Royal Highness the Duke of Cambridge, her Royal Highness Princess Mary Adelaide, Duchess and his Highness the Duke of Teck and Prince Adolphus, Prince Francis, and Prince Alexander of Teck, their Highnesses Prince and Princess Edward of Saxe-Weimar, his Serene Highness Prince Louis, and her Grand Ducal Highness Princess Louis of Battenberg, her Grand Ducal Highness Princess Alix of Hesse, her Serene Highness Princess Victor of Hohenlohe Langenburg and the Countesses Valda and Feodore Gleichen, Count Gleichen, his Royal Highness the Grand Duke of Mecklenburg Strealitz, his Imperial Highness the Czarevitch, his Imperial Highness the Archduke Franz Ferdinand

First section of two full columns of guests

Morning Post 3rd July 1894

The clipping here, is just the start of two lengthy columns in the Morning Post of 3rd July 1894, providing particulars of the guests with Luke among them. Even though the guests named are just a small fraction of the total, it can be seen that they must have been another 'Who's who' of the Royal families from many places at home and abroad.

But look who, in this shortened extract, is the very last guest to be mentioned. None other than his Imperial Highness, the Archduke Franz Ferdinand who's assasination on 28th June 1914, was a cause to the start of World War 1. In other newspapers, the reason for his visit to England was to thank Queen Victoria for her hospitality in India and the Colonies during his tour of the previous year. That sounds like a good excuse for a party invitation!

With all these Levees, reunions and garden parties Luke attended and was to attend, it becomes bewildering as to how he had maintained his excellent figure as depicted in all his photographs, despite his consuming, what must have been mountains of the richest of foods on offer.

(Or perhaps his discipline was greater than the author's!)

This party was, of course, just a matter of weeks away from 20th September 1894, which was to mark the 40th anniversary of the Battle of the Alma. The full story of it, and in particular, Luke's involvement, was not only carried in many newspapers within the British Isles, but world wide. No need to try and read this clip below as it is just a clip of the top of two very long columns in this Boston's Daily Globe newspaper of 20th September 1894. Yes, that's Boston Massachusetts and not Lincolnshire. This wasn't just because it was a 4th decade anniversary, similar reports were made on each and every anniversary.

Luke was back in Ireland only 8 days later, arriving at Kingstown on September 28th.

ST GILES PARISH CHURCH, WREXHAM

The importance of local parish churches to the regiments and units of those soldiers and airmen who were billetted in their nearby barracks, has been known for many years. Unfortunately, due to amalgamations resulting in fewer military units, their significance has been less apparent in more modern times.

These people naturally became 'localised' members of their communities and their officers traditionally, selected local churches which became their places of worship. In particular, they were 'shrines' where the names of individual senior officers were erected upon their 'passing' and where memorials listing many who had fallen in the various battles they had fought, were erected.

In the case of St Giles, this Wrexham church had played a truly magnificent part in its association with the 23rd Regiment. It was, and remains their shrine, even though, for all intents and purposes, the Regiment became amalgamated with others. The church has a fine reputation and even today, it is referred to as one of the seven wonders of Wales.

It remains a most welcoming church with a warm and comfortable aura and it would have been such for its local regiment, then at their 'Hightown' barracks, which, in 1873, became the Regimental District's Headquarters, known as 'The Depot'.

Although this practice continues today, with sad losses of military personnel in their fight against terrorism, hand to hand battles, are thankfully no more. Hence, and with the inception of national memorials and in particular, the national memorial arboretum at Alrewas in Staffordshire, the number of churches used in this way, have sadly reduced.

This change has also resulted from the organisational and structural changes of the military units which have taken place over the years. Resultant changes have witnessed a severe reduction in the number of barracks in use and hence, the number of churches used by their former occupants.

At Wrexham, in 2006, the Royal Welsh Fusiliers Regiment was merged into what became the Royal Welsh Regiment. Hightown barracks became the home of a small reservist company with command assumed by members of the 101 Battalion Royal Electrical Engineers. (REME) In 2016, fears that the barracks would close caused ministerial pressure from the town's member of parliament for it to remain open and for the time being, there are no plans to close the barracks.

There was indeed, a sad note in the voice of St Giles's vicar, the Reverend Dr. Jason Bray, when he told me that the church's military part to play, was no longer what it was. Almost the whole of the north side of the church had been given over to the Fusilier's past which now, has the death knell echoing in it, so far as the regiment and its 'shrine' is concerned.

Otherwise, he and Ann Owen, his church administrator who kindly hosted a visit by the author, were justifiably proud of the church and its 'community / family spirit'. They couldn't have selected a more welcoming church for their place of worship and its 'regimental shrine'.

On the 20th September, 1895, the 41st anniversary of the Alma battle, the regiment presented a new west window to the church, where the tower is located and where once, the organ and its gallery was housed. It's removal in 1894, presented the opportunity for the Regiment to propose the donating of the window and where, in a partially closed off space immediately below the tower, the Regiment created its Regimental Chapel.

The proposal was accepted by the vicar, the wardens and the parishoners in vestry. Whilst many brass plates and a memorial mentioned below, remain in dedication to fallen officers, the area is no longer used as the Regimental chapel.

Returning to the dedication of the window, the 1st Battalion were in India and the 2nd in Manchester. Colonel R.B. Mainwaring, commander of the 2nd Battalion, who, had fought at the battle of the Ashanti in West Africa with Luke, accompanied by the colours guarded by 100 men of his battalion, travelled from Manchester to Wrexham by train where they took part in a service and an unveiling and dedication ceremony. The new west window cost £600, this money being partially raised by every man in the Regiment donating one day's pay.

Of interest, according to the CPI's Financial Calculator, £600 in 1895 would be worth £79,412 in today's values (2020). Luke was, of course, a special guest whose gallant heroism was mentioned in the Bishop's service. He was now surrounded by many officers and men of the current battalion which had been under his command during his last five years of service, 1880 to 1885. They were all joined by many local dignitaries. The hundreds of members of the public who, despite the large size of the church, were unable to gain entry, assembled outside with flags waving and bunting strewn. It was a joyous occasion.

In marching to the church wearing their smart red ceremonial uniforms and busby helmets, the colour party was accompanied by a large choir. The 'offering of the window' ceremony was then performed and the Reverend vicar, Canon Fletcher, accepted the window and the responsibility of looking after it. The Bishop of Asaph took the service and finally, dedicated the window: -

This is a magnificent West Window, only one of two of its size in the church with five lights, (columns) the other being at the opposite 'Chancel' East end of the church.

'To the glory of God, and in memory of those who have faithfully served their Sovereign and Country in the Royal Welsh Fusiliers, this Window is erected by their Comrades and Friends, 1895.'

All guests were entertained to lunch at the barracks and a garden party was held in the grounds in the afternoon.

Along with an account of the proceedings, an etching of a like form and character of a similar window lodged at the British Library, was published by the local newspaper, the Wrexham

Advertiser the following day. Although it did not say so, it would have been assumed by those reading the newspaper, to be the window presented, but it wasn't, it was a similar design. The Rev. Dr. Bray, confirmed the fact that the newspaper may have used a facsimile of the type of window, as opposed to the actual one.

The actual window, shown above, is made of five lights (columns) by the celebrated stain glass window manufacturer, Clayton and Bell of London. The main panels depict Welsh Saints, Edward the Black Prince and St Giles. It is a huge window which made it impossible for a clear photograph of it to be obtained.

It was pleasing to discover that the fund raising committee included General Crutchley, Colonel of the Regiment and Luke's friend, General Sir Daniel Lysons. Others present, with whom Luke served, were Major General Savage Mostyn, from whom he was to inherit the Colonocy of the Regiment and Lieutenant Colonel Howard Vincent, another of Luke's friends who was with him at Westminster, when the new building belonging to the Queen's Westminster Volunteer Corps was opened.

In addition to the huge West window presented by the Regiment, almost the whole of the north aisle is taken up by numerous other brass memorial plates and other regimental memorabilia.

Included in this aisle, is yet another Royal Welsh Fusiliers memorial windows as seen below.

The more modern window installed in 1989 for the Regiments 300th Anniversary.

This is the most recently installed window, and was installed to celebrate the 300th anniversary of the Royal Welsh Fusiliers from its 1689 inauguration. Note the display of old and new uniforms and, of course, the regimental goat.

116

Apart from the brass plates in memoy of their very senior regimental commanders, such as the one above in memory of Luke, a further memorial monument was installed in the church in 1903. More on that below.

There were, of course, many other similar plaques on display, in what had been, the regimental chapel beneath the new West Window. Luke's date of birth has still not been established properly, though 1831 has obviously been preferred by the military, which possibly manged to get him into the Army, a year earlier than he should have. A very similar plaque remains in the Church of the Immaculate Conception, Farm Street, Berkley Square, London, which Luke frequently attended and where his funeral took place.

EAGLE FLIES IN LONDON.

FOURTH OF JULY DULY CELEBRATED ACROSS THE WATER.

Three Hundred Present at the Independence Day Dinner Given by the American Society — Bishop Potter Makes an Eloquent Address, While Ambassador Hay and Whitelaw Reid Discuss the Relations Between the United States and Great Britain.

[SPECIAL CABLE BY FRANK M. WHITE.] London, July 5.—[Copyright, 1897, by W. R. Hearst.]—" The American society in London " celebration of Independence day through the medium of a dinner at the Empress rooms of the Royal Palace Hotel to-night had the true American ring. All the diplomatic corps, special and otherwise, with the exception of Admiral Miller and staff, who were kept away by the sad death of Miss Miller, were in attendance, and the Pan-Anglican conference of the Episcopal Church was responsible for the attendance

CUT

Other distinguished Americans among the 300 at the other tables were J. L. Taylor, F. C. Vanduzer, J. Walter Earle, Frank W. Jones, Benjamin F. Stevens, Colonel M. J. O'Brien, Major James B. Pond, Edwin H. Low, Professor A. B. Poland, John Hays Hammond, Edward M. Fox, Imre Kiralfy and son Charles, Hiram S. Maxim, Major General Luke O'Connor, David Manning, Dr. A. H. Chamberlain, David Seligman.

Mention has already been made about Luke's travelling activities; in addition to Ireland, the West Indies, Egypt and the South of France, to name but a few destinations.

In February 1897, he set sail from Tilbury, with 170 other passengers on the Royal Mail Ship 'Ophir' of the 'Orient Line'. The ship called at Gibraltar, Naples, Port Said, Ismailia and Australia but it is not known which of these destinations, he disembarked.

However, wherever it was, he was certainly back home on 31st May 1897 which is when he once again, attended St James' Palace for the Queen's Levee which, as normal, was hosted by Queen Victoria's son, Albert Edward, the Prince of Wales, the future King Edward 7th.

TOASTING AMERICA'S INDEPENDENCE

This newspaper clipping is just the heading and start of a much longer account taken from the Chicago Tribune, Illinois, published on the 6th July 1897.

The 'American Society in London' was founded only two years previously in March 1895. It is now the oldest American society in the UK. It was inaugurated and exists now, to promote patriotic and social life amongst Americans residing in London, and good fellowship between the people of the US & UK.

117

They say, *"One way we do this is by organising celebrations of major American holidays such as Independence Day and Thanksgiving".*

Apart from Luke being in communication with his siblings in America, no obvious association connecting him with our American allies, can be found..

He had served in Canada but that would hardly associate him with the USA. It can only be assumed that his VC celebrity status, may have come to the notice of the American Embassy, whose ambassador and other high ranking officials, would have also attended the Royal Levees.

The dinner was held at the Empress Rooms of the Royal Palace hotel where "The American Society in London" gathered. Over 300 Americans including a dozen or so, American Bishops and many other distinguished guests attended. It was interesting to discover in the clipping above, that Luke was regarded as a 'Distinguished American'

> Bishop Potter of New York made the most eloquent speech of the evening, and did not hesitate to declare the most vigorous Americanism. Referring to the glories of the British Empire, he reminded his hearers that it had required a thousand years to gain them. " Give us," he said, " half that time and we will show colonies equal to these."

Toasts were given to honour the Queen, the President, the Ambassador, Diplomatic staff and many others. Humerous anecdotes were given and one in particular, contained a 'side swipe' at the British Empire as shown in this clipping.

No doubt this brought a partisan response by the assembled, with hopefully, the exception of Luke O'Connor, but I'm guessing he would have been too polite not to have applauded.

THE DEATH OF GENERAL SIR DANIEL LYSONS

Gen. Sir Daniel Lysons

1898 was to be the year when Luke visited America to meet his siblings. However, the year didn't start on a happy note because his ex commander and comrade at arms and latterly, friend, General Sir Daniel Lysons died on 29th January 1898, aged 81.

Given what Luke had said about him in his autobiography, and their close associations in later life, there is no doubt that they held each other in the highest esteem. Sir Daniel had given Luke, a helping hand in the progression of his career and they fought together at the Alma when Sir Daniel was Lukes Major and at Sevastopol when he was his Colonel. In 1869 Lysons became the General Officer Commanding for the Aldershot Military District and in 1872 he became GOC for Northern District. In 1876 he was made Quartermaster General to the Forces.

From 1880 to 1883, Sir Daniel commanded the Aldershot Division. This would be at the same time as Luke was commanding the 2nd Battalion of the Royal Welsh. He being 15 years older than Luke, he retired in 1883, four years before him.

Since his retirement, Sir Daniel had been appointed the 'Constable of the Tower of London' (The person in charge of it on behalf of the realm) and was resident in Picadilly, not far from Luke's home. In their retirements, they were almost always found at the same functions. Above all it was Luke himself who called Sir Daniel, the bravest of the brave. It was Sir Daniel Lysons who recommended Luke for an honour. There is no doubt that this man had been an inspiration to Luke and as such, he would be sadly missed by him. Sir Daniel had been raised in the small village of Rodmarton Gloucestershire and although he died in London, at his request, a simple funeral service was held there on 3rd February 1898. His body and the mourners were then conveyed by train to Gloucestershire, where, following a family service, his body was interned at Redmarton Church where many of his ancestors were also buried. He came from a long aristocratic family line.

Such incidents would obviously put a temporary stop to any holidays that Luke would have had in mind, however, if we reflect back to Luke's voyage on the RMS Ophir, which set sail to Australia via Gibraltar, Naples, Port Said, Ismailia and Colombo in mid February 1897, then almost exactly to the day, one year later, we find that he is on another vessel of the Orient Line, the RMS 'Austral' setting sail from the same Tilbury and Plymouth ports on the 4th and 5th of February, 1898. Major General Sir John McNiell VC was also a passenger but they are not listed as travelling together.

But hold on! This sailing day was the day following General Sir Daniel Lysons funeral!! This was cutting things short but if he can win a VC 44 years ago, whilst fighting the Russian Army against all odds, there was nothing to stop him dashing from a funeral in central London on one day, to getting to Tilbury Docks on the next?

This time, however, Marseille had been included in his trip. He had also been there in May 1894 and even though no details are provided as to where passengers disembarked on route, on this particular voyage, Marseille does feature again later in the year, when Luke was in America. It was said that it was hoped he would enjoy his visits there as much as he did in Marseille where he had been enjoying the sun on previous occasions.

The other strong possibility, concerns the fact that he may, on this trip, have then continued on to Egypt because Luke's brother, Daniel in Wilmington, North Carolina, might well have read in the 20th March 1898 edition of the local Wilmington 'Morning Star' newspaper, that his brother, Luke was staying at the famed hotel de Angleterre, in Cairo, Egypt.This was only about six weeks after the 'Austral' had embarked from England, so in all probability, he was more likely to have heading for Cairo, though there was nothing stopping him calling at Marseille, before hand?.

The Morning Star had connected their own famed hero, Major Daniel with his brother, Luke and had spotted that piece of news from a Cairo newspaper, 'The Sphinx' (actually spelt Sphnix) Due to the poor quality of the print, it is transcribe thus: -

> *"The Sphinx, a handsome paper published at Cairo, Egypt, thus refers to a brother of Maj. D. O'Connor, of Wilmington "One of the guests whom Egypt delights to honor, and a distinguished one indeed, is at the Angleterre. Major General Luke O'Connor, V.C."*

The very fact that the clip mentions that he was one of the distinguished guests that **Egypt delights to honor,** is proof enough that he had travelled there before. Yet there was no way of me discovering such trips other than through this media method. He having been recently networking with members of the 'Americans in London Society', suggests maybe, whether he hadn't seized the opportunity to enquire about the logistics of him reaching his siblings in America.

To have found this item in an American newspaper, was very lucky and this, probably is a good indication that Luke would have spent more time travelling than was able to have been discovered in many other countries, all around the world.

However, Luke would have returned to London from Cairo before setting off for the USA because, on 13th of June 1898, he was at St James Palace, enjoying yet another Queen's Levee. Also, on 14th July 1898 because, as is mentioned in the clipping here, Luke had been in attendance at yet another grand feast at the 'Mansion House' at the invitation of the Lord Mayor of London, Sir John Voce Moore.

Again, the clipping is just a short piece of the start of an extremely long article which contained details of all the toasts and the contents of most of the speeches made.

The contents of the article could be interpreted as being much of a 'back scratching' and morale boosting exercise for the senior Army officers present, in the light of shrinking budgets and other 'matters military' that required a boost of confidence to the three services. (Does anything change?) A similar banquet was organised for the Navy and now, it was the Army's turn.

THE ARMY AT THE MANSION HOUSE.

The Lord Mayor, who recently entertained at the Mansion House a number of representatives of the Navy, last night invited to the City some three hundred and fifty Military officers and officials, among them his Royal Highness the Duke of Connaught, the Marquis of Lansdowne (Secretary of State for War), Viscount Wolseley, (Commander-in-Chief), Generals Sir Æneas Perkins, Sir F. FitzWygram, M.P., Powlett Bingham, Sir J. Glyn, Sir C. Shute, Sir J. Raines, Sir R. Harrison, Sir J. H. Gordon, Sir Martin Dillon, Sir J. Ross, Sir H. Prendergast, Sir E. Newdegate, Sir John Adye, Sir S. Edwardes, Sir Arnold Kemball, Sir Collingwood Dickson, Sir E. A. Holditch, Lord Mark Kerr, Sir A. Taylor, Sir H. Gough, Sir W. Olpherts, Sir Henry Norman, Sir Michael Biddulph, Sir G. Willis, Sir S. Browne, Sir G. Higginson, Sir Evelyn Wood, the Hon. P. Fielding, Sir E. G. Bulwer, Sir W. G. Cameron, Sir J. Davis, and E. H. Clive; Major-Generals Sir W. Butler, Sir E. F. Du Cane, Sir C. Du Plat, Viscount Falmouth, Viscount Frankfort de Montmorency, Clery, the Hon. R. A. Talbot, C. J. Burnett, Sir J. Ardagh, Sir Coleridge Grove, Sir Owen Burne, Fryer, Sir O. Newmarch, C. W. Robinson, Luke O'Connor, Sartorius, Barnard, Borrett, Sir H. Colvile, F. S. Russel, M.P., Campbell, Kelly-Kenny, Upton Prior, M'Calmont, M.P., Byam, Swaine, Protheroe, Salis-Schwabe, Stewart, Abadie, Hutchinson, Fraser, Paton, Fitzroy H...

record on her 2nd voyage.

THE VISIT TO AMERICA

So now, its time to explore Luke's 1898 visit to America, to reunite himself with his siblings. Readers may recall a brief mention above of how he had primarily based himself with Daniel's family in North Carolina and how he must have been utterly devastated when learning of Thomas's death, a month prior to reaching his home in Omaha, Nebraska.

He had embarked on Cunard's Royal Mail ship, 'Lucania' at Liverpool, reaching New York at 6.20pm on 21st October 1898.

At that time, 'Lucania' and her sister ship, 'Campania' were the most luxurious ocean going vessels of their time. They were built and launched in Govan, Glasgow in February 1893 when they were both the largest and fastest passenger vessels afloat. Lucania broke the 'Cross Atlantic' speed

In their day, both ships offered the most luxurious first-class passenger accommodation available and were said to represent Victorian opulence at a level that would never be matched by any other ship.

All the first-class public rooms, and the en-suite staterooms of the upper deck, were generally heavily panelled, in oak, satinwood or mahogany; and thickly carpeted. Velvet curtains hung aside the windows and portholes, while the furniture was richly upholstered in matching design. Lucania's capacity was 2,000 passengers and 424 crew. Her top 'Blue Riband' speed was 27 mph.

Wilmington Morning Star 5 Jan 1899

Wilmington Morning Star 8 Jan 1899

Cunard's Steamer Lucania

First Base with Daniel

Having disembarked, Luke would be making his way south for 126 miles from New York to Wilmington, North Carolina, where he would base himself with his brother, Daniel. He arrived there, during the evening of 28th October, a week after his arrival in New York. He may, of course, have wanted to stay a few days in New York or even stay a while in Philadelphia, where friends were located.

The fact that this was his first visit to the 'Southern' states was reported in the Wilmington 'Morning Star' newspaper, on 29th October 1898. The same copy also reported that he normally spent his winters in the South of France and Egypt but he was now determined to try the climate of the USA.

This early press announcement below, was to be the first of many and it wasn't long before many editors had picked up on the fact that one of their own favoured sons, Major Daniel O'Connor, was hosting his brother Luke, an even more famous soldier of the British Army. The many accounts of Luke's sojourns with his brother's family, became lost in the accounts of the battles in which he fought, and, of course, the fact that he was one of the first to be presented with the Victoria Cross, really hit the headlines.

With Daniel being the youngest and Luke the 2nd youngest of the siblings, it is not surprising that Luke made his 'base' with Daniel and his family. No doubt, they would have spent hours talking over their respective soldiering careers, their lives and their family and, of course, that fateful voyage from Ireland to Canada.

Whilst some of the trips taken would have escaped the press, the first found of them, is as indicated in the clip below here: -

Southern Pines was a winter spa health resort located 120 miles north west of Wilmington often visited by people from the northern states. It was obviously the place to be, because only three months earlier it had been declared a 'Sundown' town.

What on earth was a 'Sundown' town?

Well, this was a term indicating an 'all white' town practising a form of segregation by a combination of discriminatory local laws, intimidation, and violence.

PINEY WOODS INN, SOUTHERN PINES, NORTH CAROLINA.

The term came from signs indicating that coloured people had to leave town by 'sundown'. The practice was not restricted to the southern states, at least until the early 1960s. Northern states could be nearly as inhospitable to black travellers as States such as Alabama or Georgia in the deep south.

This is surely unbelievable when considering that the civil war had emancipated slaves, yet 33 years later, they were creating 'white only' towns in what was, a southern state.

Of course, Daniel fought for the Union to free the slaves but his wife, Mary's father was a Confederate Major who wanted to retain slavery. Perhaps Luke would have been diplomatically indifferent, but wouldn't it have been exciting to have been a 'fly on the wall' at that conversation.

Other newspapers indicated that they had spent the first New Year's week at the Piney Woods Inn, which, by the look of the image below, appears to be a tiny village pub – I don't think!! Clearly Daniel's folk wanted to impress.

It was the Wilmington Morning Star newspaper which disclosed this visit and the article finished, as shown below. As we established earlier, Daniel was a very successful and wealthy business man himself. It may well have been for this reason that he was content to get on with his business life whilst he placed Luke in the capable hands of his wife and his only daughter, Maie.

General O'Connor and Confederate Veterans at W. L. I. Armory To-night.

General O'Connor, of the British army, who is spending some time in the city, the guest of his brother Major D. O'Connor, has accepted an invitation to attend the regular weekly drill of the Wilmington Light Infantry to-night at the W. L. I. armory. Quite a party of Confederate Veterans are also expected to attend and it is probable that a sort of informal reception will be held after the drill to afford the military men an opportunity to meet the distinguished British general.

Wilmington Morning Star 31st Jan. 1899

Daniel's wife Mary, was then aged 48 but she was only one, when Luke was winning his Victoria Cross at the battle of the Alma. Daniel's only child, his daughter Maie, who at age 21 was about to marry and was a brilliant musician who had received a first class education.

The fact that Daniel had fought in the Union Army and now living in a Confederate State, and had married the daughter of a Confederate Major, makes this visit particularly bizarre. More so, when it can be seen that Daniel had introduced Luke to his local Wilmington Light Infantry base. And it looks like a Confederate 'knees up' occurred after the event.

It was the same newspaper that revealed the next visit which was to New Orleans *"to attend the Mardi Gras. They will also make a tour of Florida before returning to Wilmington".*

Domestic flights weren't introduced in the USA until 1914 and so, this being a trip of not far off 1,000 miles, there is no indication about how they travelled. Motor vehicles weren't fully integrated until around 1893 and therefore, it would be an unlikely mode of transport.

The railroad would have been their most likely option, otherwise they would travel by horse or by ship. The latter was likely for at least part of the trip. Of course, a sea voyage would have been possible from Wilmington to New Orleans, by sailing around the Florida Peninsula into the Gulf of Mexico and landing at New Orleans. However, they were to take in a visit to Florida on their return journey from New Orleans. Whatever, their journey would have been something of an expedition.

It is doubted whether the youg ladies of the Mardi Gras would have been 'showing their all' in 1899, as they do these days, but by then, the carnival had taken a regular hold and the city was full of colour, electric lights, fancy dress, decorated street cars, pony hauled floats and an abundance of visitors enjoying themselves. However, that would not compare with New Orleans' of today, with their vast black majority population and with that of the all white 'Sundown' town in which they had not long ago, chosen to stay.

A smile also appeared on the author's face when reading in the Daily Picayune dated 12th February 1899, that Luke was going to attend the Mardi Gras. He chose to emphasise the point that he wasn't visiting New Orleans, just to see the Mardi Gras because he had seen other carnivals when visiting Southern France. The Mardi Gras just happened to be in full swing whilst he wished to explore the south!

In a later press interview, Luke disclosed that he had been as far south as St. Augustine, Florida, which

"General O'Connor and his party are guests of the St. Charles Mansion on St. Charles street, and will be here several days."

"I wanted to see New Orleans and the south," said the general. "That is what brought me and not the carnival, which I have seen a great many times in the South of France."

The trip is one of pleasure strictly. the general devoting most of his time since retiring from the English army service to traveling.

General Luke O'Connor, Mrs. D. O'Connor and Miss Maie O'Connor have returned home from a trip to Florida, visiting all the places of interest in that state.

Wilmington Messenger 2 Mar 1899

Three More Siblings to Visit

Major General Luke O'Connor, V. C., of London, England, who has been here since October visiting his brother, Major D. Oconnor, left yesterday to visit relatives in the North and West

Wilmington Messenger 7 April 1899

isn't that far into Florida State. So in the below clipping, the mention of all the places of interest, couldn't have been that 'all embracing'.

According to the above clip, it appears that Luke left Daniel's family on 6th April 1899, to visit relatives in the north and west. He arrived at his brother Thomas's in Omaha on 27th April.

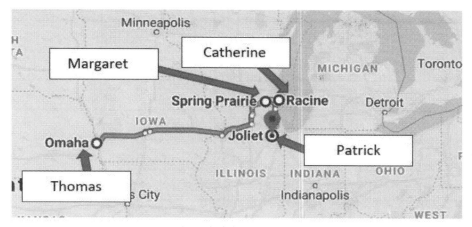

Luke's Siblings –
Thomas in the West and his sisters in the North

This clip is very helpful because, as can be seen in the map above, that his intentions were to visit all of the remaining siblings, Thomas, Catherine and Margaret.

Being in Omaha, Thomas would have been the furthest west and the two sisters, living close together in Wisconsin would have been those in the north. Luke's deceased brother Patrick's family were still in Illinois as indicated, though Patrick had died in 1869 of typhoid fever.

GENERAL LUKE O'CONNOR

Arrives From England Too Late to See His Brother Alive

Major General Luke O'Connor, V. C., of London, England, arrived in Omaha yesterday on a visit to the family of his brother, the late Thomas O'Connor, pioneer resident of this city. General O'Connor is on the retired list of the British army. His principal service was in India, and he received the Victoria cross from the queen herself for bravery at the storming of the heights of Alma in the Crimean war. General O'Connor is a great traveler and generally spends his winters in the south of France and in Egypt.

He came to this country to visit his brother, whom he had not seen since childhood, and the news of his unexpected death was a sad surprise to him. The general returns to England in a few days.

Omaha World Herald, 28th April 1899

MAJOR GENERAL O'CONNOR

Distinguished Veteran of the British Army is Visiting for a Few Days in Omaha.

Major General Luke O'Connor, V. C., of London, England, is one of Omaha's distinguished visitors at the present time. He is a brother of the late Thomas O'Connor of this city, who was one of the oldest and most respected citizens of this city, was the first register of deeds of the county and a member of the first city council. General O'Connor is visiting at the residence of Miss Ella O'Connor, daughter of Thomas O'Connor, 1616 Kyner street. General O'Connor has been on the retired list of the British army for the last dozen years, having been placed there after a long, active service, most of which he saw in India. He received the Victoria cross from the queen herself for bravery at the storming of the heights of Alma in the Crimean war. He has been an extensive traveler since being retired. He will return to England in a few days.

Oh, how sad that must have been. Thomas and Luke hadn't seen each other since being separated in childhood and now, Thomas's death had kept them apart for ever more. Hindsight is a marvelous science, but why, oh why, didn't he make that trip earlier? He had been in the country for months but just had got his itinerary the wrong way around! He must have been heartbroken to learn that his brother, Thomas had died 43 days previously on the 15th. of March, whilst he was still at Daniel's home having returned from New Orleans.

Maybe he went to see Patrick's widow, and his five nephews and nieces who had all remained in the Joliet area. This was the family with whom Daniel was living when he sold his businesses and took off to join the Civil War. Although both clippings have been shown and were only published one day apart, they provide different information.

It is the last of the clippings above which informs us that Thomas lived at 1616 Kyner Street, Omaha. The 1900 census indicates that his four single adult children, Luke's nieces, and a nephew, Evelyn, Ella, Theresa and Edmond had all been living there with him.

Luke would have travelled directly from Omaha to see his sister Catherine, whose husband, John Hute, had died about eight years earlier. His other sister, Margaret lived only 11 miles away and, of course, it was one of them who had taken Luke back to Ireland, all those years ago.

Although dates of birth of all the siblings have been suspect, the probability that Catherine would be the eldest of all seven children on that fateful voyage, seems to be favoured, however, the uncertainty remains, as it was Margaret who married first.

The clip here, mentions that Luke visited the 'Hute' home **'last week'**, which ties in exactly with him being in Omaha at the end of April. Although there is no mention in the clip of him also visiting his sister Margaret, living at Spring Prairie, so close to Catherine, he must have done.

Maj.-Gen. Luke O'Connor, V. C., of London, Eng., was a guest at the Hute home last week. The Maj.-Gen. has been on the retired list of the British army for the past ten or twelve years. His principal service was in India. He received the Victoria cross from the queen herself for bravery at the storming of the heights of Alma in the Crimean war. The general is a great traveler, and generally spends his winters in the south of France and Egypt. This being his first visit to the United States.

Racine Journal 4th May 1899

At the time of Luke's visit, Catherine was in her 7th decade and had been widowed for 8 years but her four children, were all alive. Jane was 51, David 49, Belle 47 and Charles 45. The three eldest children never married but the youngest, Charles, had been a brilliant scholar, had graduated in law from Wisconsin University and at the time of Luke's visit, he was a judge and the Mayor of Aberdeen, Brown county in South Dakota. It was he who had married at Niagra Falls in 1888.

It was obvious that when Luke left North Carolina to travel north to see relatives, he wouldn't be returning there, before his return to England on 7th June. However, just like there being no press mention of him visiting his sister, Margaret at Spring Prairie, equally, no mention of his visiting any of Patrick's family in Joliet, Illinois, can be discovered. However, such a visit was, indeed, unearthed later.

So far as press mention of him is concerned, the next time Luke's head is raised, is in Philadelphia on May 22nd 1899 when he was interviewed by a journalist. This is included in the 'Wilkes-Barre Record' newspaper, dated 23rd May 1899, the day after the interview. This is mentioned here, because until that time, there had been a gap of around three weeks when no mention of him can be found anywhere.

It is an 840 miles trip between Rochester, Wisconsin to Philadelphia and his route would have taken him through the Joliet, Illinois area. This is what might indicate that he would have sought out Patrick's widow and some of Patrick's family.

It may have been just bad luck that the press had not picked him up until he arrived in Philadelphia. There was no reason why they should, it's just that up until then, it had been amazing how they captured his movements on those occasions. cluded here, is the full excerpt from that newspaper, of their story about Luke and how he felt about America and its 'fighting ability'. Some of the revelations they mention, do not sound at all like Luke, but all that can be said was that the story, was indeed, published.

KNOW HOW TO FIGHT

Gen. O'Connor of the British Army Talks of Americans.

DISTINGUISHED VISITOR PRAISES THE WORK OF OUR ARMY AND NAVY—HE THINKS AFFAIRS IN THE PHILIPPINES ARE BEING HANDLED IN A SUPERIOR MANNER.

Philadelphia, May 11.—A distinguished arrival in this city is Maj. Gen. Luke O'Connor, V. C., of the British army, a veteran of the Crimean War, of the Indian Mutiny of 1857, and of the Ashantee War. He was one of the first men to receive the Victoria cross at the hands of the queen after the institution of the order. On the occasion of the last reunion of the heroes of Alma the British Army and Navy Review had this to say of him:

"In these days, when regimental colors are no longer carried, it is worth while recording the gallantry of a very distinguished officer still living, and who earned the Victoria cross at the battle of the Alma for protecting the colors. When the formation of the line of the Royal Welsh fusileers was for a time in disorder, Sergt. Luke O'Connor advanced between the two officers who were carrying the colors. One of the officers was mortally wounded, and the other so dangerously that he was carried from the field. Young O'Connor snatched up the colors and almost immediately fell to the ground wounded. He struggled to his feet and bravely bore the colors throughout the fight, though repeatedly urged by the officers to retire. This brave young Irish sergeant is now a major general."

The regiment of the Royal Welsh Fusileers, with which the general's name is associated, is a regiment with a history. It is over 200 years old, and took part in the battle of Bunker Hill. The regimental mascot has always been a goat, and history says that not enough soldiers of the regiment could be found after the battle to saddle the goat.

It is considered something of a joke in military circles in England that an Irishman should command a regiment of Welshmen. It is something the general is very proud of, however, for he enlisted in that regiment as a private and fought his way to the head.

The general was at the relief and capture of Lucknow, and bears many medals and other honors for brave deeds done in action. He is a tall, well built man, looks every inch a soldier, and, like most brave men, is very reticent about what he has done. It is history, however, that he commanded a storming party at Sebastopol, where he was dangerously wounded.

In conversation with a reporter today he said: "I was in Philadelphia just after your Civil War was over, visiting some friends. I would scarcely know the city to-day, there are so many changes. I left England last October to come over and see the country again, and have been as far South as St. Augustine, Fla., and New Orleans, and West as far as Omaha. It is a great country."

Asked about the late war, Gen. O'Connor said there was but one opinion about it in British military and naval circles, and that was that it wouldn't last three months. "Dewey's victory surprised us, of course, but it was a foregone conclusion that you would have used up the Spaniards anyway."

In regard to the Filipinos, the general said he had met them at close range, having been in Hong Kong and Manila. There was very little fight in them, and he thought our affairs in the Philippines were handled in a very superior manner. The trouble there will soon be over, he said, and you have come into a valuable territory. The general has a very friendly feeling for this country, as he not only has many friends here, but also has a brother, who fought all through the Civil War, and is now a resident of Wilmington, N. C. Gen. O'Connor will stay with friends in Philadelphia for about two weeks, when he will return to England.

Luke says that he had previously visited friends in Philadelphia just after the Civil War ended. (1865) He said that he had left England in October to see the country again and had been as far south as St Augustine Florida and New Orleans and as far West as Omaha (Where brother Thomas had lived until his recent death).

126

He also made comment about the Spanish American war. He had met the Philipinos in Hong Kong and Manila and thought there was little fight in them and also, that he had many friends in Philadelphia and was staying with them for about two weeks before returning to England.

First of all, for logistical purposes, we know that he would have arrived in Philadelphia sometime on or before 22nd May and with his ship sailing back to England on 7th June, plus the fact that a little later on, there is proof that he arrived back in New York on 2nd June, then what he says right at the end of this clip concerning his staying with friends for a couple of weeks, all fits together.

However, within the right hand section above, he says that he had visited the city just after the civil war and had now noticed how it had changed. That was, indeed, an unexpected statement coming from him because no where in that era, or at any other time, had any indication been found, that this visit was other than his first trip to America.

If it was a mistake, why else was it reported, if he hadn't said it? He had been serving in Canada, of course, not long after the Civil War. The only other suggestion offered is that he may have attended his brother, Patrick's funeral in 1869 or that he had visited some of his colleagues, many of whom had immigrated into the East Coast after their fighting days were over.

Whatever, the below clipping from the Buffalo Evening News dated 2nd June 1899 confirms the above interview in that they report that Luke had checked into his 5th Avenue hotel in New York in time to see the Memorial Day procession from the hotel.

There is one error in the report in that it records that Luke had been travelling in the country since "last November". In fact, he had arrived in New York on 21st October 1888.

Maj.-Gen. Luke O'Connor, late of the Royal Welsh Fusileers, arrived in New York from Philadelphia in time to see the Memorial Day procession from the Fifth Avenue Hotel, where he is stopping. He has been traveling in this country since last November. Gen. O'Connor served in the Crimean war, the Indian Mutiny and the Ashantee campaigns. He was honored with the V. C. for valor.

Buffalo Evening News 2 June 1899

TRANSATLANTIC TRAVELLERS.

Among those who will sail to-day on the American liner St. Paul for Southampton are Mr. and Mrs. William Alexander and Miss Alexander, Mr. and Mrs. H. T. Ambrose, E. M. Barton, Miss Clara May Barton and Miss Barton, Mrs. C. N. Bovee, jr., and the Misses Bovee, Mr. and Mrs. Hunter Brooke and the Misses Brooke, Mr. and Mrs. Richard Harding Davis, the Rev. Dr. J. H. Eccleston, Mr. and Mrs. L. M. Fields, Lord Fincastle, Dr. H. S. Hersey, Mrs. A. L. La Montagne and Miss La Montagne, Miss Gwendoline Moss, Miss Olga Netheroole and Louis Netheroole, Colonel M. J. O'Brien, Major-General Luke O'Connor, Mrs. A. W. Kipling and child, Baron R. Nothomb, Henry Sewell, Mrs. F. S. Witherbee and child, Mrs. C. S. Witherbee and the Rev. T. A. Worrall.

New York Tribune 7th June 1899

And so, when he set sail on the liner, St Paul for Southampton, on 7th June, Luke had been in America for over 8 months.

A NEW CENTURY AND LUKE'S FINAL 15 YEARS

Luke had served in the Royal Welsh Fusiliers during the Victorian era which included the later, and most productive period of the Industrial revolution. Indeed, whilst the whole of his service had been during Victoria's reign, he had become the friend of her eldest son, Albert Edward, Prince of Wales who became King Edward VII in 1901 when his mother died.

In just about all the hundreds of press clippings read about Luke, the story of how he won his Victoria Cross has been repeated, almost as a mandatory element when any references about him were made. Wilst that may have been expected, the human element of his life, about how his family was forced to emigrate and how he and his siblings were made orphans, has comparatively, hardly been mentioned.

Had it not been for the little known M.A.P. newspaper published 120 years ago and Jenny Cropper, the young Reveille newspaper reporter, this fact seems to have been ignored by all others, most probably, because they had been unaware of these publications. The M.A.P. newspaper was more like a specialist military newsheet than a newspaper and even Jenny Croppers story was carried many years after Luke had become newsworthy, in 1967 and that was one hundred and thirteen years after the battle of the Alma had been fought. The Reveille was a popular newspapers not widely read among the upper classes but it wouldn't have attracted the attention that it would have received, had it been published within Luke's lifetime.

In short, the human interest in his family appears to have remained well below the radar and even when touched upon by observers, has often been unaccuratelyreported. That is found to be amazing and the author has felt privileged in being able to unfold what has been a massive jig-saw puzzle to reveal a remarkable story which has porovided a great deal of pleasure to him. Luke was separated from his siblings by the Atlantic Ocean but in his retirement, he must have often sat back with a realisation of where he had come from and what he had achieved. With the whole of his adult life being within the army, his retirement would have placed him in a completely different world, and it started a new life for him.

With his visits to Marseille, Egypt and now his eight month American tour, not to mention his constant visits to Ireland in between all those invitations and other high society dinners, he had obviously been enjoying himself in his new social environment. No sooner had he arrived in Southampton on 14th June 1899, then he was on the ferry to Kingstown, Dublin for a couple of months. He had sailed from England on 20th August 1899 and returned on 30th October. The existence of a loved one still lingers, yet there is no evidence of this at all, so what on earth was he up to over there?

So, having seen the 20th century 'tick over', he wouldn't be missing the Queen's Levee which was held at St James' Palace on 6th July. On this occasion, it was hosted for the Queen by the Duke of York.

The Boyle Connection Again

In addition to the 1875 presentation of the silver 'centre piece', there began to emerge other clues to indicate that his trips to Ireland, were probably involving the making, or re-making of acquaintances at Boyle. The main evidence suggesting this, rests on an extremely kind gesture made by Luke in 1901, when he donated a baptismal font to St Joseph's Church in Boyle.

Unfortunately, neither the font, nor the church in its original form, can be seen today because, as can be seen on the next page, both were destroyed by a fire on 6th April 1977.

At the turn of the century, Luke was one of only eight living, of the 62 recipients of the VC of those presented in the first batch by Queen Victoria. The 50 years jubilee of the Crimean War was fast approaching. This was also the era when larger ocean going vessels had been introduced, mainly due to the introduction of steam turbine engines.

Although many smaller vessels, often wooden ones, were in operation, with some still operating with part sail and part steam, only the very rich could afford long haul luxury voyages. But by the first decade of the 20th century, twelve years before the Titanic was launched, metal clad mail steaming vessels of considerable size began to emerge and the rich were taking voyages all over the world.

Remains of the Baptismal Font donated by Luke to the old St Joseph's Church Boyle in 1901 following the fire in 1977.

On 17th March 1900, Luke set sail on the Orient Line's 'Mail Steamer, 'Ortona' which left Plymouth bound for Australia. Unfortunately, it cannot ascertain whether Luke was booked to take the complete journey to Australia or whether he was to disembark during it's ports of calls at either Gibraltar, Marseilles, Naples, Port Said, Suez or Colombo, before reaching Australia. It is known that the South of France and Egypt were two of his favourite locations, so maybe it would have been Marseille or Port Said, or even both, that he was heading for.

R.M.S. Ortona – Orient Line

Having calculated his annual income earlier, whilst Luke wasn't the wealthiest of bachelors, he would have been comparatively wealthy during these last 15 years and most likely, long before that. With only his apartment to maintain, he would have had plenty of funds with which to sail around the world, and with no more wars to fight, why shouldn't he?

In addition, Luke was a bachelor and therefore, additionally free to be able to travel at his leisure. It wasn't until the Victoria Daily Times published the below subject on 23rd June 1900, which mentions his marital status, that I had had placed any relevance to the subject at all:-

> *….It is, however, conceded on all hands that the man who marries while yet a mere "non-com,"* (non-commissioned) *forfeits all future hope of a combatant commission, so our typical ranker resists the blandishments of the fair daughters of the regiment, sticks tight to his bachelor quarters, and in due course becomes colour sergeant. He is then a very important personage indeed, having entire charge – under his company, equivalent to one eighth of a battalion. The company has frequently been alikened to a family, of which the colour sergeant is the father. What the men eat and drink; the manner in which their meals are served and cooked; how they are clothed and shod; whether well or ill; all this and much more depends in a great measure upon the fitness or otherwise, of the colour sergeant for his duties.*

The article continues by explaining further benefits bestowed on the good 'colour sergeant' and I fully appreciate that there will be many exceptions to this general principle, which I doubt will be found in any Army regulations. However, it does make one think whether, in fact, Luke chose his bachelorhood for the sake of his career's progression.

This same article also explained the financial rewards on offer, for those who sought promotion. Readers must bear in mind, that the amounts of pay quoted, would be the 1900 rates and that Luke had retired on full pay, some 13 years earlier. I suspect the dividing gaps of the amounts of remuneration between the different ranks, would, however, be about the same.

For those readers, unlike the author, who are fortunate to be young enough not to have slogged away at school, attempting to calculate all types of arithmetical problems under the old 'non-metric' system, then suffice to know that there were 12 pennies in a shilling and 20 shillings to a pound. It's hard to believe that without the 10x metric system, calculators did not exist.

A shilling was the equivalent of 5 new pence in todays metric measures. Therefore, the colour sergeant's 3 shillings a day, would then be 15 new pence per day now, and the Colonels £3 per day would be 60 shillings, so, coincidentally again, £3 in todays money.

The nominal rates of pay in the army are: Private, 1s. a day; lance-corporal, 1s. 3d. a day; corporal, 1s. 8d. a day; lance-sergeant, 2s. a day; sergeant, 2s. 4d. a day; color-sergeant, 3s. a day; sergeant-major, 5s. a day; 2nd lieutenant, 5s. 3d. a day; lieutenant, 6s. 6d. to 7s. 6d. a day; captain, 11s. 7d. a day; major, 13s. to 17s. a day; lieut.-colonel, 18s. a day; colonel, £2 a day; brigadier-general, £2 10s. a day; major-general, £3 a day; lieut.-general £5 10s. a day; general, £8 5s. a day; field marshal, commanding an army, £16 a day.

Obviously, the spending power bears no comparison but it is the difference of 15 pence and £3 per day that is identified and highlighted. What a jump that was!.

We can, of course, recognise that whilst Luke wouldn't have fallen into that mere **"non-com"** category, marriage might well have curbed his steep climb up the promotion ladder.

The Autobiography is Published

So, returning to the beginning of the 20th century, we can assume that at some time soon, Luke would have been penning his story *'In the days of my Youth'* which was going to be published in the M.A.P. magazine on 6th October 1900. The article was, in fact, one of a series of similar ones written by people of similar note and standing. The editor and owner of the magazine, Mr. T.P. O'Connor, who, as previously mentioned, was a friend and countryman of Luke's but not a relative, wasted no opportunity in advertising Luke's story in editions published just prior to it being actually printed. It is worth reproducing T.P. O'Connor's words here, when he describes what was to come:-

"It is certain that his narrative – which is the first he has ever given to the world – will be read with pride by his fellow countrymen and fellow soldiers, and with eager interest by all, as the story of a noble career, nobly achieved, and recorded by one who, though ever a keen soldier, was and is, ever and always, a simple-minded and lovable man."

We must remind ourselves that this was forty six years after Luke had won his V.C. The gendre of the magazine was more 'military' than anything else and as such, there was a tremendous reaction from those who knew, and had fought with Luke in the Crimea and India.

Each one could not have reflected more highly on their admiration of the man. Having produced some of them previously, there is no need to duplicate them here, though the description of Luke being a 'lovable' man, reverberated around many columns of newspapers both on the mainland and in Ireland. Men are not normally described as 'lovable' (especially when they are bachelors!). For example, the editorial of the Ballymena Observor of 2nd August 1901 includes,

"...and yet today, he is still just the same simple good-hearted man as when he was a raw Irish recruit "a man" as one of his own brother officers had described him, "whom no-one ever knew without loving".

So far as Luke's remaining siblings were concerned he had lost his brother Patrick, back in 1869 and his brother Thomas had died just a matter of days before he reached his home during his 1888 / 99 visit to America. Whilst his two sisters' dates of birth were never precisely identified, the circumstantial evidence unearthed, resulted in the belief that it was Catherine who was the eldest, however, the realisation that their mother's name was Margaret Catherine, the names of both her daughters, was a set back to that notion.

Margaret was to leave her six adult children behind. Thank heavens that Luke had been re-united with her a few years ago. And so, without forgetting the baby James who died along with his mother in Canada, there remained just Catherine and Daniel as Luke's only surviving siblings.

Things Regal

The relationship Luke had with the Prince of Wales, Albert Edward, or as the press had daubed him, 'The Prince of Society' or the 'Party Prince', has been well documented.

Albert Edward as Prince of Wales and as King Edward VII

With his mother, Queen Victoria, having reigned for 63 years, her death, on 22 Jan 1901, saw her son, the Prince of Wales, crowned the next Sovereign, King Edward V11. His friendship with Luke never waned. In so far as the new King was concerned, in their book, 'Kings & Queens' by Richard Cavendish and Pip Leahy they record that :-..."*he was not allowed to see state papers until he was in his fifties, and with little of any importance to do, he devoted himself to love affairs, gambling, cards, horse racing, hunting, shooting and eating.'*

Could this be an indication of his intelligence or his 'laissez faire' attitude? Probably the latter.

The photographs above are evidence that his uniform would have been made a few sizes bigger, as he grew older. How his way of life, in particular his infidelity, would have sat with Luke, is something which is hard to understand. However, as a devout Catholic, Luke would not have approved, but with his 'friend' being the Prince of Wales, and the Commander in Chief of his Regiment, his behaviour was, at least, performed in situations far removed from Luke's otherwise, domestic life.

It was around this time that Luke began frequenting the Naval and Military Club, Picadilly. This was illustrated in a copy of the Pearson's Weekly newspaper in August, 1902. It recorded that : - *"when he happened to be up in town, he resembled every inch an officer and a gentleman of the old school, gracious, courteous and stately. Yet he only put in about two years at an ordinary Irish village school...."*

Comment in the same article, was made that he may have made use of military schools, but no authority on that subject, can be found. The article also compared Luke with his equally famous contemporary, the Scotsman, Willie McBean V.C. who had also been a 'ranker' and at the time of his attestation, according to a colleague, *"didn't know a 'B' from a Bull's foot.* It is on record, that when he enlisted, he was *"without shoes or stockings, a shock headed, raw Highland Laddie, who understood no English and who could neither read nor write".*

However, as uneducated as they were, both had risen to become commanders of the Regiments they had first joined. Like Luke, Willie McBean's first experience of battle was in the Crimea. He had enlisted in the 93rd Highlanders as a private and he too, displayed such bravery as to be given a commission.

It was at Lucknow, during the Indian Mutiny, that Willie distinguished himself by single handedly, killing eleven Sepoy soldiers at one time, when they had surrounded him. It was said that when he had been congratulated by a comrade, he replied, *"Toots man, It dinna tak' me twenty minutes".* Sadly, he sold theVC he won and was said to have squandered away the money he received for it.

And so, Luke had met the current King many times whilst, as Prince of Wales, he was Commander in Chief of the Regiment. He was also to meet his son, George, who became the Prince of Wales following his father's coronation.This too, would be as the new Commander in Chief, at many Royal levees and Regimental dinners and also, at ceremonial occasions such as at Wrexham Parish Church on 3rd May 1903.

Luke had sojourned in Egypt and had returned on the ship Oriziba which he boarded at Port Said. His return to London on 20th April 1903, was only two weeks prior to him again being at the Parish Church in Wrexham, on this occasion, for the unveiling of a monument by the Prince of Wales, in memory of those killed, wounded or died of disease in South Africa and China. He was lucky that he had disembarked Oriziba when he did, because, 22 months later, she was wrecked off Freemantle.

The wreck of the SS Orizaba off Freemantle on 17th February 1905

The 1st Battalion had lost 153 men killed or died of disease in South Africa and the 2nd Battalion, likewise, lost many on active duty with the 'Boxers' rebellion in China. The Regiment held the distinction of being the only Regiment with separate battalions in active service at the same time, in different countries.

The monument, is on the north wall near the West end of the church juxtaposition to the new west window, presented eight years earlier.

The Prince of Wales and Princess Mary of Tech, had driven from Chester where they had been staying with the Duke and Duchess of Westminster for a few days. On their arrival at Wrexham, they drove in open carriages and then walked along Church Street to the church with the 23rd in their swanky crimson uniforms and busby headgear, flanking them, as a guard of honour.

In Memory of those who fell in South Africa and China

Wrexham hadn't received a royal visitor since Queen Victoria 14 years earlier; it can be imagined what an extraordinary public spectacle this was and which, thankfully, took place in glorious weather, with all the pomp and ceremony it deserved.

All the bunting and decorations had been out in every village along the route, which was packed with onlookers from near and far. The town centre was also packed with loyal subjects waving their flags and cheering as the Royal party passed. Following the welcoming speeches, the Prince of Wales unvailed the memorial to the sound of three volleys being fired by a firing party outside.

The white English alabaster monument bears the following words at the foot of it: - *'This monument is erected by all ranks serving in the Royal Welsh Fusiliers'*

Following the Bishop of St Asaph's solemn dedication of the memorial, and further speeches being made, the royal party and entourage moved to the church yard for the planting of commemorative Yew trees. They were then driven through the still thronged streets to the 'Depot' at Hightown, where they were introduced to officers of the Regiment. Luke was, of course, present as a guest at the church and later, at the 'depot'.

It was shortly after this event, on 8th June 1903, that the Prince of Wales, presided at the annual Regimental Dinner being held at The Whitehall Rooms in the Metropole hotel, London. General Sir Edward Bulwer KCB was the honorary Colonel of the Regiment and Sir Howard Vincent, secretary of the Regimental Club. They were in attendance, together with many other senior officers.

According to various press reports, Luke had been embarking on the more luxurious ships than he had hitherto been used to during his military career. It was in an Illinois newspaper dated 23rd May 1907 that mention was made that, three years previously, he had visited Patrick's family at Joliet, Illinois. That would indicate that the visit was made in this year, 1904, when Patrick's wife was still alive.

Mention was made earlier, that when in Philadelphia during his 1898-99 visit, he told a reporter, that he had, indeed, visited there previously. It was also suggested that he may have visited his brother Patrick's funeral or retired colleagues, but no evidence can be found of that either. In short, no evidence of a previous visit can be found at all, but that is not to say that there wasn't such a visit.

The clipping on the next page, mentions a book placed in the Joliet Library called, 'The Book of the VCs' in which Luke is mentioned. The few lines missed off the article at the end of the next page, merely mentions that Luke, badly wounded himself, but shouted, "Come on 23rd!" and that he refused to go to the rear to have his wounds dressed until he had carried the Queen's colours, to the conclusion of the battle.

Unfortunately, the book, nor its author, cannot be traced though the article correctly mentions the names of his nephews and nieces and therefore, there is no reason to dispute it, though with Patrick's death being in 1869, then any visit by Luke, would not have been for his funeral. Otherwise, there are no indications of a 1904 visit to America.

In this year, 1904, he was to take at least two cruises. Those found, included a trip to Egypt in February and then, on 12th March, he boarded the steam ship 'Gaika' of the Union Castle Line, at Southampton, for Tenerife.

The month of June was approaching and once more, Luke found his way to the Whitehall Rooms at the Metropole Hotel, London where, on 16th, he attended the annual Regimental Dinner. This was always a lavish affair with current and retired senior officers travelling some distances in order to attend. Luke was now 73 years of age and there were signs appearing of his failing health, although that didn't often get in the way of such events or holidays.

Although he had a busy social schedule in 1904, there were periods when he could have visited Patrick's family, but it appears that if had paid them a visit, then he had kept them well under the radar.

As expected, Luke attended the annual regimental dinner on 16th June 1904, as he did for the next two dinners in 1905 and 1906, both of which were held at the same venue. The 1905 dinner was, however, a little special because as the Commander in Chief, the Prince of Wales was present and presided over the proceedings.

As might be expected by now, Luke's trips across the Irish sea were now pretty constant and he arrived at Kingstown on the cross channel steamer ferry on 18th November 1904. Unfortunately, there are no clues as to his final destination or for how long, he was to stay. The same trip, however, was made on the 8th October 1905, but again without details of any return sailing.

KINSMAN WEARS VICTORIA CROSS

New Book in Library Tells of Valor of General Luke O'Connor.

IS UNCLE OF LOCAL FAMILY

Hero of Crimean War in Joliet Three Years Ago.

Three years ago Brigadier General Luke O'Connor, on the retired list of the British army, visited Joliet, the guest of his nephews and nieces, John, James, Ambrose, Mary and Kate O'Connor. The distinguished soldier wore upon his breast a little bronze medal.

This was the Victoria Cross, the highest decoration for valor bestowed by British sovereigns. The cross and its wearer are recalled by a book, lately placed in the Joliet library, called, "The Book of the V. C.," in which the name of Luke O'Connor is found among the first group to receive the cross at the hands of the young Queen, Victoria, at the close of the Crimean war.

Announced Feb. 5, 1856.

In early days a mention in dispatches was the highest reward British bravery might receive, but after the Crimea, when so many deeds of heroism thrilled the hearts even of those who wept, it was determined that more than this was needed, and the new decoration made of the cannon taken at Sebastopol and bearing by her special desire the name of the queen, was announced in the London Gazette on February 5, 1856.

Queen Victoria Gives Cross.

The first presentation, at which Gen. O'Connor was decorated, took place June 26, 1857, the year after the close of the Crimean war. The scene was Hyde Park, and a large body of troops was drawn up under the command of Sir Colin Campbell, together with a party of blue jackets, while a vast crowd of people looked on.

Just before 10 o'clock to the sound of cannon, Queen Victoria, the Prince Consort, the Crown Prince of Prussia, the Prince of Wales and his brother, Prince Albert, all on horseback, rode into the park.

The little band of sixty-two heroes, headed by Lieut. Knox, of the rifle brigade, stood at ease until the signal was given and then, one by one they came forward as Lord Panmure, secretary of war, read their names.

The forty-sixth to receive the cross from the hands of the queen was Lieut. Luke O'Connor, afterwards rising through the grades to be the rank of brigadier general, which he now holds. This was fifty-one years ago, and now, at the age of 75 years, the retired hero is still enjoying life. His headquarters are in London but he spends much time in traveling.

Why He Wears the V. C.

The deed for which he received his commission and his decoration was performed at the battle of the Alma when the 23rd Royal Welsh Fusileers formed one of the regiments on the left wing. Lieut. Anstruthers, a lad o feighteen, carried the colors for the Fusileers almost to the Russian earthworks when a bullet pierced his heart and the banner was caught from his hand by Sergeant Luke O'Connor, himself

The Fighting Soldier

In all the years of researching Luke and his family, the author has always admired the fact that, although having risen to the higher echelons of society, including often being in the presence of the Royal family, he has always demonstrated a self-effacing personality.

Luke's friend, T.P. O'Connor who once said of him, that it was difficult to engage him in discussion about religion or politics. This is why surprise resulted from the article relating to his alleged stance concerning the Irish 'Home Rule' situation, though, that was when he 'fell into the lap' of a journalist who recognised him as he arrived back in England off the Irish ferry.

On other instances, he delighted in counselling the youth of society, whether they had been in the Army or in the youth organisations he supported. It is these youngsters who may have regarded him as something of a role model or a mentor.

His stature in the Army had placed him in positions where he has been expected to make speeches and he has never shirked that responsibility. I have noticed, however, that the content of his speeches, normally followed the same themes. They have been on the lines of the importance of doing one's duty and obeying supervisors and discipline codes. He also frequently mentions that what young soldiers will learn in the army, will be of benefit for any future career in civil society.

There was one instance in 1906, however, which shocked observers a little because whether he intended to or not, he found himself praising the soldiering skills, especially the fighting fibre, of Irish soldiers. This, of course, led by inference, that he wasn't so enamoured with the soldiering performed by those of other nationals. Now that, coming from an Irish Major General of a Welsh Regiment, was never going to go down well with other nationals, whether or not, they were in the military.

The first seen of this, was in an article published in the Hartlepool Daily Mail of 16th February 1906. However, the un-named author, included in it, the fact that it was a quote taken from Luke's article within a magazine or journal called 'Tales and Talk'. Whilst no record could be found of such a magazine, the name of it has aroused suspicions, but the content, appeared genuine, and I suppose, the term 'Fake News' hadn't been heard of in those days.

The clipping is of poor quality and once again, because of this, it is transcribed below: -

The Irishman as a Fighter

The Irishman is a born soldier. In the days of Wellington and Marlborough the English Army was largely recruited from the Emerald Isle, and finer troops the world has never seen. The son of Erin loves fighting, for fighting sake. He is full of dash and fire, he is resourceful in difficulties, and seldom gives way to panic. But he must be well led, officered by men whom he both likes and trusts. The Irishman has the faults of his temperament. Once let dissatisfaction spread its cankered roots in his heart, once let him lose faith in his leaders or in his cause, and his fighting value is terribly depreciated. The doggedness of the Englishman and Scotsman is not inherent in his character. Retreat, defeat, and disaster sour his spirit, and although they cannot sap his courage they weaken his fibre.

The inclusion of *"the Irish Soldier must be well led and officered"* etc., wasn't the Luke which the author had come to know from his research. It does not, of course, mention the Welsh but on 7th April 1906, a follow up article was published in the Weekly Mail concerning this subject but it unfortunately referred to an article, it says, which was published "a few days ago". In that article, it is alleged that Luke mentioned the Welsh. Unfortunately, such a passage cannot trace it but this is what the latter edition said about it: -

Welshmen as Soldiers - Colonel Ivor Herbert on his Fighting Compatriots.

A few days ago we quoted the opinion of Major General Luke O'Connor that the Scotsman is the best soldier, who combines the dash of the Irishman and the dogged unswerving defence of the Englishman. "I do not think," adds the gallant general, that the Welshman is at his best as a soldier. He is too home-loving, too much the child of his mountains and valleys. He will fight as well as any of his contreres when the demand is made upon him, but his heart does not go out to the profession of the sword".

And so, the very obliging newspaper thought that they would convey Luke's remarks to the notice of Colonel, Sir Ivor Herbert, who was also an M.P. and who eventually retired as a Major General.

Although Sir Ivor served as a Grenadier Guard, he came from Llanarth, Monmouthsire, from a family with deep Welsh roots. His resultant retort was, just as expected :-

> *"I have bad Welshmen under my command, but never anything that could be described as a characteristically Welsh body of soldiers and what I know of the Welsh character, I am satisfied that the highest qualities that Welshmen possess as soldiers, and they are very high, would only be properly developed in a corps which was fully national. My experience of the Welsh soldiers who have served under me has shown me that their qualities of devotion is especially shown towards a leader who has a thorough knowledge of the Welsh character, and is able to appeal to his national feeling in his own language. The Welshman's adaptability to strange circumstances and his facility in acquiring foreign languages, were I believe, reognised by the Duke of Wellington in the Peninsula, and those qualities are as strong today as they were one hundred years ago".*

In attempting to promote the worth of his kinsmen, he had left himself open to the contrary view. Sir Ivor might as well have said, "What do you expect with an Irishman who can't speak Welsh, leading a bunch of Welshmen who speak little else?"

However, in trusting that no duels were fought, when examining the successes of similar soldiers who came from humble backgrounds and who had risen to higher ranks, could it have been coincidence that both Major Generals Willie McBean and Richard Wadeson were both VC holders from humble parentage? They also, had risen from the non-commissioned ranks. In addition, Major Generals John McKay and James Campbell, both Scotsmen, had achieved similar success. McKay commanded the 2nd Battalion of the 12th and afterwards, a 'Regimental District', while Campbell was Colonel of the Coast Brigade Artillery.

The remarkable thing was, that all these men were either of Scottish or Irish origin. Let's hope that Luke rested his case there, before he got into any further troble!

IT'S AN HONOUR

For many years previously, newspaper editors and notable people mentioned in them, weren't backward in coming forward to express their belief that it was about time that Luke should be bestowed a further honour.

They had, of course, a knighthood in mind, and much comment was expressed, that nothing less would do. Some newspapers had even seggested that other, less known and less worthy individuals had constantly pushed infront of the queue. One newspaper had also suggested that Luke had excluded himself from being bestowed a Knighthood, because he had accepted a full pay pension in 1887, when he was also given the honorary rank of Major General. That really doesn't add up and appears to be just an excuse, and not a reason.

Whether the rules and regulations to which the 'Honours Committee' were bound, supported that concept, is not know, but the next King's Birthday honours were to spring further controversy over this issue. This entry in the Supplement to the London Gazette of the King's Birthday Honours, 1906, as shown below on the left, indicates, that he was awarded a C.B. He was to become a Companion of the Bath.

This was the lower of three classes of military 'Honours of the Order of the Bath', a series of promotions which would lead to a knighthood, but many thought that he should have been propelled higher up the ladder to be awarded a knighthood directly, instead of having to take this, preparatory step.

In that context, and as a reminder, reproduced below on the right, is a small section of a clipping inserted when commenting on this subject raised many years ago. Yes, it had taken all that time for it to to finally happen, but even then, in 1886, it was regarded as being well overdue.

<table>
<tr><td>

To be Ordinary Members of the Military Division of the Third Class, or Companions :—

Surgeon-General William Simson Pratt, Army Medical Staff, Principal Medical Officer, Southern Command.

Honorary Major-General Luke O'Connor, V.C., retired pay, late Royal Welsh Fusiliers.

The London Gazette 29ᵗʰ June 1906

</td><td>

It is surprising how the name of Luke O'Connor still lives among the rank and file of the Royal Welsh; it is even more surprising that one who has done so much in his time for his regiment and the service should have been entirely overlooked in the recent Bath selection. If ever a man deserved a C.B., Luke O'Connor did; and he has got nothing.

Army and Navy Gazette 5ᵗʰ June 1886

</td></tr>
</table>

However, an honour, indeed it was, and it was followed with much celebration. Newspapers were full of praise and unlike, as would have occurred in modern times, little was mentioned about him being overlooked for so long.

Luke's Faith

If ever there was one iota of Luke's character which was not in dispute, it would concern his complete commitment to the Roman Catholic faith. His family, including the 'Gannon' uncles who had a hand in his upbringing, were all of the same persuasion and he would have been expected, no matter where he settled, or where he happened to be in the world, to have carried his faith with him.

One only has to return to his autobiography, to realise that he had only been a cat's whisker away from following a path which could have ended in him becoming a parish priest, as was his cousin, Peter.

The following paragraph acts as a reminder : -

> *"It was at first to make me a priest, and this notion sometimes took hold of my fancy. My uncle, however, wished me to return to Canada to join my people, but all at once, he died."*

Such a statement, and the ensuing path, he actually took, falls exactly into the realms of the author's strong belief in fate, in as much as how it serves to mould the paths we are to take in life's long journey. The question should be asked, "how would his life have run if he had, indeed, selected the path leading him to the cloth"?

It is as well that we shall never know the answer, and whilst it exercises the mind, it probably illustrates what a futile and worthless interest this 'fate' business generates. Whilst we are unable, of course, to have expected Luke to physically practice his faith in all of the situations he found himself, there would be no doubt that he would have called upon it, whenever, or wherever, he could.

When exactly Luke moved to Clarges Street or when he joined the congregation of the Church of the Immaculate Conception, only a short walk away in Farm Street, is unknown. It would, of course, have been a necessity to have moved out of barracks when he retired, but he may have occupied his house at 34 Clarges Street, much earlier.

Being in the Berkeley Square / Mayfair area, the church was attended by many of the local 'high society'. Others who frequently attended with Luke were, Lady Tweedmouth, mother of the Countess of Aberdeen and of the First Lord of the Admiralty, Lady Dimsdale, Baroness Gudin and the Very Rev. Canon Lynch, Parish Priest of Blarney, county Cork. Indeed, with Luke's attendance, there would have been a fair flavour of Irishness among the congregation.

The Church of the Immaculate Conception [Google Street View]

It was at this time, in 1906 when a Protestant Clergyman and a subsequent author, Bernard Vaughan, caused quite a stir with his sermon concerning Christian ethics. He called the sermon, and indeed the book he was about to write about it, 'The Sins of Society'. It was reported that a large number of non-Catholics, including many Protestant Clergyman were among the most attentive listeners.

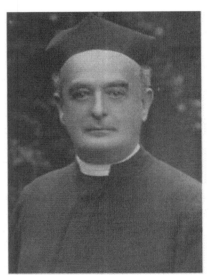

Born in 1847 in Herefordshire, Father Bernard Vaughan was educated at the 'Stonyhurst' Roman Catholic Independent School, Lancashire and became a member of the Society of Jesus.

For 18 years, he was priest at the Holy Name Church in Manchester, where he took a conspicuous part in the religious and civic life of that city.

In 1901, he went to London and worked among the poor of Westminster and the East End. It was his sermon on 'The Sins of Society' in 1906 which attracted large audiences. He preached in the USA, Canada, Alaska and lectured in China, Japan, Italy and France.

During WW1 he became Chaplain to the Catholic Troops serving with British forces on the Continent. He died in 1922.

Father Bernard Vaughan

The only newspaper article found regarding the upsurge of interest in this sermon, was contained in the Londonderry Journal of 8th August 1906 in which it was reported: -

> *"In far and near, at dinner parties, in drawing-rooms, at afternoon calls, one hears unstinted approval of the famous Jesuit's exposure of wrong-doing that is nothing less than a social cancer. Many Ulster people are included in this chorus of praise. One of these, a lady of position and great intelligence, who is well known over here (London) as well as in the North of Ireland, told friends that, although not a member of the Church to which Father Vaughan belongs, she thanked God for his splendid courage in unmasking the wickedness that exists in a certain section of society."*

As a regular attendee at the church, especially in his retirement, it was no wonder that Luke's funeral service was held there. Luke was obviously such a regular attendee, that he recognised it in his will.

He bequeathed the sum of £500 to the church and this, apart from being quite a large sum in those days, was one of the highest amounts of the many donations he bequeathed. (*CPI calculator states £500 in 1906 has a purchasing power of £61,195 in 2020*)

The Victoria Cross's Golden Anniversary

The first Victoria Crosses being awarded on Friday, 26th June 1857, meant that the 50th anniversary of that memorable day, would fall in 1907. We have already established that Luke's VC winning deed at the Battle of the Alma, was the first to be performed by a member of the Army, but the first winning deed of all, was performed by a sailor pictured here, on board the ship, HMS Hecla. He was the 'ship's 'mate' Charles David Lucas.

As mentioned when dealing with the VC presentations, Lucas's deed occurred during the British Navy's attack on the Russian controlled fort Bomarsund, in the Baltic Sea in August of 1854. During the battle, a live Russian shell landed on the upper deck. As the fuse burned, instead of diving for cover, Lucas picked up the device and carried it to the side of the ship and threw it over board. It exploded before it hit the water. Had it exploded on the deck, it would have killed a number of those there, and injured many others. The ship's Captain William Hutcheson Hall, promoted Lucas to Lieutenant on the spot.

Being born at Pontzpass, Northern Ireland on 19th February, 1834, he was therefore three years younger than Luke. He is mentioned because, on this 50th anniversary of the presentations, 60 of those first 62 recipients had already died.

In a sense, it would have been somewhat of a unique event if Lucas had been both the first to have won the VC and the last survivor of those 62 who first received them. However, with Luke being the eldest of the two, his chances of being the last of them to survive, was pretty remote.

Well, both lived to ripe old ages and with Lucas eventually becoming a rear admiral, it became a closely fought affair. Admiral Lucas was another example of a military officer not marrying, at least not until he had retired. And then, who did he marry? Well, she happened to be his old Captain's daughter; the very same captain who had promoted him on the spot in August 1854. She was Frances Russell Hall.

Lucas sadly lost his VC after he left it on a train and because duplicates cannot be issued, he was given a blank one instead. Also, he sadly died on 7th August 1914, around 6 months before Luke. Yes, not only was Luke the first soldier to win the VC, he was indeed, the sole survivor of those 62 heroes who were first presented with that most coveted medal.

Sadly, it was just prior to this 50th Anniversary of the VC presentations, that Luke was to receive news from America that his sister, Catherine died on 19th January, 1907.

We can be sure that he was made aware of that fact because communications between his brother, Daniel were still on-going. Whilst the short notice of her death below, appeared in her local Racine newspapers, the article below that, was published in Daniel's Wilmington Morning Star on 22nd January, just three days after her death.

Catherine's correct date of birth has never exactly been established. From the various official records available, it could have been anything within a 10 year span. The evidence, however, pointed to an 1816 birth which would have made her 91 when she died. But who's counting now?

However, with Catherine probably being the eldest, it was probably her who accompanied Luke back to Ireland to be cared for by their uncles. On a more alarming note, which Catherine's death brought with it, was the fact that these two boys, Daniel and Luke were now the only two siblings, of those

An Only Sister Dead.

Friends in this city of Major Daniel O'Connor will sympathize with him in the death of his only living sister, Mrs. Catherine O'Connor Hute, widow of the late John Hute, which occurred on Saturday at her home in Rochester, Wisconsin. Mrs. Hute had reached the advanced age of 90 years.

seven children and their parents who set sail on that fateful voyage to Quebec, and who were alive at that time.

So, on a more pleasant subject, the forthcoming King's Levee at St James' Palace, was, to coincide with the King's birthday and it was to be an unusual gathering, in so much, that all veterans of the Indian Mutiny, were to be invited, albeit a quick glance at the list of guests, reveals that they were more likely to be the officers as opposed to the 'other men'.

In another clipping, it was reported that Lieutenant General, Sir Gordon Pritchard introduced to the King, Sir Godfrey Clark, Lieutenant General F. Green-Wilkinson, Lieutenant General Sir Brian Millman and Major General Luke O'Connor. It continued,

A SURVIVOR OF THE MUTINY.

At the King's Levee on Monday there were present, at his Majesty's special request, the survivors of the Indian Mutiny, of which this year marks the fiftieth anniversary. General O'Connor's Victoria Cross was gained twice over in the Crimean War—at the Alma on the 20th of September, 1854, and at Redan on the 8th September, 1855. General O'Connor is one of the three survivors of the 62 gallant men

Major-General Luke O'Connor, V.C.

upon whose breasts Queen Victoria pinned the Victoria Cross in 1857, the other two being Admiral Lusk and Capt Jones, of the 7th Fusiliers. On the outbreak of the Mutiny, O'Connor went to India with his regiment. He was the first wearer of the Victoria Cross to arrive in India, and there was very great curiosity on the part of all his comrades on the march to the relief of Lucknow under Lord Clyde to see and examine the then newly instituted and already, of course, much coveted decoration.

Cardiff Times 8th June 1907

"The King kindly shook the hand and gave a word of welcome to each of the veterans presented to him. Many of the veterans wore the Victoria Cross."

These 'Mutiny' invitees were, of course, in addition to the many aristocratic and otherwise, 'titled' selection of attendees, who normally attended them.

In early September of this 1907 year, the summer season at Harrogate was rapidly drawing to a close, but it still had an important part of its course to run. The hotels and hydro were all full and working at high pressure. Whether Luke was once again drawn there due to the cures and treatments offered by the waters, or whether it was because the large hotels were now becoming accustomed to providing their own entertainment and orchestras, is unknown. But for whatever reason, Luke was among the many Lords and Ladies, and other very senior military officers who were reported to be in the town at the same time as himself.

There could well have been another attraction which may have drawn Luke to his hotel because, of all people, Father Bernard Vaughan, who had recently preached at Farm Street, had left this Harrogate hotel two weeks earlier but was expected to return imminently, to complete his 'cure'.

The Death of Sir Howard Vincent

As the Autumn of Luke's life approached, the years of Luke's life were becoming less eventful. Apart from attending yet another King's Levee and the annual regimental dinner in 1908, (at which he presided) he could expect to attend an increasing number of funerals and memorial services. Indeed, on 9th April 1908, such a sad occasion occurred following the death of Sir Charles Edward Howard Vincent KCMG CB DL, better known as Howard Vincent or C. E. Howard Vincent.

Sir Howard had been one of Luke's colleagues in the Royal Welsh Fusiliers, but he was of a much different ilk, for not only did he become the first director of the Metropolitan Police's Criminal Investigation Department, but it was said, though unconfirmed, that he could well have been a British spy.

Being a product of Westminster School and Sandhurst, his commission had been purchased. However, being a soldier, was just one interesting aspect of his life. He was also a barrister, police official and a Conservative party politician who sat in the House of Commons from 1885 to 1908 and he also studied Russian and other languages.

It may also be remembered that Sir Howard was the colonel of the Westminster Volunteers which Luke had also associated himself with. He died in Cannes France, but his body was taken by funeral coach to London the next day, and the memorial service was held on 11th April at St Margaret's, Westminster. The King was represented and all of the 23rd's hierarchy, both veterans and current commanders were present. He was another, who had been **'born to lead'**.

Sir Howard thought very highly of Luke and was a good friend. It will be remembered that a few pages back, mention of him was made regarding a letter he had written to TP O'Connor when he read that Luke's autobiography was about to be published. The clipping below followed the actual publication and again, signifies exactly what he thought of him. It is very necessary that it is included here, because, almost at the end of this book, the various reasons which separate heroes from the rest of us is discussed. One reason briefly touched upon, was the question as to whether, in his daring deeds, Luke could have been trying to show that as a perceived 'posh boy' with a 'monied' uncle, he was trying to prove that he was just 'one of the boys'.

Perhaps this quote below, written by Sir Howard about Luke, throws a different light on the subject. The title is difficult to translate but it might be something like, 'Take what you have earned', which does make sense.

Bene Meruit de Patriâ.

"You can look back upon the past with pride. You can look upon the present with satisfaction. Rest assured that your name will always be remembered by the Royal Welsh Fusiliers, be always surrounded in the annals of the British Army by the laurel wreath you won so well—and as in the battles of the British Empire in 1900, so in the future, brave and successful soldiers will emulate the deeds of Luke O'Connor, Major-General. All may not have equally good fortune, though they may deserve it. But all may win it, and the Sovereign and the Army will look upon them, as upon you, as deserving well of their country."

C. E. HOWARD VINCENT.

If not surprised, Luke would surely have been proud of such an accolade. However, nothing further of interest occurred with Luke in 1908, perhaps other than his being a little surprised that after reading in the 1907 newspapers that it was only himself and Admiral Lucas of the 62 first VC medal recipients, who were then alive, he was to read a year later, there were four of them still alive, and in another, there were five! At least there were no similar reports following Luke's death.

Apart from attending the King's Levee, at which future Prime Minister, Sir Neville Chamberlain attended, Luke's 1909 diary contained details of a holiday at Bournemouth, but otherwise, it confirmed his commitment to motivate young men and encourage them in their desired pursuits. The Church Lads' Brigade was one such organisation and on 24th June 1909, Luke attended their 'Festival Dinner' at the Hotel Cecil. It was presided over by Field Marshall the Duke of Connaught who managed to raise donations of £1,135 towards their expenses, a very large sum in those days. Apart from the Duke, other speakers included Field Marshalls Lord Grenfell and Sir George White and a host of other 'top brass' officers, were present, besides Luke.

On 14th August 1909 reinforcing Luke's support for the youth of the nation, he had the honour of being asked to inspect the Catholic Boys' Brigade at their camp near Effingham, Surrey. The brigade consisted of about 900 boys drawn chiefly from Liverpool, London and Birmingham. Fittingly, so far as the 'Colours' were concerned, the lads carried three standards which had been blessed by the Pope. Luke considered that the 'Lads' bearing and appearance were very good.

King Edward 7th died on 6th May 1910 and his son; George 5th succeeded him. His 16 year old son, Prince Edward who was later to become King Edward 8th, became the Prince of Wales and his investiture occurred on 13th July 1911.

The Indian Mutiny Reunion

1910 was to be a year of more notable events. This was particularly so, on 6th July 1910 at the Chelsea hospital London when the governor of the hospital, Field Marshall Sir George White, was celebrating his 75th Birthday. No less than 80 Officers, 70 Chelsea Pensioners and 5 civilians had been invited, in addition to 160 survivors of the Indian Mutiny.

Following many group photographs taken on the courtyard, more photographs were taken on the terrace of the hospital. This included a group of six Victoria Cross winners, all of who had been associated with Sir George over the years and whose photograph is shown below.

Excluding their individual accreditations for the honours bestowed upon them, they were, from left to right, otherwise known as Lieutenant General Sir James Hills–Johns, Luke himself, Field Marshall Sir Evelyn Wood, Field Marshall Rt Hon. F. S. Earl Roberts, Field Marshal Sir G.S. White and Colonel Sir E.T. Thackeray.

With so many of these veterans getting together after long periods of time, this must have been a really jolly occasion but unfortunately, the first group photographs taken, had included an 84-year-old colour sergeant Wells, formerly of the Cameron Highlanders and who was known as the 'father' of that regiment. He sadly collapsed and died just after his photograph was taken.

Copies of this photograph appeared in most national newspapers and the one shown below, was published on the front page of The Daily Mirror on 7th July 1910. The original photograph is held at the Wrexham archives and the above is a photograph of that original which, contains Luke's handwritten note on the reverse, dated 24th July 1911. He had written that note just over a year following the photograph being taken.

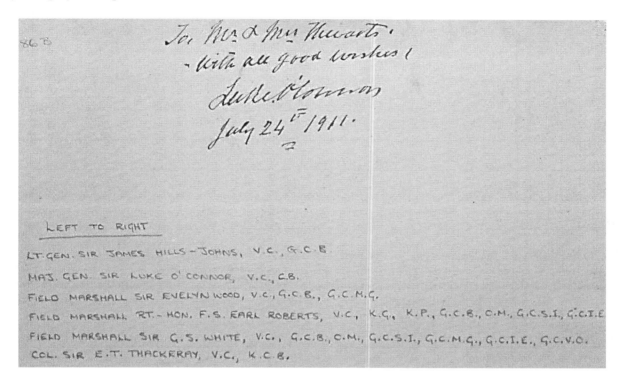

He must have been of a pedantic nature to have included all of the subjects' honours accreditations following their individual names; this being another reason why they have been excluded from the front of the photograph on the previous page.

Daniel and Family's Visit

Excluding all his battles, it was almost immediately following this occasion, that Luke was to experience, perhaps one of the most exciting events of his life. He was to receive a visit from his brother Daniel, his wife, Mary, their daughter Maie and Maie's husband, the Judge Egbert Kedar Bryan. It was over ten years past, when Luke visited America and stayed with Daniel and his family.

As indicated in the newspaper clipping below, they left their home in Wilmington, North Carolina, on 19th June 1910, for a two month tour of Europe. They were to return home on 22nd August. Nothing is mentioned of their intention to visit Luke in London. Their visit with him, was not carried by the

Wilmington Morning Star 21st June 1910

British press but was just a reference referred to as described in the below clipping dated 6th August 1910, published in Wilmington.

Luke had indeed, been recorded in the press as being a visitor at the Old Ship hotel, Brighton on 13th August. Bearing in mind the reports above, this would have been around the timee when Daniel's family would have been with him. No doubt he was entertaining them with what he may have thought as a 'quid pro quo' visit, on similar lines to that which he had received on his visit to the USA.

SIR LUKE O'CONNOR.

London Illustrated Publication Has Account of Celebration.

Mr. R. N. Sweet, of this city, has received from Major Daniel O'Connor, of Wilmington, who is visiting his brother, Sir Luke O'Connor, V. C., in England, a copy of the Daily Mirror, published in London, which contains on its front cover an excellent group photograph of a notable gathering of heroes in honor of the seventy-fifth birthday of Field Marshal Sir George White, the hero of Ladysmith. The group includes Sir Luke O'Connor and five other wearers of the Victorian Cross, who were guests of honor at the great celebration. Sir O'Connor, on a recent visit to Major O'Connor in Wilmington, made many friends here, one of whom was Mr. Sweet, who prizes the likeness of Sir O'Connor very much. Sir O'Connor's military rank is that of major general.

6th August 1910

Maj. Daniel O'Connor and Mr. and Mrs. E. K. Bryan, who have been spending the past two months abroad, returned home yesterday morning and were cordially welcomed by their hosts of friends who were delighted to know that they have had a most pleasant sojourn abroad. They visited all places of interest on the Continent and reached New York on the White Star Liner three days ago. After spending a few days North, they returned to Wilmington. While abroad Maj. O'Connor had the pleasure of spending some time with his brother, General O'Connor, of the British Army, retired, and who was recently given the Victorian Cross for his distinguished services.

23rd August 1910

The Death of Florence Nightingale

Florence Nightingale, OM, RRC, DStJ
Born: 12 May 1820 Florence Italy.
Died: 13th August 1910 Mayfair
The Pioneer of modern nursing
Educated at Kings College London
and at Cambridge University.

Daniel and his family arrived back in New York on 20th August 1910, which was the same day on which a memorial service was held at St Pauls Cathedral for the 'Lady of the Lamp' the nurse, Florence Nightingale. Florence had died a week earlier, at her home in Mayfair which was just half a mile from

Luke's home. She had arrived in the Crimea on 4ᵗʰ November 1854, the eve before the Battle of Inkerman. She had brought with her 38 nurses, including 14 Anglican sisters, 10 Catholic sisters of mercy and 3 trained nurses.

Luke had been nursed by Florence after he had been shipped out of the Crimea on the vessel, Columbo, following his being wounded at Alma. Having been treated at the hospital at Scutari, he intended to return to his regiment, but caught a fever on board the ship, was landed at Balaclava and returned to Scutari where he was once again, treated by her. He wrote in his autobiography, " *"I was sent back to Scutari, where I received much kind attention from Miss Nightingale and the Sisters of Charity"*.

Little was he to know, that around 50 years later, they would be living so close to each other. She was apparently, quite a shy lady during her early career days, but she had blossomed as her career developed and, in addition to her receiving the freedom of the City of London, many honours were bestowed upon her. Among these, she was the only woman to receive the 'Order of Merit'. One journalist wrote, "Indeed, she was the only woman who has deserved it of the twenty distinguished people with whose name it is associated. She sounds like another, who was **'born to lead'.**

Miss Nightingale was not only a marvellous nurse and leader, she was also a social reformer. So many people wanted to pay their last respects to her, that the 'War Office' had arranged the memorial service on behalf of, and with permission of the family. In fear of there being insufficient room to accommodate the 'upper crust', they had 3,000 tickets distributed to the aristocracy and military commanders who they knew would want to attend. The members of the public who were not invited, were allowed, so far as possible, to enter by the side doors to stand in the aisles.

The King, the Queen and Queen Alexandra, were all represented and the Archbishop of Canterbury attended. Numerous ambassadors, military personnel, Chelsea Pensioners, politicians, representatives of the medical profession, all combined to fill every seat in the Cathedral and leave many standing outside.

News of her death and of her memorial service, was published in 768 different newspapers in just about, all counties of the British Isles, not to mention British national newspapers and those others published abroad. Among them, was a very long and detailed account provided in the Newcastle Evening Chronicle. It reads: -

> *"One of the most interesting figures at the service, was Major-General Luke O'Connor, who won his Victoria Cross in the Crimean campaign in which he was intimately associated with the quiet Miss Florence Nightingale".*

LUKE'S FINAL FIVE YEARS

The past decade had witnessed Luke's attendance at numerous Royal Levees, reunions and other civic and social events, all of which would have been tinged with a good dose of military flavour and, which would have indicated that his retirement had done little or nothing, to dampen his association with his Regiment.

Since the battle of the Alma, many annual parades had been held on 20ᵗʰ September each year, not only in celebration of the Regiment's victory, but also, of course, in recognition of the gallant and brave sacrifices, Luke's colleagues had made.

Even though 1910 was the 56ᵗʰ anniversary of Alma, and the Battalion was located at their Royal Barracks in Dublin, this year's parade was going to be no exception. It was also specifically held in honour of Luke who had been invited to attend; indeed, to inspect it. It assembled in 'Review Order', he having been received by them, with a salute. 'Quarter Column' was then formed and he gave the assembled parade an address in which he recalled with pride, the part taken by the battalion at Alma and how it resulted in further honours for the regiment.

On the more leisurely side, the 1911 census indicated that Luke was taking it easy at a top class hotel, The Imperial at Meyrick Street, Bournemouth, was among the best there was in the town. There were 93 occupants in the hotel that night, 37 of which, were staff.

This year's annual regimental dinner was again held at the Princess Restaurant, London, on 30th May 1911. It will be recalled that 36 years ago, in 1875, after Luke had returned from West Africa, he was presented with a magnificent 3 feet high silver centre piece by his Roscommon friends at Boyle.

As a bachelor, heaven knows what he did with it, because, as was mentioned by T.P. O'Connor in his M.A.P. magazine, with the remains of his own family being in America, this superb trophy had barely an intrinsic value to him. An image of it is reproduced here, as a reminder. I guess that with age catching up with him, it was for this reason that he chose this annual dinner at which to present that centre piece to the officers mess.

It seems that the regiment were so proud of Luke and the 'centre piece' that at the national Eisteddfod of Wales on 20th August, 1912, they placed it as the centre piece of their public display.

1911 was, of course, the 57th anniversary of the Alma battle and Luke was still regarded as something of a celebrity, He was now the only survivor from his regiment who had fought at Alma. Although many newspapers also reported that he was the only remaining person from the 62 who were presented with the first Victoria Crosses, they were incorrect, because there were, in fact, two of them, the other being Admiral Charles Lucas of the Royal Navy. (His death has been mentioned earlier)

For this year's annual 'Alma Battle Day' parade, the 2nd Battalion was in India but the 1st Battalion was still at Dublin and Luke was, once again, present. He would now be around 80 years of age, though there were signs of his health declining.

Only three days later, the Daily Telegraph & Courier, reported that he was lying dangerously ill at the Junior Constitutional Club, Piccadilly. That situation continued until in another newspaper, the Islington Gazette of 15th April, it was reported that - *"having been dangerously ill for some time, he was now practically recovered"*.

This good news was to get better, indeed, in August, 1912, he was reported to be a guest at a fashionable wedding at St Mark's church, Milverton, Leamington Spa on 7th August. The bridegroom was Commander Humphrey Walwyn, the 2nd son of Colonel James Harford Walwyn who Luke succeeded as Colonel of the 2nd Battalion, the Royal Welsh Fusiliers in 1880. Humphrey was to marry Eileen Mary Straubenzee, daughter of Major General – van Straubenzee. The list of guests was like a who's who of all military dignitaries. Even listing the gifts given by each of them – Luke's was a silver rose bowl.

As a matter of interest, Humphrey became Vice-Admiral **Sir Humphrey Thomas Walwyn**, KCSI, KCMG, CB, DSO. He died in 1957 and served during the 2nd Boer War and the 1st World War. He was also the Commander in Chief of the Royal Indian Navy from 1928 until his retirement in 1934. He then served as Governor of Newfoundland from 1936 throughout the 2nd World War until 1946.

Is this further evidence of how success often breeds success, or is it simply a matter of success being 'in the genes'? Or were they just **'born to lead'**?

Unfortunately, before the year 1912 was out, evidence of Luke's ill health again appeared. This was doubly sad because, on 4th October 1912, the inaugural meeting and dinner of the Royal Welsh's 'Old Comrades Association' took place in the Assembly Rooms, at High Street, Wrexham. This was a huge event in the history of the regiment at which 180 past and present warrant and non-commissioned officers and other men were present.

As this was the inaugural meeting, the constitution was proposed and accepted and the officers and committee members were elected. Following the business, the meeting moved to the Wynnstay Arms hotel to enjoy the dinner. The only toast was for the health of the King and a telegram was sent to him, saluting the new King, ' George 5th'. A reply came from Balmoral Castle on the following day :-

"Please convey to the 180 past and present members of the Old Comrades Association of the Royal Welch Fusiliers, his Majesty's best thanks for their loyal message."

(Signed) STAMFORDHAM

Luke also sent a telegram apologising for being unable to attend because he was 'indisposed'. No other reason, other than maybe, his poor health, which might have caused his indisposition, can be found.

The Knighthood

Luke would have been delighted in the knowledge that he was to be included in that year's June honours list. This good news was later published in the London Gazette of the 3rd June as hereunder:

SIR LUKE O'CONNOR IS HONORED IN BRITISH ARMY.

Many Wilmington friends of Sir Luke O'Connor, of the British army, who has several times visited his brother, Maj. Daniel O'Connor, of this city, will read with interest the following from a recent issue of the Army and Navy Gazette, a journal of the Reserve and Territorial Forces, published in London, England:

...... while of those who have attained the dignity of a K. C. B. no name will give greater general satisfaction than that of Sir Luke O'Connor, V. C., whose great career is thus worthily crowned.

To be Ordinary Members of the Military Division of Second Class, or Knights Commanders, of the said Most Honourable Order—

Colonel and Honorary Major-General Luke O'Connor, V.C., C.B. (retired).

The London Gazette 3rd June 1913

News of this honour was to spread like wildfire around the world. It appeared in numerous British newspapers but the one catching the eye, was from North Carolina, the Wilmington Morning Star that obviously wanted to link Luke's brother, Daniel, their own local hero, with his brother's success.

It is suspected that the comment relating to Luke visiting 'several times' stemmed from the very long visit he made with Daniel in 1888/89 during which sojourns were taken away from Wilmington, with him returning there, on more than one occasion.

Owing to the very long list of other recipients contained within the below newspaper column and the fact that the Morning Star duplicated it word for word from the British edition, the centre of it has been deleted, just to concentrate on Luke's achievement.

In the eyes of many in this world, Luke's Companion of the Order of the Bath (CB) should have been a KCB way back in 1906. That wasn't to be, but although he wouldn't have made his feelings known, that injustice had now been corrected, albeit in the autumn of his life. He was now Major General Sir Luke O'Connor, VC KCB, but it was such a pity that he couldn't have enjoyed his knighthood for longer than he did.

The 59ᵗʰ. Alma Day, 1913.

The 59ᵗʰ Anniversary of Alma Day, was held at the 'Victoria' barracks, Windsor, home of the 1ˢᵗ Battalion. Luke is seated immediately behind the goat mascot's horns.

His recent knighthood meant that he was to be the guest of honour. He took the salute and inspected the parade. The battalion marched past, first in slow, and then in quick, time. He finally addressed the battalion and expressed his great pleasure and pride in again being asked to inspect the regiment on 'Alma Day'.

Such was Sir Luke's celebrity status that the clipping from The Times below, turned out to be a forerunner to their story carried on 8th October 1913.

SPEECH BY MAJOR-GENERAL SIR LUKE O'CONNOR.

Major-General Sir Luke O'Connor, V.C., K.C.B., was present on Saturday at a special parade of the 1st Batt. Royal Welsh Fusiliers at Victoria Barracks, Windsor, to commemorate the Battle of the Alma, where, as a sergeant, he caught the colours as they fell from the dying hands of young Anstruther and planted them on the heights of Alma, for which service he obtained his commission. There was a full parade of the battalion in review order under the command of Lieutenant-Colonel H. O. S. Cadogan. The goat given to the battalion by the King led the troops, his horns being specially gilded for the occasion. The general public were admitted to witness the ceremony, and there were several distinguished officers present. The colours of the battalion were escorted to the parade ground, and afterwards the battalion marched past Sir Luke O'Connor.

Sir Luke O'Connor, in addressing the battalion, said it was a great compliment to him to be present at the ceremony. He joined the Royal Welsh Fusiliers as a private and had had the great honour eventually of commanding the battalion. At the battle of the Alma he only did a soldier's duty. Six weeks after he joined the battalion he gained his first stripe and he ultimately became a major-general. He saw in their ranks that day intelligent and smart-looking young soldiers, and they ought to be proud that they belonged to such a distinguished regiment. Army training was splendid for young men, and they could make themselves fit in that service to take any appointment in civil life when they left the regiment. It was the happiest time of his life when he served in the battalion. He wished them, on their forthcoming departure for Malta, health and happiness, and he hoped he would see them all again. At the call of Colonel Cadogan, the men put their bushies on their bayonets and gave three cheers for the veteran soldier. Subsequently Sir Luke O'Connor had a talk with three Chelsea pensioners who had served in the battalion, one veteran, named Brown, who possessed several medals, having been in the regiment when General O'Connor commanded it. Sir Luke O'Connor afterwards lunched with the officers.

Luke's desire to follow his mentor, Daniel Lysons' wish, namely to encourage the youth of society, to put their very best efforts into whatever they chose to do, has been mentioned previously.

To emphasise the point, it was pleasing to discover an essay written by Luke on his thoughts of how one should always do their duty. It could well have been a speech, except that many similar contributions were made and printed in a Canadian newspaper, *'The Edmonton Journal' (Edmonton, Alberta, Canada)* on 6th December 1913.

Luke's was not the only contribution. Others written with the same 'inspirational flavour' were written by:-

1. Mr. J. Fergus Cunningham about the Boy Scouts,
2. Mr. W.I. Tait about the Y.M.C.A. and
3. By a Scout Patrol Leader, Hardy who recounted a Baden Powell inspirational story entitled   . 'If I was a Boy Again'.

The stories were aimed at inspiring young men, in the way Luke had done throughout his adult life. What seemed unusual, however, was that although featured in a Canadian newspaper, they were all written by British contributors.

It is because, with few exceptions, he had always refrained from making comment himself, that the author wished to include the full clipping of his article.

This was not the first time he had expressed his passion for 'Doing one's Duty'. The excerpt is on the next page below:-

150

WHAT LIFE HAS TAUGHT ME.
By Maj.-Gen. Sir Luke O'Connor, V. C., K. C. B.

Speaking as an old soldier, I say without hesitation that the first and greatest lesson life has taught me is that one should strive to do one's duty always, and under all circumstances.

"Thank God, I have done my duty!" exclaimed our greatest sailor, Nelson, as he lay dying after Trafalgar; and Gordon, one of our greatest soldiers, used almost the same words shortly before he was killed at Khartoum.

I am quite sure that you lads, just starting the battle of life, cannot do any better than take to heart the example set you by these two heroes, and act upon it.

Duty first, last and all the time! That is the keynote of success in life, as it is also of true happiness and contentment. Duty to one's God, to one's King, to one's country, to oneself, to one's fellow-men! These are the ideals I have set before myself, and tried to act up to. Do the same yourself. You will never regret it. Take an old man's word for that.

And do not forget that when you have achieved success—as you almost certainly will if you follow my advice—it then becomes your duty to help others to achieve it. When I am asked, as I often am, to inspect boys' brigades, and other similar organizations, and say a few words to them, I always consent, even thought it entails inconvenience, or even hardship, upon me personally. I have risen from a bed of sickness to comply with a request of this kind, and that upon more than one occasion. This I do because I conceive it to be my duty.

The truest happiness lies in performing faithfully this kind of duty. Looking back on a long life, crammed full of incident and adventure, I can truthfully say that what gives me the greatest satisfaction is the knowledge that through my influence and exertions many of the young men of my regiment were helped to higher and better ideals of life than perhaps they would have attained to otherwise, while three of those I trained and was interested in followed so closely in my footsteps that they succeeded in gaining their army commissions.

Acting on my advice, they did their duty faithfully and well, and in due course they received their reward.

In the same way I received mine, when I carried the Queen's colour throughout the battle of the Alma river, after my officers had been killed and I had been severely wounded.

I did this because it was my duty; but, all the same, I did not disdain my reward, and it was the sweeter when it came, in that I knew that I had well and truly earned it. In the same way, when, a little later in my career, I led my men to the second assault on the Redan, and was again severely wounded, it was the knowledge that I had done my duty that softened and sweetened the pain, and added happiness to the possession of the little bronze cross "for valour" with which my efforts were afterwards rewarded.

The short inspirational essay was written by Luke in a Canadian Newspaper.

151

LUKE'S FINAL YEAR

In 1914, Luke contracted pneumonia but there had been a previous occasion when he suffered with that, and now, January wasn't a good time of the year to suffer it again. On this occasion, his condition necessitated a move into a Care Home but as he improved, he transferred to the St James's Palace Hotel in Bury Street, London. Here, he could summon assistance at the sound of a bell and receive all the attention his illness demanded.

Thankfully, by 29th January, newspapers were reporting that he was beginning to recover though on 5th February, he was still a guest, being nursed at the St James Palace Hotel.

On 2nd March 1914, newspapers were commenting that at age 83, his condition was 'an anxious thing'. In doing so, the Belfast Telegraph also commented that Luke had been a great friend of the late, King Edward 7th.

On a brighter note, he was able to attend the annual regimental dinner on 26th May at the Princess Hotel, London. He was also at the King's Levee on 10th June. His 'activity' days were, of course, over. The very poor photograph of him here, shortly after having attended the Levee, is possibly the last photograph taken of him.

Major-General Sir Luke O'Connor, who attended the Royal Levee, yesterday, enjoys the distinction of being the first winner of the Victoria Cross, the reward for a daring deed at Alma.

Appointed Colonel of the Regiment

Major General Sir Savage Lloyd-Mostyn was not only a friend and colleague of Luke's, but he had been the Honorary Colonel of the Royal Welsh Regiment for some years. Commissioned with an Eton education, he had served with Luke at the Redan, during the Indian Mutiny and in West Africa.

Sir Savage sadly died on 2nd June 1914, just eight days before the levee. His death was a real shock because he had been found submerged in his bath, with the hot tap running. With a scald mark to his chin and with the bath not having overflowed when being discovered by his wife, the inquest arrived at the conclusion that he had been in the bath and had wanted to top it up with hot water. He must have fainted and suffocated after submerging beneath the water.

Sir Savage's death created the vacancy for the appointment of the Honorary Colonel of the Royal Welsh Fusiliers. Although purely a titular title, this was the highest post available in the regiment and due no doubt, to Luke being a few years older that Sir Savage, he could not have dreamt that he would ever succeed him, though, he would have given his right arm, to do so.

Luke, was duly appointed and was later to refer to his title, as the greatest honour and achievement he had made. Having joined the regiment in 1849, he had loyally served it for 65 unbroken years. The newspapers were awash with these facts and although it was now 60 years since the Battle of the Alma and 57 years since he was presented with the Victoria Cross, if ever his celebrity status had diminished, it was certainly resurrected now.

The Sheffield Daily Telegraph placed the news beneath a heading: - **'AT LAST'** – The clipping is of poor quality, so the start of it is transcribed as thus: -

Major General Sir Luke O'Connor V.C., K.C.B., one of the gallant veterans of the British Army, has been gazetted Colonel of the Royal Welsh Fusiliers in place of the late Major General, the Hon. Sir S. Mostyn". "This is the regiment which Sir Luke joined as a private soldier as far back as 1849, and one of the chief ambitions of his life, has now been attained."

No more can be said that as is contained within the below 'Broad Arrow' clipping. Luke would have been informed of his appointment, before the Levee took place.

Sir Luke O'Connor, K.C.B., V.C.

At the age of eighty-three an honour has come to this gallant old soldier, an honour it is probable he appreciates more than any other it is in the power of his King to confer on him. He has been gazetted colonel of the Royal Welsh Fusiliers, in which he enlisted more than sixty-five years ago. Little can he have imagined on that far-off-day when he took the Queen's shilling that later on he would command his regiment, still less that in his old age he would be its full colonel. Sir Luke O'Connor's career shows that, even in days gone by, the Army could offer something substantial to the man who enlisted in the ranks, and that advancement could be obtained by means of true soldierly bravery. Promoted sixty years ago for bravery at the battle of the Alma and awarded the Victoria Cross, he fought in the Indian Mutiny and distinguished himself in Ashanti, being rewarded with a brevet lieutenant-colonelcy; later he commanded a battalion of his regiment and retired with the honorary rank of Major-General just twenty-seven years ago. To few, if any, men has the honour of colonel of the regiment come in like case—that is, to a man who enlisted as a private soldier. Many men have been given commissions for service in the field, but where they were men without means or interest they usually dropped out, either owing to age or, in the old days, through inability to purchase; he was only twenty-three when he got his commission, and the other difficulty of promotion does not seem to have interfered seriously with his career. We offer Sir Luke O'Connor our sincerest congratulations on his appointment, especially as we feel sure no honour could have been more gratifying to him, and wish him many years of life and health.

Broad Arrow 19ᵗʰ June 1914

With all deference to Sir Savage and his family, it was such a shame that Luke had to wait until the autumn of his life, to receive his knighthood and now, the colonelcy of his regiment, but alas, even that wasn't to come until 6 months prior to his death.

153

Luke's allegiance to his regiment had now been repaid after all those years. He would have been tremendously proud and to repeat, he commented that he cherished that honour, more so, than any of the honours he had hitherto, been awarded.

World War 1

We can be assured that even in his retirement at 83, Luke would not be far away from his uniform. Apart from travelling abroad, he was settled in London at 34 Clarges Street, Mayfair, not far from his beloved Farm Street Church and he would still be accepting invitations to just about each and every 'high society' event.

The assassination of the presumptive heir to the Austrian throne, Archduke Franz Ferdinand and his wife Sophia occurred whilst they were on an official visit to Sarajevo, Bosnia on 28th June 1914. Whilst riding in an open top carriage, a 19 year old Serbian nationalist shot them at point blank range with a semi-automatic pistol. Luke would have met this couple at the Clarence House garden party in 1894.

The ensuing World War 1 naturally demanded the recruitment of a large number of able bodied men and the Secretary of State for War, Lord Kitchener, became the well-known face of the poster created to attract them.

Naturally, the numbers also required men of officer quality as supervisors and because of the numbers of them required, the system of producing them, was going to have to change. It had been most unusual for officers like Luke to be promoted from the ranks without purchasing a commission, but those that had, had demonstrating the skills and bravery required, to be so promoted.

Lord Kitchener was soon to learn that those who were best suited to train the new recruits were the sergeants and colour sergeants who were already in the regular army. He was reported to have said,

"there are few genuine 'rankers' in the army today, holding commissions. I mean men of the type of General Luke O'Connor, VC and the late Hector Macdonald, who won their laurels by sheer force of merit and character. There are, without doubt, plenty of men in the ranks who would make excellent officers, and they cannot be overlooked. Their time is coming, and shortly, and when the new army is complete many men who have been tried and found trustworthy and gallant will get the promotion which they deserve".

The giant obstacle in the way at that time, was that to purchase a commission, required at least £100 per year, more than the normal income from pay. (Nearly £12,000 in 2020 – CPI)

A soldier would need to find this for some 6 – 10 years and there weren't many who could afford it. Lord Kitchener was making his views known in the People's Journal published on 26th September 1914, an advertisement hoping to attract the right characters who would earn a promotion to an officer rank in the same way as Luke had done. Not only did he quote Luke among another half dozen examples, but it was nice to see that it was Luke who came to his mind first.

It is not, however, the pride which Luke would have felt by Lord Kitchener mentioning him, that causes it to be written about here. It is because one cannot help wondering what he would have thought about himself and the war, from a personal perspective. Whilst he couldn't have helped being proud, it is suspected that even at 83, he had possibly wondered whether he could be of any help to the war effort.

It was possibly his attendance at many recruitment meetings where he gave his normal inspirational talk, which, helped to swell the queues in the recruitment offices. He was famous, and young boys hung on to his every word.

Indeed, it wasn't long before Luke was present at a recruiting parade at a United Irish League meeting held at Westminster on 19th October. It was organised and chaired by that friend of Luke's, the Irishman, T.P. O'Connor, the owner / editor of the M. A. P. magazine which carried Luke's autobiography back in December, 1900.

At the Chairman's request, the audience rose, and with uplifted hands, took the pledge to restore freedom to Belgium. Luke was introduced by the chairman and received a great reception when he appealed to the manhood of the country to join the ranks to defend the liberation of the Empire. A resolution pledging Irishmen to support the Allied force, was carried. This was an excellent example of Luke not being able to take part in the war, but doing his level best to ensure other, more able men, were.

The Death of Rear Admiral Lucas

A further death which would undoubtedly impact on Luke's status in life, was that of Rear Admiral Charles Lucas. He was that brave sailor who had thrown a live Russian shell into the sea, it having landed on the deck of his ship and which exploded before it hit the water.

Sir Luke and he, were the only two recipients of that first batch of 62 V.Cs presented by Queen Victoria, who were still alive. He was now the only survivor of them all.

Unfortunately, Luke fell ill with pneumonia again in November and was unable to attend the funeral of Lord Roberts who had died aged 82 on 14th in St Omer, France. Newspaper reports said that Luke was suffering a 'serious' illness and that he would be represented by Colonel Stanley-Creek.

"Sir Luke O'Connor, like Lord Roberts, has always had the soldier's cause at heart and has agitated continuously for more pay for the ranks, as well as for the officers, for he maintains there are scores of non-commissioned officers who cannot accept commissions because they could not live on their pay, yet who would make ideal officers. Sir Luke is a great believer in the inestimable value of the 'non-commissioned man.'"

Wilmington Morning Star 7 December 1914

Field Marshal Frederick Sleigh Roberts, 1st Earl Roberts, VC, KG, KP, GCB, OM, GCSI, GCIE, KStJ, VD, PC, FRSGS became the last Commander-in-Chief of the Forces. Ironically, he contracted his pneumonia whilst he was visiting British troops.

It is hoped that Luke hadn't contracted it from him.

Once again, amid numerous British newspaper reports about Luke, the above snip from the Wilmington morning Star, North Carolina, carried brief details of Lord Roberts' death and linked Luke with his friendship. Surprisingly, no mention of Luke's brother Daniel, was made.

THE FINAL ROLL CALL

The fact that reports of Luke's death mentioned that he had been ill for some time, tends to indicate, that he never recovered from that bout of pneumonia, mentioned above, which he contracted in November, 1914. After all, it was quoted that he had been 'seriously ill' for some time. He died at his home, 34 Clarges Street, Piccadilly, on 1st February 1915.

Just as quickly as Luke had been gazetted the Colonelcy of the Royal Welsh after Sir Savage Lloyd Mostyn's death seven months ago, as indicated in the London Gazette below, Luke's replacement was found the day following his death, on 2nd February 1915. However, these consecutive dates, may well have been backdated to provide seamless periods of the Colonelcy.

MEMORANDA.

Major-General Sir Francis Lloyd, K.C.B., C.V.O., D.S.O., Commanding London District, to be Colonel of The Royal Welsh Fusiliers, in succession to the late Major-General Sir Luke O'Connor, V.C., K.C.B. Dated 2nd February, 1915.

London Gazette 12th March 1915

Luke's home - 34 Clarges Street, Piccadilly, London

As has been mentioned before, it was such a shame that Luke hadn't been given more time in which to justifiably share in the glory of his fine achievements. News of his death was published over several weeks in numerous newspapers both at home (including Wales and Ireland) and abroad. All contained the same material relating to Luke's heroic acts. In addition to the content of the London Times shown immediately below, others, from America and Canada are included below, so as to give an international flavour to the tributes.

DEATH OF SIR LUKE O'CONNOR.

V.C. HERO OF THE CRIMEA.

Major-General Sir Luke O'Connor, V.C., K.C.B., who rose from the ranks to command the regiment in which he enlisted some 65 years ago, and was one of the first to receive the Victoria Cross, died in London yesterday, in his 84th year. He had been seriously ill for some time.

Born in February, 1831, at Elphin, County Roscommon, O'Connor enlisted in the 23rd Royal Welsh Fusiliers at the age of 17. With his regiment he landed in the Crimea early in 1854, and they came under fire immediately afterwards on the heights of the Alma. O'Connor had at this time attained the rank of sergeant, his promotion having been exceptionally rapid for th se long-service days. Scarcely had the closely contested action of the Alma begun— the 23rd had but just come within range of fire— when Lieutenant Anstruther, carrying the Queen's Colour, fell mortally wounded. O'Connor, marching by his side as one of the Colour party, was struck in the breast, and had also fallen. Finding, however, that the officer's condition was hopeless and the position demanded prompt action, the young sergeant picked himself up, pulled himself together, took the Colour, rushed forward with a desperate effort in face of a murderous fire, and planted the emblem of victory on the redoubt before those of the enemy who were near at hand could realize their peril. The effect on the advancing battalion was instantaneous. Seeing what had been done by the valour of one man, all ranks of the gallant 23rd pressed onward to his support, and within a few seconds the position had been carried at the point of the bayonet.

This having been accomplished, O'Connor was urged to place himself under medical care; but he pleaded so earnestly to be allowed to do his duty to the end that his wish was acceded to. Thus he and the Colour he had borne so nobly did not part company until the battle was over and he had received the praise and thanks of Sir George Browne and General Codrington on the field, before his assembled comrades, and been told that he would be recommended for a commission. His own simple comment on his exploit in later years was that he "only did a soldier's duty." He was gazetted to an ensigncy whilst in hospital. But an honour was to come which he valued even more than his promotion: that was the Victoria Cross, conferred upon him when the decoration was created, largely as the result of his own act of valour. The Cross was pinned on his breast by Queen Victoria at a great military parade in Hyde Park, in June, 1857.

The Mutiny and Gold Coast.

O'Connor obtained his lieutenancy in February, 1855, and had returned to duty in time to be present at the siege and fall of Sevastopol, the attack on the quarries, and the assaults of June 18 and September 8. On the latter occasion he again distinguished himself by what was spoken of as his "cool heroism and the splendid example he set to all about him." But he was again seriously wounded—this time in both thighs. For his service in the Crimea, besides receiving his commission and the Victoria Cross, he was decorated with the medal and two clasps, the Sardinian and Turkish medals, and the 5th Class of the Medjidieh.

The 23rd, which had returned home at the close of the war, at once embarked for India when the Mutiny broke out in 1857, and there O'Connor had the good fortune to see service under Sir Colin Campbell in the operations for the relief of Lucknow. He was present at the defeat of the Gwalior contingent at Cawnpore, at the siege and capture of Lucknow, the operations across the Gomtee under Outram, and in several minor affairs. For the Mutiny Captain O'Connor—he was promoted in August, 1858—received another war medal with clasp. After several uneventful years he accompanied the 2nd Battalion Royal Welsh Fusiliers to the Gold Coast for Sir Garnet Wolseley's expedition to Kumasi at the end of 1873, having then reached the rank of major. For this service he received a brevet lieutenant-colonelcy, and the medal with clasp.

On June 24, 1884, he succeeded to the command of the 2nd Battalion Royal Welsh Fusiliers, and in 1886 he went on half-pay with the rank of colonel. He was granted a Distinguished Service reward, and retired on March 2, 1887, with the rank of major-general. He was made a C.B. in 1906, and K.C.B. in 1913; and only last year he had the satisfaction of being appointed honorary colonel of his old regiment.

This clipping below is just the start of a similar report contained in a Wilmington newspaper in North Carolina of 4th February 1915. Much of the text cut, is a repetition of the brave actions he performed at the river Alma, Sevastopol, India and in West Africa.

Below is the Canadian sample, together with an additional one.

VALIANT IRISH KNIGHT HAS DIED

Brother of Maj. Daniel O'Connor, of This City Passes In London.

Major General Sir Luke O'Connor, V. C., K. C. B., brother of Maj. Daniel O'Conor, of this city, died at his home in London, England, last Sunday and was to be buried today, according to advices received here yesterday from relatives in Illinois and a cable today from London.

Sir Luke O'Connor was in Wilmington on a visit to his brother in July, 1889, and is remembered by many friends he made while here.

Poor Copy but just first section from the 'Morning Star', Wilmington, North Carolina. Daniel's local newspaper.

LATE SIR LUKE O'CONNOR

Personal Reminiscence of Officer Who Formerly Lived Here

An interesting personal reminiscence of the late General Sir Luke O'Connor V.C., K.C.B., appears from the pen of a friend in the London Daily Telegraph: When quartered in Montreal forty-four years ago I had the privilege of knowing Captain Luke O'Connor, V.C., of the Royal Welsh Fusiliers, a friendship which has lasted since then; and there must be many still living in Montreal and many Canadians of that generation now residing in London, who knew him well and mourned his death. He was at that far-off period a conspicuous figure in the garrison of Montreal, owing to his having risen from the ranks of his distinguished regiment and having won the Victoria Cross, and he was one of the most popular officers of the garrison and the spirit of all the bright social functions for which Montreal was then so noted.

How he won the Victoria Cross at the battle of the Alma and afterwards distinguished himself in the Crimea and the Indian mutiny and the relief and fall of Lucknow, and subsequently rose to the command of his regiment and became a general and was made a K.C.B., forms a noble tradition in the glorious annals of the British Army. And he has left a heritage of heroic example that should inspire many a young soldier in the army today to try and follow in the footsteps of his brilliant career. Since his retirement Sir Luke lived principally in London, and was a familiar figure in the West-end, and the clubs and his charming Irish personality endeared him to everyone who knew him. He was a devout Catholic, and devoted a great deal of his means to Catholic charities, especially an Irish orphanage in which he took a deep interest.

He was greatly affected by the war, and used to say, "it is not war at all but wholesale murder." He was an intimate friend of Lord Roberts and the night before he died he told his faithful nurse that he had a most vivid dream that he was speaking to him about the war. And in a few hours he joined his illustrious comrade in the land of deathless heroes. He used always to say that he had extraordinary presentiments and premonitions manifested to him in his dreams, a characteristic of his Celtic nature. The writer had the privilege of seeing Sir Luke in his last peaceful sleep, the rugged lines of his features were effaced and smoothed by death, his hands—those hands which had valiantly planted the standard of victory on the heights of Alma—clasped on his breast, holding his blessed rosary, and his soul, his heroic soul at rest in the bosom of his Savior and his God.

The Gazette, Montreal 18th March 1915

The first paragraph explains who the author was but his estimate about when his contact with Luke was made, is a little mistaken as it was in 1866-1867 when Luke was there.

Whoever this person was, reports that his London based friend, saw Luke, as he says, "*in his last peaceful sleep*" ...

He must therefore, have been close to him, and in the absence of other sources concerning the times when Luke would have 'let his hair down', it is a pleasure to read at least a glimpse as to how that was achieved by him.

161

An additional clipping from Canada has been included, which had also been printed in the Montreal Gazette, just prior to the one above. This one, includes more of a personal reminiscance. The writer recounting being quartered with Luke in Montreal 44 years ago. (It was actually 49 years previously) The author was slightly out with his dates but it was so many years ago.

Sir,—Your interesting article on the late Sir Luke O'Connor awakened past reminiscences of the writer.

As Capt. O'Connor, he was with his regiment, the 23rd Royal Welsh Fusiliers, when stationed in Montreal, about 1864 or 1865.

Shortly after the close of the Civil War, General Meade, of the U. S. Army, who commanded the Army of the Potomac—and was commander of Federal forces at the battle of Gettysburg—when visiting Montreal, expressed a wish to see a British regiment inspected.

The 23rd R. W. Fusiliers were arriving here on that day, so General Lindsay ordered them to march straight from Bonaventure Depot to the Champs de Mars, where they were inspected. They were in full marching order, and I never saw a finer regimental exhibition.

With the historic goat led in front, the officers with a sort of pigtail lapels, and the magnificent marching, it was a most picturesque sight.

The writer, then a mere boy, felt a glow of patriotic pride in their performance before a foreign general.

Col. Bell, V.C., was a pronounced Martinet—and they were always in a state of drilled perfection. There were four V.C. officers in the regiment, viz., Col. Bell, Capt. Cary, Capt. Lawrence, and Capt. Luke O'Connor, who lived here for many years later.

The officers of the regiment had very exclusive ideas, but the old-time prejudice against "rankers" did not exist among them.

They were too proud of their captain, Luke O'Connor, V.C., later General Sir Luke O'Connor, V.C.

Yours truly,

H.

Montreal, March 5, 1915.

The Gazette, Montreal 13th March 1915

162

As mentioned earlier, the perceived snobbishness of commissioned officers, may have effected Luke's ambitions, particularly, the fact that against all expectations, his knighthood appeared to be 'held back' for some considerable time. However, in Luke's case, the last two paragraphs of this clip tend to refute that, certainly in so far as those who knew him and had worked along side him. If such divisiveness existed, then it would be from those, perhaps of a higher status, who were not close to him.

There were numerous other accolades given to Luke in countless reports of his death but the line must be drawn somewhere.

THE FUNERAL AND LUKE'S WILL

Luke's funeral, officiated by the Rev. Father Considine, was held on Thursday 4th February, three days following Luke's death. It was a Requiem Mass held at his 'Church of the Immaculate Conception' in Farm Street, Berkeley Square. The King was represented by his Aide-de-camp, Colonel Norie.

The coffin, which had been placed on a catafalque overnight facing the altar, was draped with the Union Jack with his 'cocked' hat and sword placed on it. It was carried on a gun carriage drawn by eight horses of the Royal Horse Artillery to St Mary's Catholic Churchyard, Kensal Green for internment with military honours. It was preceded by drums and fifes and a firing party of fiftymen of the Scots Guards.

The author has experienced many wills which invariably reveal the character of the person making them. Luke's will was no exception. He had left an estate of £10,528 gross, £10,340 net.

According to the Office for National Statistics composite price index, £10,340 in 1915 is equivalent in purchasing power to about £1,069,948.76 in 2020. Let's make it easier and round it to £1,070,000. That's a huge one million and seventy thousand pounds! No wonder Luke was hopping aboard the luxury liners of the day. It is not know whether 34 Clarges Street was his own property, but if it, or an apartment in it, was, then it is presumed that it would have been included in his estate.

So back to the beneficiaries and what might have been going through his mind when he wrote his will. If asked to guess, one might have predicted three areas in his life which he would have held dearest. They would be, 1. His Catholic faith, 2. The Army and 3. His family. Let us see who, or what it was that Luke had decided to leave his money to.

So, according to the Consumer Price Index and the average inflation rate which the index provides at 4,25% since 1915, the following table has been compiled: -

BENEFICIARY	PROPERTY OR 1915 £ AMOUNT	2020 £ VALUE
Wrexham Depot of Royal Welsh Fusiliers.	Medals, Decorations and Swords	VC App. £1m+?
Brother Daniel's Family	Miniature medals	
Rev. Emanuel Bans - Incorp. Society of Crusade of Rescue, Compton St. Russell Sq. London towards expense of annually emigrating 1 boy and 1 girl to Canada £3,000		£310,430

General Objects of the above Charity	£500	£51,738
Manager of St Hugh's House Kings Ave. Clapham Park for Catholic cripples	£500	£51,738
Superiors of St Joseph's hospice Mare St Hackney for the dying.	£500	£51,738
Superior of Nazareth House Hammersmith	£500	£51,738
Rector of The Church of Immaculate Conception, Farm Street.	£500	£51,738
Superior of the Sisters of Charity, Boyle, for the very poor.	£500	£51,738
St Mary's Asylum for the female blind, Merrion, Dublin.	£500	£51,738
Superior of the Convent of Poor Clares, Galway.	£300	£31,043
Superior of the Convent of Poor Clares, Notting Hill.	£300	£31,043
Superiors of the Sisters of Charity, Elphin, Co. Roscommon for the very poor.	£300	£31,043
Superior of the Sisters of Charity Carlisle Place, Westminster for the very poor	£300	£31,043
Superiors of the Sisters of Charity, Lower Seymour Street, London for the very poor.	£300	£31,043
Superiors of the Little Sisters of the very poor, Portobello Rd.	£300	£31,043
Superior of the Helpers of the Holy Souls, Gloucester Rd Regents Park.	£300	£31,043
The Rev. Arthur H. Powner of the Church of Warwick Street, London.	£300	£31,043
The Benevolent Spociety for the relief of the aged and infirm poor.	£300	£31,043
Catholic Soldiers Association	£200	£20,695
Residue to other deserving Charities nominated by his executors		See below

Of the net £10, 340, the above figures account for £9,850. This leaves £490 to be dispersed by Luke's executors. However, the £3,000 bequeathed to the immigration of two children to Canada annually, was reported as being £1,000 in other media. The other slight question remaining, concerns the retrieval of information during the process of research, some time ago, that Luke had left his niece, Isabela (Belle) Hute, the sum of £200.

Belle was the spinster daughter of Luke's sister, Catherine. He would not have met her before his visit to the Hute home in America in 1899. At that time, Catherine was a widow and Belle was the third eldest of four children, aged 47. She was a member of the Order of the Eastern Star which was a Freemasons Club, one of few that admitted ladies. Above all, she was a respected pioneer teacher. She must have caught Luke's eye as a very highly respected member of her community, as was made clear in her obituary. She was the only member of his surviving family who had received anything in his will.

With reference to the executors' duties to disperse the remainder of his assets among good causes of their choice, one such donation which had been made to the St Andrew's hospital, Dollis Hill, London, has been discovered. In 1914, this hospital became a military hospital to treat injured British, Australian, Belgian and Canadian wounded soldiers.

The report found, was printed in the *'Hendon and Finchley Times'*, dated 2nd March 1917, which concerned the publication of their 4th annual return and hence, the hospitals struggle to balance the books. The financial year closed with a deficit of £68 15s 3d. It was reported that £20 had been received from the executors of Luke's will.

In so far as his other donations are concerned, they most certainly emphasise his religious and charitable nature, and in addition to the thoughts expressed above, he ensured that it was the poor Catholics and the crippled catholic youth that were going to benefit. Also, with regard to the sending of two youths to Canada each year, he makes no comment on the religious faith they should be.

THE EPILOGUE AND CONCLUSIONS

Without duplicating most of what has already been said about Luke, there are no qualms at all, in again, emphasising the level from which he had risen. Though his ancestors may have been from the highest echelons of Irish descent, his parents had fallen on tough times during the onset of the *'An Gorta Mor'* (The Great Hunger) and the early stages of the potato famine was almost upon them.

From being the child of a poor Irish family who, together with six siblings, had been left as orphans in a foreign land around 76 years before his death, Luke had become a friend of the King, the Colonel of a Regiment in the British Army, had been offered the position of Governor General of Canada and had been urged to become a candidate for a parliamentary constituency in Ireland. It was for the sake of his family, (which, to him was his regiment), that he declined these latter accolades. He was respected by the aristocrats, politicians and other upper crust of society he met, but most of all, by the men who he commanded who not only respected him, but 'loved' him. He was such a rare breed.

These were the amazing levels to which he had risen and which left others, not at all concerned that he had been a non-commissioned officer who had reached those dizzy heights.

His ancestors, were said to have been descended from the pre-Norman Kings of Connaught and the last High Kings of Ireland. So despite the hard times on which his family had fallen, was there some hereditary gene which may have been introduced to the mix and which played a part in producing such a brave, courageous and lovable character?

Within his current family, discounting Luke's youngest sibling James, who, as a baby, on reaching Canada, died with his mother, both his sisters had married successful men after they settled in America and their success gene, appears also, to have been transmitted to their children. Luke's brothers, Patrick, Thomas and Daniel were each hailed as among the most respected and talented members of the communities in which they settled. Patrick and Daniel were successful businessmen and Daniel was also a hero who had been left for dead on a battlefield during the American Civil War. He survived and rose to be a Major and later became a multi millionaire estate agent and developer.

Thomas was a hero in other spheres. He had been the first recorder of land and property in the state in which he chose to settle. He was a leader within the Catholic church.

In Luke's case, without meeting his siblings, he had shown so much courage and bravery in situations which so very few of us have experienced. History tells us that there are men who fear and men that don't. Were his actions 'brave' or was he simply imprudent? In the few public comments that Luke had made during his lifetime, after being asked if he thought cowardice could be cured, he said that whilst nervousness maybe overcome with experience, he thought that cowardice could not be cured. So, what drove him to become a hero?

Was he saying that whilst some were either made of the stuff that blots out dangers, whilst others simply do what they can to escape their fears, for their own safety? Perhaps the following true example, helps to describe how we are divided within these behavioural spheres.

In November 2019, only seven weeks prior to this being written, people were being stabbed by a terrorist who wore a fake suicide vest and had strapped knives to both hands. He was a free but convicted terrorist, attending an offender rehabilitation conference held at the Fishmongers' Hall, at one end of London Bridge. He had been invited to the conference as a previous offender and participant in the programme. Although banned from entering London under the terms of his release, he was granted a one-day exemption to attend.

It was during the conference that he declared that he would blow up the building and he commenced to stab people. In a frenzy, he was hell bent on trying to kill as many as he could. Most of the people who were in close proximity fled, screaming for their very lives. Wouldn't you?

However, some people attacked and tried to disarm him. Although semi-overpowered, he managed to escape the venue and the scenario extended to London Bridge where his presence and the ensuing melee, caused people to again scream and run for their lives. Two, or maybe more from the conference, including a chef and a convicted murderer, continued their pursuit. The chef had taken a 1.5 metre whale's tooth displayed in the hall as a weapon and another, a fire extinguisher. This was certainly a dangerous situation with the offender managing to kill two innocent people and injure others.

Why was it then, that the vast majority saw immediate danger and fled, while a very small number by comparison, attempted to disarm the terrorist and over power him? The pursuit of their objective was so strong that they had to be pulled away so that the police could shoot the terrorist.

It is early days in that example and as this is written, those who attacked the offender have yet to be honoured for their bravery, though most probably they shall be. However, having posed the question, it's not surprising that the answer is difficult to find.

But both Daniel and Luke were the siblings who faced similar dangers. They were both in uniform and being paid to be there. They were expected to do what they had to do. (In Luke's words, '**Their Duty'**) If, in any way, they had turned their backs as some did, they would be called cowards. According to some accounts of the Alma situation, there were some soldiers who held back and were loitering among the buildings in the burning village. Also, it will be remembered that as soon as they could, both Luke and Daniel, quite independently of one another, immediately set to organising the recruitment of volunteers to fight in their respective wars.

In short, they were the type who had no compunction in going forward. They were clearly driven and wanted to fight for what they perceived as their cause. This is an attitude which is suggested is a necessary ingredient in one's psyche, which must be present, and which may well have been handed down as an hereditary element. It was uncanny that both had wars to fight and both fought in similar fashion, yet they had been apart for many decades. It surely demonstrated that they were 'made of the right stuff' and were **'born to lead'**.

In those situations, another factor can emerge and that is, our spontaneous reaction. How many times have we done something which, as an afterthought, we regarded as stupid or dangerous? Spontaneity may well have been present in the example above, but in Luke and Daniel's cases, these were planned acts of warfare which, maybe were never expected to appear; but wait! Could Luke have simply wanted to persuade the colour bearer, Anstruther to get beneath the shadow of the redoubt at Alma, as a means of self-preservation?

In the context of spontaneity, we witness heroes many times being interviewed on TV when they respond to the inevitable question about why they acted with such courage. They typically respond in such terms as "I didn't think, it was just on impulse" or, "it was the natural thing to do".

It is suggested that it would be highly improbable that anyone would intentionally go out having planned to win any recognition, let alone a medal for any type of bravery. These acts of courage seem to have occurred without any pre warning or following any encouragement. In Luke's case, the Victoria Cross did not even exist! It was the various acts of courage that were emerging from the Crimean War, which led to it being established on 29th January 1856, some 16 months following Luke's deed at the River Alma.

The George Cross wasn't introduced until 1940 and the Conspicuous Gallantry Cross was only introduced in 1995. So, it appears that so far as can be established, there were no medals or rewards, at all in existence when Luke acted as he did at the Alma. In his case, the word, 'spontaneous' seems appropriate, yet he would have insisted on doing his duty.

Another characteristic also emerges. Having eventually been cared for by a 'monied' uncle in London, a retired naval surgeon, evidence exists that he may well have been regarded as the 'posh boy', with him being able to buy additional food and of a higher quality when he first was in barracks at Winchester. Could it be that this type of discrimination became a motivational factor in him wanting to prove to his less 'well-off' colleagues, who might have been perceived as more capable of jumping into dangerous situations, that he was nothing special and just 'one of them'?

On reflection, it wasn't long, of course, before he was singled out to drill his colleagues and was sent to drill various units of the Militia. In other words, his superiors had already identified him as something special and so, any signs of that being a motivational factor behind his courageous actions, cannot be found.

It seems, therefore, that we should settle on the gene being an influential factor in the O'Connor family and that he, like his immediate and past family, were all pretty remarkable and spontaneously courageous. Whatever, it has been a pleasure to have delved into his courage and compassion.

The most expert witnesses in this epilogue, will be the men who served side by side with Luke. The men who knew him as a colleague and as a leader whom they would faithfully follow. Readers will recall that many pages back, was reproduced the reactions following Luke's article, 'In the days of my youth' story in T.P. O'Connor's, M.A.P. magazine.

It contained numerous complimentary letters; however, one of them has been kept back, the one which the author felt was submitted from the heart and which aptly and honestly painted his portrait.

As seen below, it was from the pen of a colleague who joined the Royal Welsh 14 years after the battle of the Alma but sadly, he was not named in the edition which published it. So, this will be his thoughts of Luke, not in battle but as a 'leader' of men. Even without knowing of his antecedent history, he must have thought that Luke was, indeed, something special and was **'born to lead'**.

"But Luke O'Connor, you were among the first, if not the first, of our time. I joined the Royal Welsh Fusiliers fourteen years after you had been promoted – wounded – bleeding – on the banks of the Alma. You commanded 'B' Company. These thirty years I have known you. A finer or keener soldier never had the cross swords of a general upon his shoulder. You had enough and to spare of record and of honour to turn your head. But you remained the simple soldier; the good nature, which in the year that I was born made you popular among the boys of Boyle, and, with the drill sergeant at Winchester, made you popular with all who met you. I am proud to have soldiered with you. This story, though of yours, I learn now for the first time in connected narrative, although we have known each other all this time. If you had not won the Victoria Cross at the Alma, you would have won it at the Redan."

GALLERY

Sergeant O'Connor wounded, while in the act of taking the colour from Corporal Southey
Courtesy of the Illustrated Naval and Military Magazine

Sergeant Luke O'Connor – VC at Centre Bottom
Courtesy Wrexham Archives

Courtesy Wrexham Archives
Is this Luke without moustache?

Courtesy Wrexham Archives
Visiting Card

The younger soldier

Wearing his VC

With fellow officers of the Royal Welsh Fusiliers.   (RWF Museum)

An oil painting by Algernon Smith -

Reproduced from the Regimental Records of the RWF – Vol. 2

This is Luke but his brother Daniel earned the reputation of being 'The Posy Captain' due to him wearing a flower in his buttonhole. It looks like he wasn't the only brother to do so!

ABOUT THE AUTHOR

Brian Humphreys is a retired senior police officer resident with his wife in Worcestershire. They have two daughters and four grandchildren living nearby.

He spent most of his service in the Criminal Investigation and Operations Departments and was trained as a 'hostage negotiator'. Having been a Detective Chief Inspector, head of the Criminal Investigation Departments of the Malvern and Worcester Divisions, then head of Operations and a Detective Superintendent, based at West Mercia Force Headquarters, he became the Sub Divisional Commander at Bromsgrove, Worcestershire from where, on promotion to Chief Superintendent, he undertook a two year secondment to the Home Office with H.M. Inspectorate of Constabulary.

At the conclusion of his secondment, he was appointed the Redditch Divisional Commander, then Head of the Traffic and Operations Division. After 34 years in the Police Service and when head of the Operations Department, he retired in 1994 to form his own business and became involved in the project management of the first computerised 'Automatic Fingerprint Identification Service' (AFIS) in England and Wales. Following its successful conclusion, he took part in an Interpol project introducing AFIS as a 'Proof of Concept' throughout the inhabited Caribbean Islands.

At the conclusion of the project and running a successful Private Investigator's business, he formed a business association on a troubled industrial estate and became the manager of a large Secondary School in Worcester.

When fully retired, he launched into a hobby of local and family history, including researching those from his village, who had fallen in World War 1. This resulted in him writing his own family history books and a 'My Family Hero' story published in the 'Who do you think you are' magazine. He also wrote three local history books for consumption within his village.

On the discovery that Luke O'Connor may have been his wife's ancestor, he spent several years of researching his life and family, culminating in writing this book.

He continues to play golf, bowls and table tennis and says that he watches too much rugby.

BIBLIOGRAPHY

Ashcroft, Michael : *Victoria Cross Heroes,* Headline Review 2007

Cary & McCance, '*Regimental Records of the R.W.F. Vol. II:* Naval & Military Press, 2015

Cavendish, Richard and Leahy, Pip: *Kings and Queens,* David and Charles Ltd., 2006

Journal of the Connaught Rangers Association The. No. 4. Vol. 1. January 2007,

Cropper Jenny: *A Lonely Road to Glory:* Reveille Newspaper 9th to 15th Feb. 1967 pages 13 & 14.

Dawson, Anthony: *Voices from the Past – The Siege of Sevastopol 1854 – 1855.* Frontline Books 2017

Draper, John William: *History of the American Civil War: Containing the events from the Proclamation of the Emancipation of the slaves to the end of the war.* Harper 1870

Glover, Michael: *That Astonishing Infantry,* Leo Cooper, 1989

Goodacre, Major David 1st Scots Guards: 'The Colours - The Symbol of a Regiment. BBC News Web page 2011

Grunting, William: *Cass Street Sketches,* C.B. Hayward, 1897

Indiana University: *The Iowa Journal of History and Politics Vol. 45,* State Historical Society of Iowa, 1947

Kinglake, Alexander William, 1809 -1891: '*Kinglake's History of the Crimean War'.* 1854-1868 - Cambridge University Library. GB 12 MS.ADD.9554

Swan, James B: *A Chicago's Irish Legion (The 90th Volunteers in the American Civil War)* 2009. Southern Illinois University Press 2009

The Iowa Journal of History and Politics. The Annals of Iowa6 (1903), 69-70. Available at: https://doi.org/10.17077/0003-4827.2914 Hosted by Iowa Research Online

Vaughan, Bernard: *The Sins of Society*, K. Paul, Trench, Trubner, 1907

Williams, W. Alister: *Heart of a Dragon 'The VCs of Wales and the Welsh Regiments'* Bridge Books 2006.

Woodruff, George H: *Fifteen years ago, or The Patriotism of Will County,* BiblioBazaar 2016.

http://www.allworldwars.com/Battlefields-of-the-Crimean-Campaign-1854-55.html

Printed in Great Britain
by Amazon